ISRAEL
The Key to World Revival

© 1999 Avner Boskey
Final Frontier Ministries
Box 121971
Nashville TN 37212-1971
USA

www.davidstent.org

ISRAEL: The Key to World Revival by Avner Boskey
Published by DAVID'S TENT PUBLISHING

Final Frontier Ministries
Box 121971
Nashville TN 37212-1971
USA
www.davidstent.org

ISBN-13: 978-0-9898428-0-8

Library of Congress Catalogue Registration TX 7-744-782

Cover Design & Typesetting: Voyage Media Group

Printed in the United States of America
First Edition 1999
Second Edition 2015

Contents

Acknowledgments

Thanks go to the many people have participated in the birthing of this book. John Paul Jackson first encouraged me about writing books. David and Ferne Kiddie were the divine catalysts for this one. Dr. Gershon D. Hundert, Segal Professor of Jewish Studies, McGill University, led me to research more carefully than I thought I needed to. John Wimber helped reveal the Father's heart to me. Bob Jones has consistently spoken the truth in love. Jim and Michal Ann Goll are friends, counselors and encouragers. Charles Lynn has lightened our load. Those who have prayed this book into existence (especially Tom and Dee Weber) and who have contributed to its production - thank you!

My four children Daniel, David, Asaph and Elisha have donated many hours of their father's time to this project. Their sacrifice has made this book possible. My wife and dearest friend Rachel has enriched this book with helpful editorial comments. Her encouragement, faith and cheering me on are the greatest human blessings I have known.

Avner Boskey
Omer, Israel
June 1999

Note to the Reader

This book is written from a Messianic Jewish perspective and with a Jewish flavor. Certain terms are used throughout the book which may be new to some readers. The Hebrew personal name *Yeshua* is used instead of the more common translation from the Greek *Jesus*. Both names refer to the same Messiah. The Hebrew title *Messiah* is used instead of the Greek derivative *Christ*. Both words refer to the same Anointed One of God. The personal name of the God of Israel, the *Tetragrammaton*, is basically not used in this book. Instead, the term 'the Lord' has been substituted. In all Scripture translations used the terms *Jesus* and *Christ* have been replaced by the terms *Yeshua* and *Messiah*.

A.B.

Introduction

The Jewish people are a living paradox - fascinating to study, yet difficult to comprehend. Their recorded history is the longest and oldest of any people on the face of the earth. Their Bible, both Old and New Testaments, is the world's most influential book. Their land of Israel is the country where many Christians believe the campaign of Armageddon will erupt, and Jerusalem is the city to which Jews and Christians believe Messiah will return. Even early Islamic tradition mandated prayer in the direction of the Jerusalem, 'the House of the Holy Place.' Which one of us feels that his or her handle on the significance of the Jewish people is adequate?

The Bible does claim to give adequate answers concerning Israel. The writers of the Scriptures proclaim that God has chosen the Jewish people. They say that the cities and valleys, the cliffs and *wadis* of the land of Israel are the stage which will support the fulfillment of ancient prophetic promises. The Bible declares that the future redemption of the Jewish people holds the key to the liberation of Planet Earth.

This book is an attempt to communicate the Scriptures' vision concerning Israel in a clear, user-friendly and unapologetic manner. It is written primarily for believers in Yeshua (Jesus' original Hebrew name) who love the Bible and its Author. The day is coming when the Body of Messiah will understand how God's heart beats for the Jewish people, when believers will unashamedly embrace God's call on the Church to save Jewish lives. To paraphrase Paul the Apostle's rhetorical question, "How shall the Gentiles believe in these things unless they hear?"

This book is also dedicated to my Messianic Jewish brothers and sisters. The God of Israel has called our people to many mighty tasks, and one of the most challenging in our own eyes is becoming servants and lights to our Gentile brothers and sisters. This calling is doubly difficult in light of 3,500 years of anti-Semitism. May this book expand your mind, give you new vision and broaden the scope of your own calling.

Finally, this book is an offering to you - Jewish, but definitely not a believer in the Messiahship of Yeshua. You might be curious about the title and message of this book. Perhaps you are reading in order to humor a Christian friend, or to evaluate and destroy dangerously false teachings. *Shalom aleichem* (welcome) whatever be the case! It is my respectful prayer that the God of Israel will speak to you as you flip through these pages, and that He will clearly reveal to your own heart whatever truth may be printed here.

The trumpets of war are sounding across this planet. The eyes of God are examining hearts in every hidden and public place. Like Uncle Sam, the God of Jacob is looking for a few good men and women who will courageously stand up and throw themselves into the heat of battle, into the thick of the fray - into the ministry of saving Jewish lives.

Perhaps He is also calling you to stretch out your hands to Israel, calling you to turn His special Jewish key and so unlock the door to world revival!

Avner Boskey

Section One:

BIBLICAL FOUNDATIONS

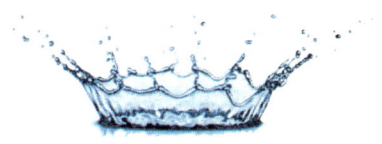

Chapter One

The Father's Heart for Israel

There is a famous story about four scholars - a German, a Frenchman, an American and an Israeli - who were once asked to present papers on the subject of elephants. The German lectured on *'Psychiatric Studies of Angst in Adolescent Elephants.'* The Frenchman lectured on *'The Love Life of the Pachyderm.'* The American gave a motivational seminar on *'Building Bigger and Better Elephants.'* The Israeli spoke on *'The Elephant and the Jewish Problem.'*

Someone once said, 'Out of the abundance of the heart the mouth speaks.' In this story, each of these scholars spoke what was on his heart. The Jewish people have seen much suffering in their long history, and every faithful son or daughter of Israel takes it to heart. But if God were asked about the Jewish people, what would be the response of His heart?

Psalm 148:14 gets to the heart of the matter. It says that "God has raised up a horn[1] for His people Israel... the people close to His heart!" God calls the Jewish people 'His people' and the whole subject of the Jewish people is close to His heart. In times past many Christians have recognized that fact, calling the Jewish people 'the Chosen People.' Why did God choose this nation? What motivated Him to extend favor to such a peculiar and intense people?

Israel - The Nation Close to God's Heart

Moses gives one of the earliest explanations about why God chose Israel in Deuteronomy 7:6-8. He proclaims to the Jewish people:

> You are a people holy to the Lord your God. The Lord your God has chosen you out of all the peoples on the face of the earth to be His people, His treasured possession. The Lord did not set His affection on you and choose you because you were more numerous than other peoples, for you were the fewest of all peoples. But it was because the Lord loved you and kept the oath He swore to your forefathers...

Like a bolt of lightning out of a clear sky comes the Scriptural justification for why God chose Israel: He fell head over heels in love with her! The God of Israel is a God of *passions*. God's choice of Israel was swayed by His own romantic nature – "because the Lord loved you." The love affair between God and the Jewish people spans 4,000 years. It's the longest recorded love affair in human history. The relationship between Israel and her God is not a dry theological treatise. It is a hot-blooded Middle Eastern love story, a divine 'Thousand and One Nights!'

Cutting to the Heart

Moses mentions that God's love for Israel is connected to a legal oath – "because the Lord loved you and kept the oath He swore to your forefathers." Centuries before Moses was found in a basket among the bulrushes, God proclaimed His love to Israel *by cutting*

---

1 A horn was carried about in ancient parades as a military banner denoting joyful victory.

a covenant (entering into a legal, contractual agreement) with the Patriarchs Abraham, Isaac and Jacob.[2] Theologians call this covenant *the Abrahamic Covenant*. It's the nuclear core of the love affair between God and the Jewish people. This Abrahamic promise of love hangs tough in every generation throughout history (love to a thousand generations).

One thousand five hundred years after the Exodus, Saul of Tarsus (Paul the Apostle) sent a circular letter to a small gathering of Jewish and Gentile believers in Yeshua (Jesus' Hebrew name) who lived in Galatia, a province of central Turkey. Paul wanted his readers to understand that the Abrahamic covenant is still in force even after Yeshua's crucifixion. The Abrahamic covenant is still ticking throughout the entire New Testament era. Paul states:

> Brothers, let me take an example from everyday
> life. Just as no one can set aside or add to a human
> covenant that has been duly established, so it is in
> this case. The promises were spoken to Abraham and
> to his seed... What I mean is this: The Torah (ed., the
> Mosaic covenant), introduced 430 years later, does
> not set aside the covenant previously established
> by God and thus do away with the promise...God in
> His grace gave it to Abraham through a promise.[3]

Paul wants believers to grasp the fact that the Abrahamic covenant is still alive and well. It still defines the relationship between God and the Jewish people, Abraham's physical chosen seed.[4] God's loving heart for Israel still beats strongly - even in our day.

The Apple of God's Eye

The Hebrew Scriptures not only describe God's heartbeat. They also talk about His eyes! Two thousand five hundred years

---

2 *Cf.,* Gen. 12:1-3, 7; 13:14-17; 15:1-21; 17:1-21; 18:14-19; 21:12; 22:15-18; 26:2-5, 24; 27:27-29, 37; 28:11-15; 32:24-30; 35:1-13; 46:1-4. *Eg.,* Jer. 34:18 for an interesting description of 'cutting' a covenant.

3 Gal. 3:15-18. The Hebrew word Torah or 'teaching' is translated into Septuagintal Greek by the word nomos, which is usually translated into English by the word 'law', as the NIV does in this case.

4 More on the Abrahamic Covenant can be found in chapter 2.

ago, the prophet Zechariah proclaimed concerning the Jewish people: "This is what the Lord Almighty says... '(W)hoever touches you touches the apple of His eye!'"[5] In this Hebrew word picture someone is attempting to poke his finger into the pupils of God's eyes. What *chutzpah* (brazenness)! God will certainly slap away those impertinent hands and punish the offender. From God's perspective, to roughly handle the Jewish people is to stick a finger into the eyes of God! Handle Israel with care!

Deuteronomy 32:8-11 also talks about the apple of God's eye:

> When the Most High gave the nations their inheritance,
> when He divided all mankind, He set up boundaries for
> the peoples according to the number of the sons of Israel.
> For the Lord's portion is His people, Jacob His allotted
> inheritance. In a desert land He found him, in a barren
> and howling waste. He shielded him and cared for him;
> He guarded him as the apple of His eye, like an eagle that
> stirs up its nest and hovers over its young, that spreads
> its wings to catch them and carry them on its pinions.

Moses is singing the words of this song under a prophetic anointing,[6] waxing rhapsodic about God's great covenant love for Israel. In the middle of the song he suddenly declares that the borders of every nation are pre-established by the Lord, and that these borders are mystically related to the number of Jews in the world at any given time! Though Israel is not a numerically significant nation, God views the Jewish people as being at the very heart of world affairs – the apple of His eye.

Moses' divine perspective certainly disagrees with the position of world bodies like the United Nations. The Security Council may one day conclude that they have the wisdom, the justice, and the military might to redraw Israel's borders. But the God of Israel sits on His heavenly throne and laughs![7] He is the One who has decided

---

5   Zech. 2:8.

6   Deut. 31:30.

7   *Cf.*, Psa. 2:1-5

where the borders of the Gentile nations should be, and Israel is the yardstick He uses in determining those boundaries. The Jewish people remain the apple of God's eye.

Since the eye is the lens through which a person perceives the world around him, could God be saying that Israel is the lens through which He gazes at and evaluates the world? Will God render judgment or blessing to the nations of the world based on their treatment of the Jewish people, the apple of God's eye?

The Heart of a Shepherd

In the ancient Near East, kings liked to describe themselves as shepherds of their people. They were responsible to provide jobs, food and security for their followers. But even in the Middle East reality can sometimes fall short of election-year promises! In his own day Ezekiel took the shepherds of Israel to task for failing to meet their divinely mandated responsibilities.[8]

In contrast, the God of Israel describes Himself as the Good Shepherd of His nation who will provide, protect, and grant peaceful grazing grounds:

> For this is what the Lord says: "I Myself will search for My sheep and look after them. As a shepherd looks after his scattered flock when he is with them, so will I look after My sheep. I will rescue them from all the places where they were scattered on a day of clouds and darkness. I will bring them out from the nations and gather them from the countries, and I will bring them into their own land. I will pasture them on the mountains of Israel, in the ravines and in all the settlements in the land. I will tend them in a good pasture, and the mountain heights of Israel will be their grazing land. There they will lie down in good grazing land, and there they will feed in a rich pasture on the mountains of Israel. I myself will tend My sheep and have them lie down, declares the Lord. I will search for the lost and bring back the strays. I will bind up the injured and strengthen the

8 *Cf.*, Ezek. 34:1-8.

weak, but the sleek and the strong I will destroy. I will
shepherd the flock with justice... They will no longer be
plundered by the nations, nor will wild animals devour
them. They will live in safety, and no one will make
them afraid. I will provide for them a land renowned for
its crops, and they will no longer be victims of famine
in the land or bear the scorn of the nations. Then they
will know that I, the Lord their God, am with them and
that they, the house of Israel, are My people, declares
the Lord. You My sheep, the sheep of My pasture, are
people, and I am your God, declares the Lord."[9]

The God of Israel bares His heart for all the world to see concerning
His affections for the Jewish people! As these Scriptures wash
across our minds, we are sensitized more deeply to the passions of
the Father's heart.

In Isaiah 40:11 God leads His scattered Jewish people back to
the reborn land of Israel. "He tends His flock like a shepherd: He
gathers the lambs in His arms and carries them close to His heart;
He gently leads those that have young." Once again we glimpse the
gentleness of God, and sense the tenderness of His heart toward the
descendants of Jacob.

One hundred years after Isaiah, Jeremiah took up the torch and
prophesied to the nations of the world about God's shepherd-heart
for His people: "Hear the word of the Lord, O nations; proclaim it
in distant coastlands: 'He who scattered Israel will gather them and
will watch over His flock like a shepherd.'"[10]

The Jewish people are not only God's tender sheep, but also His
first-born son.[11] Hosea the prophet once found himself being drawn
into a gentle daydream of God: "When Israel was a youth I loved
him, and out of Egypt I called My son...Yet it is I who taught Ephraim
to walk; I took them in My arms. But they did not know that I healed
them. I led them with human ropes (*ed.*, like a calf), with bonds of

---

9   Ezek. 34:11-16, 28-31.

10   Jer. 31:10.

11   *Cf.*, Exod. 4:22-23.

love. And I became to them as (*ed.,* a ploughman) who lifts the yoke from their jaws, and I bent down and fed them."[12] God mixes His poetic similes rather rapidly in this passage. He is the doting father letting Israel the toddler grasp hold of His pinkies as he learns to walk. And like the good shepherd, God also describes Himself as the considerate farmer gently leading his calf, or carefully pouring feed into the trough of his favorite ox.

The Womb of Compassion

The Hebrew language is earthy, like the people who speak it. The Hebrew word for compassion *rahamim* comes from the root word *rehem* or 'womb.' In the Semitic mind, a mother not only carries a baby to term in her womb; she continues to be deeply stirred within whenever she thinks of that precious little baby – even if that baby is now married with children of his own!

The prophet Isaiah, a contemporary of Hosea, heard God whispering to him that His love for Israel is softer than a mother's breast, throbbing with more compassion than a mother's womb. "But Zion said, 'The Lord has forsaken me, the Lord has forgotten me.' Can a mother forget the baby at her breast and have no compassion on the child she has borne? Though she may forget, I will not forget you! See, I have engraved My people on the palms of My hands; your walls are ever before Me…"[13]

The diamond of God's love sparkles again in Psalm 102, where God's ideal servants have compassionate hearts for the Jewish people, for the land of Israel and for Zion – the city of Jerusalem. "You will arise and have compassion on Zion, for it is time to show favor to her; for the appointed time has come. For her stones are dear to Your servants; her very dust moves them to pity… For the Lord will rebuild Zion…He will not despise their plea."[14]

Yeshua had this kind of heart. He was moved to tears when He saw Jerusalem from the Mount of Olives. As Yeshua "approached

---

12   Hos. 11:1-4.
13   Isa. 49:14-16.
14   Psa. 102:13-14, 16-17.

Jerusalem and saw the city, He wept over it and said, 'If you, even you, had only known on this day what would bring you peace - but now it is hidden from your eyes.'"[15] "O Jerusalem, Jerusalem... how often I have longed to gather your children together, as a hen gathers her chicks under her wings, but you were not willing!"[16]

These brief quotes are striking in their emotion. The heart of God is unchanging toward His people Israel. It overflows with love and is bathed in mercy. "Therefore, this is what the Lord says: 'I will return to Jerusalem with mercy... and the Lord will again comfort Zion and choose Jerusalem.'"[17]

Israel - 'God's Country'

God is a realist, intensely practical in all His dealings with mankind. The first thing He emphasized to Abram, even before He cut the covenant with him, was real estate. "Go out from your country... to the land which I will show you!"[18] Before Abram knew what the Promised Land was called or even where it was, God had already hidden the land of Israel in His heart and surrounded it by His love. Moses taught this truth to the Jewish people as they all camped on the Eastern bank of the Jordan River.

He reminds them of how God's heart is always connected to the promised land of Abraham's covenant:

> (T)he land that the Lord swore to your forefathers to give to them and their descendants, a land flowing with milk and honey...is a land of mountains and valleys that drinks rain from heaven. It is a land the Lord your God cares for; the eyes of the Lord your God are continually on it from the beginning of the year to its end...[19]

There is a special place in the heart of God for the land of Israel,

15 Lk. 19:41-42.

16 Matt. 23:37.

17 Zech. 1:16.

18 Gen. 12:1.

19 Deut. 11:9-12.

for it is the home of His beloved Jewish people. It is always His land and their land, whatever the nations may call it – *Canaan, Palestine, Greater Syria, the Occupied West Bank* – at any given moment in history.

Jerusalem, the Home of God's Heart

Many Christian and Muslim theologians deeply appreciate the spiritual role of Jerusalem. For the majority of Jewish people, however, Jerusalem is not only another significant spiritual place; it is the passion of their hearts. This state of affairs is not new. Two thousand six hundred years ago the psalmist cried out in Babylonian captivity: "How can we sing the Lord's song in a foreign land? If I forget you, O Jerusalem, may my right hand forget her skill! May my tongue cleave to the roof of my mouth if I do not remember you, if I do not exalt Jerusalem above my chief joy!"[20]

Why are the Jewish people so devoted to the City of Peace? The answer lies hidden in the heart of Israel's God: nearly 3,000 years ago the Lord appeared to King Solomon in Jerusalem and said, "I have heard the prayer and plea you have made before Me; I have consecrated this Temple, which you have built, by putting My Name there forever. My eyes and My heart will always be there."[21] God's eyes, His name and His heart are eternally bound to Jerusalem. No wonder the Jewish people declare this city to be their pearl and their prize – their chief joy!

At the close of the 20th century, the Christian world is witnessing an amazing rise in the fervor and intensity of intercessory prayer. Many of these believers look to Isaiah 62:6-7 as their 'banner' text, "I have posted watchmen on your walls, O Jerusalem; they will never be silent day or night. You who call upon the Lord, give yourselves no rest, and give Him no rest till He establishes Jerusalem and makes her the praise of the earth."[22] The same God who is highlighting this

---

20   Psa.137:4-6.

21   1 Ki. 9:3.

22   Isa. 62:6-7.

text to intercessors the world over, originally had Isaiah pen those verses to express God's own heart for Jerusalem the city and Israel the people!

The day is coming when many soldiers in this new prayer army will have what seem to be scales fall off their eyes. They will suddenly understand the original context of these verses, and clearly experience the Father's heart of intense love for the Jewish people. Then they will begin to raise their voices and intercede for Israel, a nation close to God's heart, until God makes her the praise of the whole earth.

Chapter Two

Flaming Prophets With An Attitude

At one point in 'Fiddler On The Roof' Tevye the milkman grumbles to the God of his fathers about the persecution which comes with being Jewish. "O God," he complains, "You've chosen us out of all the peoples on the earth. Just for once, why don't You choose someone else?" So why did God choose the Jewish people? Was it only for them to suffer? What are the original plans and blueprints God used in drawing up the Jewish people's prophetic destiny?

The Snake and the Seed

The original divine blueprints sketch out a majestic drama. Act One opens in the land known today as Iraq, in the Garden of Eden. As we quietly observe the stage, God has solemnly pronounced words of judgment over the serpent and now He is addressing the dark angel who empowered him: "And I will put enmity between you and the woman and between your seed and her seed; He shall bruise you on the head, and you shall bruise Him on the heel."[1] Some Rabbis of old have stated that this passage in Genesis 3:15 prophesies the coming of Messiah. Christian theologians call this verse the protoevangelium, the 'gospel in seed form.' This verse is our first prophetic key. It will open the door of understanding concerning God's purposes for the Jewish nation.

Genesis 3:15 declares that a powerful hatred for mankind would burn throughout the ages in the heart of the great serpent, better known today by the name Satan. The human race would fear and hate this enemy of their souls. Ultimately someone known as the Seed of the woman would arise and deal a lethal blow to the serpent's head. In that struggle, the great serpent would wound this champion on the heel.

The rest of the Bible fleshes out the fulfillment of this great promise. God would choose one special seed, a special people, who would give birth to the Seed of the Woman. Then, at the end of the ages, this champion would destroy all the works of Satan and deliver a death-blow to the dragon.

God had now planted an unshakable hope for a deliverer deep in the hearts of men and women. Adam and Eve now had reason to believe that some newborn baby boy in their own generation might turn out to be the promised redeemer. When Eve gave birth to Cain her first child, she remembered God's prophetic word and hoped that this son would be the special seed.[2] Later, when all of mankind perished in the Great Flood, the only adult males who survived were Noah and his three sons Shem, Ham and Japheth. Noah's three sons knew that the promised male seed would be born from one of their own descendants.

The flood waters had risen, drowning the sinful rebellion of man

---

1   Gen. 3:15

2   Gen. 4:1. The Hebrew for Cain (*qayin*) and the verb 'I have obtained' (*qaniti*) are based on the same root that Melchizedek uses in Gen.14:19 to describe God, the 'Possessor (*qone* – also 'Maker' or 'Purchaser') of Heaven and Earth.' A Hebrew word play was probably involved in Eve's mind, blending the thoughts of fashioning, owning and obtaining.*Cf.*, David L. Cooper, *Messiah: His Nature and Person*, Biblical Research Society, Los Angeles, 1933, p. 30.

for a season. But as they receded, Genesis 11 tells us that a new age arose. It raised its ugly head, again in Iraq, on the broad river plain of Shinar. There Noah's grandchildren were making the first disastrous attempt to establish a new world order, a 'city whose builder and maker was man.' The engineers of the Tower of Babel had an inkling that God wanted mankind to migrate to other lands and continents.[3] But they were comfortable where they were. They did not want to move on. The hidden rebellion deep in their hearts burst into open revolution against God's call to be fruitful, to fill the earth and to worship Him.

But God always gets His way. Before the demonic tower could be completed and before the rebellion of mankind would bring on another worldwide cataclysm, the Lord splintered mankind into thousands of people groups and language families, divisions which to this day define the face of our planet.

As God was dividing mankind, His focus was zooming in on one specific nation which would give birth to the Seed of the Woman: "When the Most High gave the nations their inheritance, when He divided all mankind, He set up boundaries for the peoples according to the number of the sons of Israel. For the Lord's portion is His people, Jacob His allotted inheritance."[4]

Shield of Abraham

Approximately 200 years after the Tower of Babel, God's plan began to kick into high gear. In the city of Ur the Lord opened the ear of a descendant of Shem named Abram. Abram heard whispered promises concerning a far-off land, an awesome people and a great destiny. At last the prophetic word birthed in the Garden of Eden was about to receive a national address. The 'Seed of the woman' would also be the seed of Abram.

> The Lord said to Abram, "Get out of your land, your
> native country and your father's household and go

---

3 *Cf.*, Gen. 11:4

4 Deut. 32:8-9

to the land I will show you. I will make you into a
great nation and I will bless you, and I will make your
name great, and you will be a blessing. I will bless
those who bless you, and whoever makes light of you
(*Hebr., qalal*) him I will curse (*Hebr., arar*); and all the
families of the earth will be blessed through you.'"[5]

There are three separate recipients in this prophecy – Abram
himself, a great nation which descends from him, and all families
(people groups) of the earth. Each one of these recipients would
obtain different and specific blessings. Abram was told that he
would receive a land,[6] worldwide fame, and a personal blessing
from the hand of God. He would also become the patriarch of a
great nation. Abram's security would be legally guaranteed by
God Almighty's covenant: those who would bless Abram would
be blessed by God, and any individual who would demean, mock,
despise or even laugh at Abram would be cursed by God.[7] Finally
Abram was told that his life would have great personal significance
in that all peoples would receive a blessing through him.[8]

Within a few chapters the second group in the Abrahamic
covenant is identified. The great nation issuing from Abram's
loins are his descendants through Isaac and Jacob, later known as
the Jewish people. The land which had been promised to Abram
personally would also forever belong to all his descendants
through Isaac and Jacob – to the whole Jewish people.[9] The exact

---

5 Gen. 12:1-3 (*my translation*)

6 *Cf.*, Gen. 12:7; 13:14-15; 15:7,18-21; 17:8; 26:3; 35:12; 50:24-25.

7 Though most English Bibles use the verb 'curse' twice in Gen. 12:3, there are actually two different
   Hebrew verbs used. The first verb, *qalal*, has the following range of meanings: to consider
   as superficial or as of little account, to treat with contempt; to make light of; to view as being a
   small matter. The second verb *arar* refers to the process of binding someone with a curse or an
   enchantment, and is used when invoking the name of God that He might cause the curse to work.
   Cf., Lexicon In Veteris Testamenti Libros, 'Arar,' 'Qalal,' pp.89-90, ed. L. Kohler, W. Baumgartner,
   Leiden, E.J. Brill 1958, p. 840.

8 *Cf.*, Gen. 18:18. Later on we learn that Abram would become the father of many different Arab
   nations as well, though these nations would not be the primary legal recipients of the Abrahamic
   covenant.*Cf.*, Gen. 17:4-6, 15-21; 21:9-13.

9 *Cf.*, Gen. 13:14-15; 15:18-21; 17:8; 22:17; 24:7; 26:3; 28:15; 35:12; 48:4; 50:24-25.

borders of Israel's homeland were drawn by God Himself. It's worth noting that these divinely mandated borders are much larger than any borders Israel has ever possessed.[10] The people of Israel would become as numerous as the dust of the earth and the stars of the sky.[11] Dynasties of mighty Jewish kings would flourish.[12] All Jewish men would carry about in their flesh a lifelong sign of this amazing covenant between God and the Jewish people – circumcision. Finally God declares that these Abrahamic covenant promises would last forever.[13]

Over the next 500 years God would re-emphasize all the clauses of this everlasting covenant with the Jewish people, with strikingly beautiful landscapes as the backdrop. On the green mountain ranges of Moriah God promised that Abraham's seed would ultimately triumph over all earthly adversaries, that the Jewish people would possess the gates of their enemies. All the nations of the earth would be blessed through the Jewish people, Abraham's descendants.[14] One hundred years after Abraham, in the ochre desert sands of Beersheba, the Lord comforted Jacob, letting him know that the provisions of the Abrahamic covenant now applied to his own generation and would be passed on to his children.[15]

Moving 400 years down the corridor of time, a Mesopotamian sorcerer named Balaam ben Be'or felt the Spirit of God rushing through his body and taking control of his tongue. Standing on the magnificent heights of Moab and gazing down into the lush Syro-African Rift valley, he saw more than three million Israelites gathered near the sparkling Jordan River, waiting to enter the promised land of Canaan at Joshua's command. By the Spirit of God Balaam prophesied that the whole Jewish nation was now under

---

10 Cf., Gen. 15:18-21
11 Cf., Gen. 13:16; 15:5.
12 Cf., Gen. 17:6
13 Cf., Gen. 17:9-14
14 Cf., Gen. 22:17-18; 24:60; 26:5
15 Cf., Gen. 27:29

the protection of the Abrahamic covenant.[16] God's mighty promises to Abraham were alive and well in Joshua's day and they are in excellent health in our day also. Though modern presidents and dictators don't know it, these Abrahamic promises are still shaping the destiny of the world and the church of the twenty-first century.

Seeing is Believing

God wanted the nations to learn about Him by observing His covenant people the Jews. By studying how God dealt with the Jewish people, the Gentiles would learn something about the very heart of God. And by recognizing and respecting God's calling on the Jewish people, the nations would receive the blessing of Genesis 12:3.

The very first Gentile to grasp this point was the Gerarite sheikh Abimelech: "Now it came about at that time that Abimelech... came to Abraham and said, "God is with you in all that you do. Now therefore, swear to me here by God that... according to the kindness that I have shown to you, you shall show to me (similar kindness)...""[17] A few years later Abimelech has received even more understanding, proclaiming to Isaac: "We see plainly that the Lord has been with you... You are now blessed of the Lord."[18]

In Jacob's day, pagan uncle Laban was aware of God's blessing on Jacob, and he pleaded with him to remain in Syria: "If now it pleases you, stay with me. I have divined that the Lord has blessed me on your account."[19] In Joseph's day Pharaoh's top security officer Potiphar came to the same conclusion as Laban.

> Potiphar, an Egyptian who was one of Pharaoh's officials,
> the captain of the guard, bought (Joseph)...The Lord
> was with Joseph and he prospered... When his master
> saw that the Lord was with him and that the Lord gave
> him success in everything he did, Joseph found favor in

---

16 *Cf.*, Num. 24:9
17 Gen. 21:22-23
18 Gen. 26:28-29
19 Gen. 30:27

his eyes and became his attendant... (T)he Lord blessed the household of the Egyptian because of Joseph. The blessing of the Lord was on everything Potiphar had...[20]

Even after Joseph was thrown into the dungeons of Pharaoh, God was committed to prospering the descendants of Abraham.

But while Joseph was there in the prison, the Lord was with him; He showed him in kindness and granted him favor in the eyes of the prison warden. So the warden put Joseph in charge of all those held in the prison, and he was made responsible for all that was done there. The warden paid no attention to anything under Joseph's care, because the Lord was with Joseph and gave him success in whatever he did.[21]

In Bible times God captured the attention of the nations by blessing Israel, granting her success and even military victory. These principles which caught the eye of Gerarites and Pharaohs hold true for Generation-X and beyond.

A Nation of Prophets

The third group on which the Abrahamic covenant aims its spotlight is the Gentiles. God wants to bless all nations through the seed of Abraham, through the Jewish people – "through you and through your seed will all the nations of the earth be blessed." The Jewish people would be God's mouthpiece to the nations. One of the reasons why God chose Israel was to raise up a nation of prophets, to create a prophetic nation. The entire Jewish people were meant to have an intimate personal relationship with God, and then to share the overflow of that relationship with the Gentiles.

The first use of the term prophet is found in a Jewish context, in Genesis 20 where it is used to describe Abraham. The Lord appeared to Abimelech in a night dream and commanded him, "Now therefore, restore (Abraham)'s wife, for he is a prophet, and

---

20   Gen. 39:1-5
21   Gen. 39:20-23

he will pray for you, and you will live."[22]

'Like father, like son.' As God had programmed a prophetic destiny into Abraham's DNA, so He also seared that calling into the collective consciousness of the Jewish people. The psalmist, describing the Sinai wanderings of Israel, explains that the whole Jewish people were anointed by God and sealed with a prophetic purpose.

"...(W)hen they were few in number, very few and strangers in (the land of promise), they wandered about from nation to nation, from one kingdom to another people. He permitted no man to oppress them, and for their sakes He reproved kings: "Do not touch My anointed ones, and to My prophets do no harm!""[23]

One simple description of a prophet is "someone who puts into human words what God brings to mind."[24] The relationship between God and Abraham reveals this dynamic. "And the Lord said, 'Shall I hide from Abraham what I am about to do, since Abraham will surely become a great and mighty nation, and in him all the nations of the earth will be blessed? For I have chosen him...'"[25] God gave Abraham and his people the calling to hear from God, to think God's thoughts after Him, to walk in God's ways and to reflect His light to the inhabitants of the earth.

God's heart to bring Israel into prophetic fullness is seen in Moses' wistful response to Joshua. Two Jewish elders, Eldad and Medad, were found prophesying inside the camp of Israel, though all of the elders were actually supposed to be present at a general meeting outside the camp, in front of the Tabernacle. Joshua ben Nun is quite upset at this lack of order, and bursts out: "Moses my lord, restrain them!" But Moses said to him with a sigh "Are you jealous for my sake? Would that all the Lord's people were prophets,

---

22   Gen. 20:7

23   Psa. 105:12-15

24   *Cf., The Gift of Prophecy in the New Testament and Today,* Wayne Grudem, Westchester: Crossway, 1988.

25   Gen. 18:17-19

and that the Lord would put His Spirit upon them!"[26]

God chose Israel to be a prophetic people. Paul the Apostle reminds us in the Book of Romans that the gifts God gave to the Jewish people and His calling upon their lives are irrevocable![27] God has never repented of choosing Israel, and He will never rescind His prophetic calling which, like an unfurled banner, flutters over the heads of the Jewish nation. No human being has yet seen Israel come into the fullness of her prophetic calling. Will that fullness come in our generation?

Why Are All These Faces Shining?

One aspect of Israel's prophetic calling is usually overlooked by modern Bible students – Israel's irrevocable calling to be a light and a servant to the Gentiles. This theme begins to bud in the Book of Numbers, as God instructs the high priestly line of Aaron about the proper way to bless all the tribes of Israel.

> Then the Lord spoke to Moses and said, 'Speak to
> Aaron and to his sons, saying, "In this way you are
> to bless the sons of Israel. You shall say to them: 'The
> Lord bless you and keep you. The Lord make His face
> shine on you and be gracious to you. The Lord lift
> up His countenance on you and give you peace!'[28]

God tells the priests to invoke His mighty name over Israel three times, and to ask Him to shine the glory of His face upon the Jewish people. Since God Himself created the words of this prayer, we know that this prayer is one He really wants to answer! In response to this prayer, God promises to pour out rivers of blessing, protection, grace and peace upon the Jewish people. God's light illuminating Israel's upraised faces will be visible proof that all the other promised blessings are on their way.

Moses had an experience like this in his own life. After he had received the Ten Commandments for the second time, the Book of

---

26 Num. 11:28-29
27 Rom. 11:28-29
28 Num. 6:22-27

Exodus tells us: "And it came about when Moses was coming down from Mount Sinai... that (he) did not know that the skin of his face shone because of his speaking with (the Lord). So when Aaron and all the sons of Israel saw Moses, behold, the skin of his face shone, and they were afraid to come near him."[29] As Aaron and the Jewish people gazed at the shining face of Moses, they saw with their own eyes that Moses had met with God and was now delivering a prophetic message from the Almighty. In a similar way, God's original plan was to have a relationship of intimacy with all the tribes of Israel, to shine the light of His favor on the Jewish people, to so bless the descendants of Jacob that all the nations of the earth would be able to look at Israel and with their own eyes see that God's promise to Abraham was true.

The Levitical blessing we looked at in Numbers 6 is actually a prophetic key which opens the door to an event of world-shaking proportions. That event is fleshed out in Psalm 67. Let's briefly look at the psalm.

Psalm 67

*Notes for the music director:
use stringed instruments; this is both a psalm and a song

May God be gracious to us and bless us
and make His face shine upon us [Selah]
That Your ways may be known on earth,
Your salvation among all nations.
May the peoples praise You, O God;
may all the peoples praise You.
May the nations be glad and sing for joy,
For You rule the peoples justly
and guide the nations of the earth [Selah]
May the peoples praise You, O God;
may all the peoples praise You.
Then the land will yield its harvest,
and God, our God, will bless us.

29   Exod. 34:29-30; cf., 2 Cor. 3:7-11,18

God will bless us, and all the ends of the earth will fear
Him.
(*my translation*)

As the psalmist puts quill to papyrus, he feels God stirring his
heart, bringing to mind Numbers 6. So, in the ancient words of the
Aaronic benediction, he asks God to bless Israel. Perhaps the author
of this psalm was himself a descendant of Aaron, interceding
according to his own priestly calling. As the Holy Spirit breathes
upon his mind, the psalmist finds himself drawing a connection
between two seemingly unconnected events – blessing for Israel on
the one hand, and spiritual enlightenment for the Gentile nations
on the other. So he lifts his voice and cries out, asking that divine
blessing might truly fall in power upon the Jewish people according
to God's promise.

"If only God's light would shine on Israel and radiate off her
face into the world!" he groans. "Then all the nations on earth
would be drawn to the beauty and power of the God of Israel." The
psalmist knew that the Gentiles would 'believe it when they see it:'
they would believe in God's saving power when they would see it
incarnated in the lives of the Jewish people and glowing on Hebrew
faces.

Psalm 67 creates a biblical connection between two events –
Israel coming into a promised place of blessing and intimacy with
her God, and the great harvest of the nations as the fruit of Israel's
revival.When Israel's face will shine with the oil of God's blessing,
all the peoples will be saved. As we shall now see, this was the
original prophetic pattern received by psalmists and prophets.

Isaiah the prophet saw a similar vision in his day. He beheld a
time in the distant future when gross spiritual darkness would
cover all Gentile nations. A smoggy cloud of materialism and
sensuality would one day blanket the whole Gentile world. Yet in
the middle of that future darkness, a blazing light would break
forth out of Heaven and cut through the soot, illuminating the face

of the Jewish nation.

> Arise, shine, for your light has come, and the glory
> of the Lord has shined on you. For behold, darkness
> has covered the earth, and thick fog has covered the
> nations. But on you the Lord will shine, and His glory
> will be seen upon you. And nations will come to your
> light, and kings to the brightness of your rising![30]

Another Scriptural example shows this principle in action. The Queen of Sheba (modern Yemen) crossed the Arabian desert to observe the Jewish people and their wise king Solomon. Deeply impressed by what she saw, she announced publicly, "Blessed be the Lord your God who delighted in you to set you on the throne of Israel. Because the Lord loved Israel forever, therefore He made you king, to do justice and righteousness."[31] A Gentile queen's heart turns to God in praise and blessing. Why? Because she acknowledges that God has chosen Israel, and she perceives His light and delight shining both on King Solomon and on the Jewish people.

Another example of this principle is found in Psalm 117.

Psalm 117

Praise the Lord, all nations!
Laud Him, all the peoples!
For heroically powerful is His covenant-faithfulness to us
And the Lord's truth is eternal!
Halleluya!
(*my translation*)

Here the psalmist encourages the world to praise and worship

---

30 Isa. 60:1-3. Though many Gentiles in the church have applied this passage primarily to themselves, Paul the Apostle sees the context of Isaiah 59-60 as referring to the Jewish people. In Rom. 11:26 he quotes Isa.59:20 with reference to Israel alone, utterly convinced that Yeshua will come back to His Jewish people in a special way, removing the sins of all those in Jacob who return to Him. Further, the entire chapter of Isa. 60 describes the physical ingathering of the Jewish people from their 2,700 year of exile, and depicts in detail the help that believing Gentiles will extend to them in days to come.

31 1 Kgs. 10:9

the Lord because His *hesed* (a Hebrew word signifying faithfulness to a covenant or love based on covenant) is overpoweringly great towards the Jewish people. It may initially surprise some readers to understand the psalm this way, to wrestle with the clear sense of the Hebrew text. Even more thought provoking is the fact that this message was chanted in Jerusalem's Temple in the Hebrew tongue only for a thousand years before the Gentile nations had any idea of what God was saying!

So why did God ask the nations to be excited and thankful that Israel has some kind of divine priority? Paul the apostle helps us to unpack this concept in Ephesians 2:11-12. He reminds his non-Jewish readers that, during the time period when Psalm 117 was composed, Gentiles were "excluded from the commonwealth of Israel, and strangers to the covenants of promise, having no hope and without God in the world." One of the reasons God called Israel His chosen nation was to bring great blessing to all nations. Another less palatable reason why God chose the Jewish people was to test Gentile hearts. Would non-Jews be willing to humble themselves, taking on the attitude of a servant, and bless God's wisdom in choosing Israel? Not everyone would be able to respond like the Roman centurion in the Gospel of Luke, who loved the Jewish nation, ministered material blessing to them, and realized that, as a Gentile, he had no automatic access to God's promises. Amazingly, Yeshua Himself proclaimed over this nameless centurion, "I say to you, not even in Israel have I found such great faith!"[32] Luke's Roman centurion is an ideal example of the heart attitude God is looking for among the nations.

Servant of All

God chose the Jewish people because He loved them and honored His word to Jacob's descendants. But God also had a job for Israel to do: He chose Israel to reflect God's light onto all the nations of the world. The Hebrews were to be God's magnifying glass, focusing

---

32   Lk. 7:1-10

the light of God's word and presence upon the nations lost in a black hole of sin. The Jewish people were to be a model society set on a hill, a community of light. Israel's happiness and blessing was to blaze brightly in a dark world driven insane by ambition and strife.

God said that Israel would be "My own possession among all the peoples, for all the earth is Mine. And you shall be to Me a kingdom of priests and a holy nation."[33] The Lord declared that the Jews were "His people, a treasured possession, as He promised you... and that He shall set you high above all nations which He has made, for praise, fame, and honor; and that you shall be a consecrated people to the Lord your God, as He has spoken."[34] Whatever light and blessing God poured out on Israel was meant to overflow to the nations as well.

In the 8th century B.C. God spoke through Isaiah the prophet, declaring that the whole Jewish nation is His servants: "But you, O Israel, My servant; Jacob, whom I have chosen; you descendants of Abraham My friend; I took you from the ends of the earth, from its farthest corners I called you. I said, 'You are My servant'; I have chosen you and have not rejected you."[35] God chose the Jewish people to serve Him by being His messengers. They would bring His truth and the good news of His love for mankind to the farthest reaches of this planet. The Apostle Paul made this same point in his Shabbat *derasha* (sermon) given at the Jewish synagogue of Pisidian Antioch. "For this is what the Lord has commanded us: 'I have made you a light for the Gentiles, that you may bring salvation to the ends of the earth.'"[36]

Yeshua the Messiah was once teaching a Jewish gathering about the high value of servanthood in God's sight. "You know that those who are regarded as rulers of the Gentiles lord it over them, and their high officials exercise authority over them. Not so with you.

---

33   Exod. 19:5-6
34   Deut. 26:18-19
35   Isa. 41:8-9
36   Acts 13:47 quoting Isa. 49:6

Instead, whoever wants to become great among you must be your servant, and whoever wants to be first must be slave of all."[37] These words are a Messianic invitation to the entire Jewish people: Israel will blossom and fill the world with fruit only when she becomes securely rooted in the rich black soil of a servant's heart.

A land, a people and a blessing; a prophetic people, a flaming nation and a servant community – all these glittering facets are part of what God intended for His amazing Jewish jewel, Israel the Chosen People.

---

37   Mk. 10:42-44

Chapter Three

Broken Branches, Broken Heart

God's intentions for the Jewish people are painted in brilliant colors in the Bible. But it's obvious that not everything in Jewish history has been peaches and cream! Two magnificent Temples have been razed to the ground in Jerusalem. The people of Israel have been scattered twice across the face of this planet. Less than sixty years ago, six million Jews were starved, shot or gassed to death by Nazi forces. What happened to God's original plan?

Sin – The International Common Denominator

When Adam and Eve sinned, there was physical fallout – the ground was cursed with thistles and thorns. There was spiritual fallout too. Humans no longer had a close relationship with God. Adam and Eve were banished from the Garden, from the presence of God their Father.

Within a few generations sin quickly increased to where "the

Lord saw how great man's wickedness on the earth had become, and that every inclination of the thoughts of his heart was only evil all the time. The Lord was grieved that He had made man on the earth, and His heart was filled with pain."[1]

God chose Abraham and his Jewish descendants to be part of the solution to sin. But since the Jewish people are also descendants of Adam and Eve, they share in mankind's sinful condition. Jews do not automatically have a personal relationship with God. King Solomon, the wisest man who ever lived, was aware that Jews are sinners just like the rest of the world. He prayed to God at the dedication of the First Temple:

> When the Jewish people sin against You – and there
> is no one who does not sin – and You become angry
> with them and give them over to the enemy, who
> takes them captive to his own land...and if they have
> a change of heart, and repent and ...say, "We have
> sinned, we have done wrong, we have acted wickedly"...
> then ... forgive Your people, who have sinned against
> You; forgive all the offenses they have committed
> against You... For You singled them out from all the
> nations of the world to be Your own inheritance...[2]

Israel was fashioned to be part of God's solution to the problem of sin. But it would come as a shock to the Jewish people to discover that they too were part of the sin problem.

If You O Lord Kept a Record of Sins...

In modern democracies politicians make use of propaganda experts called 'spin doctors.' Spin doctors use television, newspapers and magazines to make defeats appear like victories. They hush up scandals, turn slanderous attacks into savage counter-attacks, and always protest that their clients are squeaky clean. In contrast, the authors of the Bible were poor spin doctors! They prophesied to Israel's spiritual condition, warts and all.

1 Gen. 6:5, 6

2 1 Kings 8:46-53

Because the Bible speaks openly about Israel's sins, some have concluded that Jews are more sinful than other peoples. When the Scriptures say that "the sin of Judah is written down with an iron stylus, with a diamond point it is engraved upon the tablet,"[3] unfriendly observers shake their heads in self-righteous horror and say, "Aren't the Jews hard-hearted and sinfully stiff-necked? After all, they perversely refuse to follow the truth !"

The Apostle Paul is concerned that Gentiles understand why Jewish sins are detailed in the Bible. To Gentiles who feel that they are better than Jews, Paul asks: "What then? Are we better than they? Not at all; for we have already charged that both Jews and Greeks are all under sin, as it is written, 'There is none righteous, not even one...'"[4] God lets mankind take a good look at Jewish sin so that the nations might understand one simple point: Jewish sin and Gentile sin are surprisingly similar. As the psalmist said, "If You, O Lord, kept a record of sins, O Lord, who could stand? But with You there is forgiveness; therefore You are feared."[5]

The following pages describe four areas of sin in which the Jewish people participated. For centuries the prophets pleaded with Israel to turn from these destructive ways back to their God.

I Did It My Way

Moses warned Israel about trusting in themselves. God didn't want the Jewish people to boast in their own achievements, power or religious observance.

> When you have eaten and are satisfied...be careful that
> you do not forget the Lord your God ... Otherwise ...
> when you build fine houses ... when your ... flocks
> grow large and your silver and gold increase and all
> you have is multiplied, then your heart will become
> proud and you will forget the Lord your God ... You
> may say to yourself, "My power and the strength of

---

3   Jer. 17:1

4   Rom. 3:9-10 quoting Psa. 14:1

5   Psa. 130:3-4

my hands have produced this wealth for me." But remember the Lord your God, for it is He who gives you the ability to produce wealth, and so confirms His covenant, which He swore to your forefathers...[6]

After the Lord your God has driven (ed., the seven nations) out before you, do not say to yourself, "The Lord has brought me here to take possession of this land because of my righteousness." No, it is on account of the wickedness of these nations that the Lord is going to drive them out before you...not because of your righteousness or your integrity... to accomplish what He swore to your fathers, to Abraham, Isaac and Jacob.[7]

For seven hundred years God warned the Jewish people through the prophets, but the majority of Israel refused to follow God's ways of wisdom. In the days of Hosea God finally said:

But I am the Lord your God...You shall acknowledge no God but Me, no Savior except Me. I cared for you in the desert, in the land of burning heat. When I fed them, they were satisfied; when they were satisfied, they became proud; then they forgot Me. So I will come upon them like a lion, like a leopard I will lurk by the path.[8]

Seven hundred years after God warned of coming judgment in Hosea, the Apostle Paul sadly admitted that many of his own Jewish people still trusted in their own righteousness: "Brothers, my heart's desire and prayer to God for Israel is that they may be saved. For I can testify about them... (that) they did not know the righteousness that comes from God and sought to establish their own."[9]

Are You Calling Me a Prostitute?

It's not a compliment to call someone a prostitute. Yet at various

---

6   Deut. 8:10-14, 17-20

7   Deut. 9:4-6

8   Hos. 13:4-8

9   Rom. 10:1-4

times God has accused the Jewish people of prostitution. He was not only referring to sexual immorality. The Bible sometimes describes worship of a deity in terms of sexual union between the god and the worshipper. Positive examples of this can be found in Ezekiel 16 and the Song of Solomon.[10] On the down side, idol worship is described by the prophets as spiritual prostitution.

Moses first warned the Jewish people about the dangers of spiritual prostitution. One of the commandments in the Torah, to wear the *tzitzit* or fringed garments, was intended by God to be an outward token of an inward commitment. "You will have these tassels to look at and so you will remember all the commands of the Lord, that you may obey them and not prostitute yourselves by going after the lusts of your own hearts and eyes."[11] God prophesied to Moses just before his death that, even though the Jewish people wore *tzitzit*, they would soon commit spiritual prostitution. "And the Lord said to Moses: 'You are going to rest with your fathers, and these people will soon prostitute themselves to the foreign gods of the land they are entering. They will forsake Me and break the covenant I made with them.'"[12]

Israel's problem had a spiritual source. "I know all about Ephraim; Israel is not hidden from Me. Ephraim, you have now turned to prostitution; Israel is corrupt. Their deeds do not permit them to return to their God. A spirit of prostitution is in their heart; they do not acknowledge the Lord."[13]

Over one hundred years later Ezekiel and Jeremiah conveyed the anguished cry of God's heart to the Jewish people trapped in spiritual prostitution.

> But you (Israel) trusted in your beauty and used your
> fame to become a prostitute. You lavished your favors on

---

10   The Song of Songs is understood by many rabbis and pastors on two levels — as a physical description of the joys of married love, but also as a mystical description of the love affair between God and His people.

11   Num. 15:39

12   Deut. 31:16

13   Hos. 5:3-4

anyone who passed by and your beauty became his...How weak-willed you are, declares the Sovereign Lord, when you do all these things, acting like a brazen prostitute!... Therefore, you prostitute, hear the word of the Lord![14]

Long ago (Israel) you broke off your yoke and tore off your bonds; you said, "I will not serve You!" Indeed, on every high hill and under every spreading tree you lay down as a prostitute... How can you say, "I am not defiled; I have not run after the Baals"... (Y)ou said, "It's no use! I love foreign gods, and I must go after them."[15]

Heart of Stone

God also wanted the Jewish people to take a look at their own hardheartedness. Lack of compassion for people had once been the sin of ancient Sodom. But in Ezekiel's day this sin now characterized the people of Judah.

As surely as I live, declares the Sovereign Lord, your sister Sodom and her daughters never did what you and your daughters have done. Now this was the sin of your sister Sodom: she and her daughters were arrogant, overfed and unconcerned; they did not help the poor and needy. They were haughty and did detestable things before me. Therefore I did away with them as you have seen...You have done more detestable things than they, and have made your sisters seem righteous...[16]

One hundred years later in the Book of Zechariah God reminded Israel that her history of hardheartedness stretched from the Egyptian Exodus to the Babylonian Exile:

This is what the Lord Almighty says: "Administer true justice; show mercy and compassion to one another. Do not oppress the widow or the fatherless, the alien or the poor. In your hearts do not think evil of each other." But they refused to pay attention; stubbornly they turned

14   Ezek. 16:15, 30, 35

15   Jer. 2:20-25

16   Ezek. 16:48-51

their backs and stopped up their ears. They made their hearts as hard as flint and would not listen to the law or to the words that the Lord Almighty had sent by His Spirit through the earlier prophets. So the Lord Almighty was very angry. "When I called, they did not listen; so when they called, I would not listen," says the Lord Almighty. "I scattered them with a whirlwind among all the nations, where they were strangers. The land was left so desolate behind them that no one could come or go."[17]

False Shepherds in Shepherds' Clothing

In Bible days the Jewish people followed their leaders for better or for worse. When godly kings led Israel, the nation remained godly. When evil kings came to the throne, the nation quickly abandoned true worship and consorted with idols. Godly shepherds were a blessing from Heaven, but evil kings and priests brought judgment on the Jewish people. "Righteousness exalts a nation, but sin is a disgrace to any people."[18]

In the Book of Ezekiel the God of Israel took up a lament against the evil kings and priests who were abusing His Jewish people:

Son of man, prophesy against the shepherds of Israel; prophesy and say to them: "This is what the Sovereign Lord says: Woe to the shepherds of Israel who only take care of themselves! Should not shepherds take care of the flock? You eat the curds, clothe yourselves with the wool and slaughter the choice animals, but you do not take care of the flock. You have not strengthened the weak or healed the sick or bound up the injured. You have not brought back the strays or searched for the lost. You have ruled them harshly and brutally. So they were scattered because there was no shepherd, and when they were scattered they became food for all the wild animals. My sheep wandered over all the mountains and on every high hill. They were scattered over the whole earth,

17   Zech. 7:8-14
18   Prov. 14:34

and no one searched or looked for them. Therefore, you shepherds, hear the word of the Lord: I am against the shepherds and will hold them accountable for My flock."[19]

Judgment Day

God had called Israel to be a living example of faithfulness, righteousness and light. But if the Jewish people disregarded God's calling and embraced sin, they would become an example of God's impartial judgment. Isaiah said it in a nutshell, "When Your judgments come upon the earth, the people of the world learn righteousness. Though grace is shown to the wicked, they do not learn righteousness; even in a land of uprightness they go on doing evil and regard not the majesty of the Lord."[20]

Like the builders of the Tower of Babel, the Jewish people did not understand how much it would cost to turn their backs on God's calling. In Isaiah's day the Lord needed to spell it out clearly.

> You have neither heard nor understood; from of old your ear has not been open. Well do I know how treacherous you are; you were called a rebel from birth. For My own name's sake I delay My wrath; for the sake of My praise I hold it back from you, so as not to cut you off. See, I have refined you, though not as silver; I have tested you in the furnace of affliction. For My own sake, for My own sake, I do this. How can I let Myself be defamed? I will not yield My glory to another.[21]

Israel's chosenness implied greater responsibility and greater judgment: "You only have I chosen of all the families of the earth; therefore I will punish you for all your sins."[22]

Moses prophesied that judgments on Israel would come in successive waves and in increasing severity. Jewish disobedience to God would lead to drought, plague, invasion, forced resettlement

---

19   Ezek. 34:1-7, 10

20   Isa. 26:9-10

21   Isa. 48:8-11

22   Amos 3:2;*Cf.*, Isa. 40:2; Rom. 2:5-11.

and finally exile.[23] About 750 B.C. God explained how He had attempted to get Israel's attention on these matters, but to no avail.

> I gave you empty stomachs in every city and lack of bread in every town, yet you have not returned to Me, declares the Lord. I also withheld rain from you when the harvest was still three months away. I sent rain on one town, but withheld it from another. One field had rain; another had none and dried up. People staggered from town to town for water but did not get enough to drink, yet you have not returned to Me, declares the Lord. Many times I struck your gardens and vineyards, I struck them with blight and mildew. Locusts devoured your fig and olive trees, yet you have not returned to Me, declares the Lord. I sent plagues among you as I did to Egypt. I killed your young men with the sword, along with your captured horses. I filled your nostrils with the stench of your camps, yet you have not returned to Me, declares the Lord. I overthrew some of you as I overthrew Sodom and Gomorrah. You were like a burning stick snatched from the fire, yet you have not returned to Me, declares the Lord. Therefore this is what I will do to you, Israel, and because I will do this to you, prepare to meet your God, O Israel.[24]

Ultimately God would exile Israel to Assyria and Babylon which today are in Iraq. There they would have opportunity to consider their ways, repent and return to the Lord.

> Son of man, when the people of Israel were living in their own land, they defiled it by their conduct and their actions. Their conduct was like a woman's monthly uncleanness in My sight. So I poured out My wrath on them because they had shed blood in the land and because they had defiled it with their idols. I dispersed them among the nations, and they were scattered through the countries; I judged them according to their conduct and their actions. And wherever they went among the nations they profaned My holy name, for it was said of them,

23   *Cf.*, Deut. 28:15-68

24   Amos 4:6-12

"These are the Lord's people, and yet they had to leave His land." I had concern for My holy name, which the house of Israel profaned among the nations where they had gone.[25]

Sour Grapes in The Vineyard

Seven hundred years before Yeshua (Jesus) began His earthly ministry, the prophet Isaiah sang a song of mourning over the Jewish people, using the poetic imagery of a vine:

> I will sing for the one I love a song about His vineyard: My loved one had a vineyard on a fertile hillside. He dug it up and cleared it of stones and planted it with the choicest vines. He built a watchtower in it and cut out a winepress as well. Then He looked for a crop of good grapes, but it yielded only bad fruit. "Now you dwellers in Jerusalem and men of Judah, judge between Me and My vineyard. What more could have been done for My vineyard than I have done for it? When I looked for good grapes, why did it yield only bad? Now I will tell you what I am going to do to My vineyard: I will take away its hedge, and it will be destroyed; I will break down its wall, and it will be trampled. I will make it a wasteland, neither pruned nor cultivated, and briers and thorns will grow there. I will command the clouds not to rain on it." The vineyard of the Lord Almighty is the House of Israel, and the men of Judah are the garden of His delight. And He looked for justice, but saw bloodshed; for righteousness, but heard cries of distress... Therefore my people will go into exile for lack of understanding; their men of rank will die of hunger and their masses will be parched with thirst... But the Lord Almighty will be exalted by His justice, and the holy God will show Himself holy by His righteousness.[26]

When Yeshua the Messiah came to His own people, He found bad fruit. He was "despised and rejected" by Sadducean priests, and was called a false Messiah by many Pharisee theologians. Yeshua

---

25   Ezek. 36:16-21
26   Isa. 5:1-7, 13, 16

responded to Israel's false shepherds in a parable based on Isaiah 5.

> Listen to another parable: There was a landowner who planted a vineyard. He put a wall around it, dug a winepress in it and built a watchtower. Then he rented out the vineyard to some farmers and when away on a journey. When harvest time approached, he sent his servants to the tenants to collect his fruit. The tenants seized his servants: they beat one, killed another, and stoned a third. Then he sent other servants to them, more than the first, and the tenants treated them the same way. Last of all, he sent his son to them. "They will respect my son,' He said. But when the tenants saw the son, they said to each other, "This is the heir. Come, let's kill him and take his inheritance." So they took him and threw him out of the vineyard and killed him. Therefore, when the owner of the vineyard comes, what will he do to those tenants? They replied, "He will bring those wretches to a wretched end, and he will rent out the vineyard to other tenants, who will give him his share of the crop at harvest time. Yeshua said to them, "Have you never read in the Scriptures, 'The stone that the builders rejected has become the capstone. The Lord has done this, and it is marvelous in our eyes"? ... He who falls on this stone will be broken to pieces, but he on whom it falls will be crushed." When the chief priests and the Pharisees heard Yeshua's parables, they knew He was talking about them.[27]

Some of the Branches Were Broken Off

These four areas of sin would now bring judgment to Judah and Israel. When Jeremiah spoke of the coming judgments, he described the Jewish people as a beautiful olive tree. "The Lord called you a thriving olive tree with fruit beautiful in form. But with the roar of a mighty storm He will set it on fire, and its branches will be broken."[28]

The task of chronicling this process fell to Paul the Apostle. In

27   Matt. 21:33-42, 44-45
28   Jer. 11:16

Romans 11 he addresses Gentile believers in Rome, attempting to set the record straight. Yes, it is true that God broke off some Jewish branches, but also "No" – not all of the Jewish people were broken off. "(S)ome of the (Jewish) branches have been broken off... But they were broken off because of unbelief, and you (Gentiles) stand by faith. Do not be arrogant, but be afraid. For if God did not spare the natural branches, He will not spare you either."[29]

A sobering prophetic event had occurred in Israel. The false shepherds had been weighed in God's balances, had been judged and found wanting. The majority of Israel's leaders would soon discover that the candlestick of their spiritual authority had been snuffed out by God. Forty years after Yeshua's prophecy and His crucifixion, Herod's magnificent Temple would be gutted by Roman flames, and Israeli prisoners would glut the slave markets of the Mediterranean Basin. The *Hurban Bayit Sheni*, the Great Destruction of the Second Jewish Commonwealth, was God's decisive response to Israel's rejection of Yeshua.

The Broken Heart of God

It was not an easy thing for God to judge His people and let the nations violate the Daughter of Zion. The anguished cry of God's broken heart screams from the pages of Scripture. "How can I give you up, Ephraim? How can I hand you over, Israel? How can I treat you like Admah? How can I make you like Zeboiim? My heart is changed within Me; all My compassion is aroused!"[30] "Is not Ephraim My dear son, the child in whom I delight? Though I often speak against him, I still remember him. Therefore My heart yearns for him; I have great compassion for him, declares the Lord."[31]

The Bible tells us that God often puts His own plans, thoughts, concerns and feelings into the hearts of His prophets.[32] As Paul the

---

29   Rom. 11:17, 20-21

30   Hos. 11:8. Admah and Zeboiim, two towns in the area of Sodom and Gomorrah, were destroyed by God in Abraham's day.*Cf.*, Gen. 14:2; Deut. 29:23.

31   Jer. 31:20

32   *Cf.*, Neh. 2:12; 2 Cor.8:16

Apostle meditated on Israel's sins and the judgment of God, he cried out in anguish. Then he let his readers know that the anguish was not his alone – the heart-wrenching sobbing for Israel that filled his own being came from the broken heart of the Holy Spirit. "I speak the truth in Messiah – I am not lying, my conscience confirms it in the Holy Spirit – I have great sorrow and unceasing anguish in my heart. For I could wish that I myself were cursed and cut off from Messiah for the sake of my brothers, those of my race, the people of Israel..."[33]

When a parent disciplines his child, he often says, "This will hurt me more than it hurts you!" Probably few children believe their parents' words. But when the Messiah weeps over His own city, we know that the heart of God is broken over the broken condition of His own people.

> As (Yeshua) approached Jerusalem and saw the city,
> He wept over it and said, "If you, even you, had only
> known on this day what would bring you peace – but
> now it is hidden from your eyes. The days will come
> upon you when your enemies will build an embankment
> against you and encircle you and hem you in on every
> side. They will dash you to the ground, you and the
> children within your children within your walls. They
> will not leave one stone on another because you did
> not recognize the time of God's coming to you."[34]

---

33   Rom. 9:1-4a
34   Lk. 19:41-44

Chapter Four

Life from the Dead

The Ministry of Jealousy

When Israel's religious leaders turned their backs on Messiah, they were also turning their backs on the privilege of remaining on the cutting edge of God's kingdom. God was passing the spiritual torch on to the Gentile nations. During the first century A.D. Jewish evangelists spread the Good News of Yeshua's life, death and resurrection across the Roman and Parthian Empires. Millions embraced the gospel. The original Messianic Jewish movement met with such great success that it quickly became Gentile in makeup, in government, in culture and in theological expression. On the cupolas of churches across the world Yeshua the curly-headed and olive-skinned Jewish Messiah was being transformed into a blond Northern European Jesus Christ.

The transfer of the spiritual baton from Jews to Gentiles had been prophesied in the Torah:

> (The Jewish people) made Him jealous with their foreign
> gods and angered Him with their detestable idols. They
> sacrificed to demons, which are not God...The Lord...
> was angered by His sons and daughters. "I will hide My
> face from them," He said, "and see what their end will
> be; for they are a perverse generation, children who are
> unfaithful. They made Me jealous by what is no god
> and angered Me with their worthless idols. I will make
> them envious by those who are not a people; I will make
> them angry by a nation that has no understanding."[1]

The Jewish leadership's loss would be the Gentile nations' gain.
Paul announced to Rome's Jewish leaders, "Therefore I want you
to know that God's salvation has been sent to the Gentiles, and
they will listen!"[2] In the Letter to the Romans he quotes from the
Torah to show how the Gentiles would come into God's kingdom
purposes. Not only that – the Gentiles would now be used to stir
up jealousy among the Jewish people and make them hungry for
God's salvation.

> Moses says, "I will make you envious by those who
> are not a nation; I will make you angry by a nation
> that has no understanding." And Isaiah boldly
> says, "I was found by those who did not seek Me; I
> revealed myself to those who did not ask for Me." But
> concerning Israel he says, "All day long I have held out
> My hands to a disobedient and obstinate people."[3]

Originally God had wanted the Jewish people to shine His light
on a darkened world and make Gentiles hungry for God. Now the
Gentiles would have a similar calling to the Jewish nation. "Again
I ask: Did they stumble so as to fall beyond recovery? Not at all!
Rather, because of their transgression, salvation has come to the

1 Deut. 32:16-21

2 Acts 28:28

3 Rom. 10:19-21

Gentiles to make Israel envious."[4]

But Christianity's new alliance with the Roman Empire did not move the Jewish people to godly envy. Christian art, architecture and theology did not stimulate spiritual jealousy in Israel's heart. No, only real spiritual fruit and godly character among the Gentiles will move the Jewish people to spiritual hunger. Yeshua had made the same point to Israel's leaders at the conclusion of His parable of the vineyard: "Therefore I tell you that the kingdom of God will be taken away from you and given to a people who will produce its fruit."[5] As Gentile leaders stepped up to the plate and took their turn at bat, would they produce the fruit God was looking for?

In moving the leadership of His earthly purposes from Jewish to Gentile hands, God had two goals in mind. He wanted to bring in a mighty harvest of all peoples. He also wanted to bring restoration to His people Israel. For the most part the Church today is focusing on the first of these two purposes – Gentile evangelism. As the day of Messiah's return approaches, the second emphasis, the restoration of Israel, will move to the center stage of the Church's attention.

The Original Full Gospel Message

In Romans 9-11 Paul helps the Gentile readers of his day to understand God's heart and purposes for the Jewish people. One of God's end-time promises is that the entire nation of Israel will come to faith in Yeshua. But even in Paul's day the Jewish people's rejection of Yeshua still had a blessed side-effect: the gospel was now freely offered to the nations. "(The Jewish people's) transgression means riches for the world, and their loss means riches for the Gentiles."[6]

Riches had come to the Gentile world. The nations were now the proud caretakers and guardians of the 'crown jewels' of the gospel. But a danger existed that Gentiles might start to get territorial and defensively hold on to their present situation. The Jews' misfortune had become the Gentiles' good fortune, and many would prefer to

4 Rom. 11:11

5 Matt. 21:43-44

6 Rom. 11:12

leave it that way! But no – Paul wants Gentile Christians to realize that one day Israel will come into her own. On the day Israel accepts Yeshua, the Jewish people will receive the full backlog of God's promises made to them since Abraham. Paul says that this Jewish fullness will also have another blessed side-effect for the nations, something he calls *much greater riches.* "How much greater riches will their fullness bring!"[7] When the majority of the Jewish nation gets grafted back into the tree of faith, all Gentile Christians will be overtaken by incredible spiritual riches. That is worth getting excited about!

It is true that in Messiah all believers have been blessed "with every spiritual blessing in the heavenlies."[8] Yet few believers fully experience every last one of these spiritual blessings on earth today. Many of these blessings will undoubtedly be our experience in Heaven. Some blessings will only be experienced when Yeshua returns to earth. The blessings of Romans 11:12, *the much greater riches,* will shower down on the nations only when Israel comes to faith. Paul wants everyone in the Church to know that these *much greater riches* exist. They are divine incentives moving us to pray and to labor for Israel's salvation.

The Second Coming is Jewish

The Bible says that history's most exciting days are yet to happen. Perhaps the most awesome of these events is the Second Coming. Every day millions of believers whisper the words, "Thy kingdom come, Thy will be done on earth as it is in Heaven." But many believers don't yet know that the Second Coming is on hold until Israel does a spiritual 'about-face' and changes her mind about Yeshua.

In the Gospel of Matthew Yeshua quotes Psalm 118:26, a psalm which prophesies about the Messiah. "O Jerusalem, Jerusalem, you who kill the prophets and stone those sent to you, how often I have

---

7 ibid.

8 Eph. 1:3

longed to gather your children together, as a hen gathers her chicks under her wings, but you were not willing. Look, your house is left to you desolate. For I tell you, you will not see Me again until you say, 'Blessed is He who comes in the name of the Lord.'"[9] The phrase *Baruch ha-Ba b'shem Adonai* ("Blessed is the one who comes in the name of the Lord') is a Hebrew greeting to God's representative. Yeshua prophesies that the Jewish people will not see their Messiah return to Zion until they as a people cry out to Him, acknowledging Him as God's Anointed. Only then will Messiah come.

What will it take to bring Israel over the threshold of national repentance so that they cry out to Yeshua? In Hosea the Lord says: "Then I will go back to My place until they admit their guilt. And they will seek My face; in their misery they will earnestly seek Me."[10] Hosea understood that only troubles of apocalyptic proportions will move Israel to turn to Yeshua. Zechariah describes the day when Israel will turn to the Lord: "And I will pour out on the house of David and the inhabitants of Jerusalem a spirit of grace and supplication. They will look on Me, the one they have pierced, and they will mourn for him as one mourns for an only child, and grieve bitterly for him as one grieves for a firstborn son."[11] Prayer for Israel's national repentance is high on God's list of intercessory priorities!

Rejected by God or by Men?

Years ago Bailey Smith, a former president of the Southern Baptist Convention in the USA, was preaching to a large gathering. At one point in his address he proclaimed, "God does not hear the prayer of a Jew!" A media firestorm resulted, and Bailey Smith later publicly apologized for his inaccurate remarks. Actually God hears the prayer of every human being. Mr. Smith probably intended to say that no man, not even a Jew, has guaranteed access to God except through Jesus Christ. Since that time it is to be hoped that

9 Matt. 23:37-39

10 Hos. 5:15; Cf., Dan. 12:7

11 Zech. 12:10

Mr. Smith has grown in his ability to communicate Christian truth regarding the Jewish people.

But it is no secret that many Christians secretly believe that God has rejected the Jewish people. They will not always voice these thoughts, but strong currents run deep. Chapter eight of this book considers the theological origins of this belief. In the meantime, is it true that God has rejected Israel?

In Romans 11:15 Paul declares concerning the Jewish people, "For if their rejection is the reconciliation of the world, what will their acceptance be but life from the dead?" Paul sometimes packs much meaning into so few words, and we need to take the time to unpack his 'shorthand' style.

The first question to be asked is this: what does Paul mean by the term *their rejection*? Is Paul saying that God rejected the Jewish people, or is he saying that the Jewish leadership rejected God? Romans 11:1-2 offers significant help: "I ask then: Did God reject His people? By no means! I am an Israelite myself, a descendant of Abraham, from the tribe of Benjamin. God did not reject His people, whom He foreknew." Paul categorically states that God has not rejected His people Israel. He then brings personal proof. Since Paul is Jewish and God has not rejected Paul, Paul's own existence serves as supporting evidence that God has not rejected Paul's people.

The testimony of the prophets agrees with Paul.

> They will pay for their sins because they rejected My laws and abhorred My decrees. Yet in spite of this, when they are in the land of their enemies, I will not reject them or abhor them so as to destroy them completely, breaking My covenant with them. I am the Lord their God. But for their sake I will remember the covenant with their ancestors whom I brought out of Egypt in the sight of the nations to be their God. I am the Lord.[12]

This is what the Lord says, He who appoints the sun to

---

12 Lev. 26:43-45

shine by day, who decrees the moon and stars to shine by night, who stirs up the sea so that its waves roar – the Lord Almighty is His name: Only if these decrees vanish from My sight, declares the Lord, will the descendants of Israel ever cease to be a nation before Me. This is what the Lord says: Only if the heavens above can be measured and the foundations of the earth below be searched out will I reject all the descendants of Israel because of all they have done, declares the Lord.[13]

The word of the Lord came to Jeremiah: "Have you not noticed that these people are saying, "The Lord has rejected the two kingdoms He chose?" So they despise My people and no longer regard them as a nation. This is what the Lord says: If I have not established My covenant with day and night and the fixed laws of heaven and earth, then I will reject the descendants of Jacob and David My servant and will not choose one of his sons to rule over the descendants of Abraham, Isaac and Jacob. For I will restore their fortunes and have compassion on them."[14]

For neither Israel nor Judah has been forsaken by his God, the Lord of hosts, although their land is full of guilt before the Holy One of Israel.[15]

Who is a God like You, who pardons sin and forgives the transgression of the remnant of His inheritance? You do not stay angry forever but delight to show mercy. You will again have compassion on us; You will tread our sins underfoot and hurl all our iniquities into the depths of the sea. You will be true to Jacob, and show mercy to Abraham, as You pledged on oath to our fathers in days long ago.[16]

(A)s far as election is concerned, (the Jewish

13 Jer. 31:35-37
14 Jer. 33:23-26
15 Jer. 51:5
16 Mic. 7:18

> people) are loved on account of the patriarchs,
> for God's gifts and His call are irrevocable.[17]

The broad teaching of Scripture is clear: God has not rejected nor will He ever reject the Jewish people. Therefore the term *their rejection* in Romans 11:15 cannot mean that God has rejected Israel. What actually happened is this: the Jewish people, represented by their leadership, have rejected God's Messiah. The term *their rejection* in Romans 11:15 means that a majority of Jews rejected Yeshua.

The same thought had just run through Paul's mind a few verses earlier in Romans 11:12. In verse 12 Paul uses a sentence structure similar to verse 15 as he talks about the Jewish people's transgression: "But if their transgression means riches for the world, and their loss means riches for the Gentiles, how much greater riches will their fullness bring!" The parallelism of thought between v.12 and v.15 (transgression/rejection, fullness/acceptance) emphasizes the point that the Jewish people's rejection of God, and not their rejection by God, is being discussed in Romans 11:15.

Life from the Dead

Though a majority of Jews have rejected Yeshua the Messiah, their rejection has produced a wonderful side-effect, *the reconciliation of the world*. What does this term mean? Does it mean that when Israel rejected Yeshua, all Gentiles immediately found peace with God? The Bible plainly teaches that only believers in Yeshua find peace with God.[18] A closer look reveals that the term *reconciliation of the nations* is simply another New Testament way to say 'the free offer of the gospel to the Gentiles.' For example, in 2 Corinthians 5:18-21 Paul calls evangelism *the ministry of reconciliation*. Paul is saying that the Jewish people's rejection of Yeshua has created a tremendous spiritual opportunity. An unprecedented harvest of all the nations is now a real possibility!

We now turn to consider the second part of Romans 11:15, "What

---

17 Rom. 11:28-29
18 Rom. 5:11

will their acceptance be but life from the dead?" What does Paul mean by the term *their acceptance*? Since the term *their rejection* means 'the Jewish people's rejection of Yeshua', the term *their acceptance* must mean 'the Jewish people's acceptance of Yeshua.' This is an astounding concept. Israel's accepting Yeshua will usher in life from the dead. Now we must unpack the new term 'life from the dead.' What does it mean? What will it look like?

Jaffa Oranges, Anyone?

It seems that Isaiah caught a glimmer of this wonderful future when he prophesied: "In days to come Jacob will take root, Israel will bud and blossom and fill all the world with fruit."[19] God is not thinking about Jaffa oranges here, but about a blessing coming through the Jewish people which will be international in scope. That blessing will be so great, and those riches will be so vast, that this scenario can only be described as *life from the dead*.

Paul's teaching on 'life from the dead' seems to run counter to what some believers have been taught, namely that the last great event before the return of Messiah Yeshua is Israel's national repentance. According to this viewpoint, the Jewish people turn to Messiah at the end of the Great Tribulation. Their prayer of repentance ends the Tribulation within a matter of days. This teaching says that during the Tribulation period, only one select group of 144,000 Jews will be sealed for a worldwide evangelistic ministry. No specifically productive role for the rest of the Jewish nation is emphasized in this scenario. What is left for Israel is to flee to the desert and wait for a supernatural deliverance when Yeshua returns.

Could it be that God has grander plans for the Jewish people than have yet been imagined? What if the whole nation of Israel will come to faith in Yeshua not as a 'last-minute event' before the Second Coming of Yeshua but while there is still productive time left? Imagine if the whole Jewish nation then enters into a cutting-edge evangelistic ministry outstripping what happened in the Book

---

19 Isa. 27:6

of Acts! When Paul says *life from the dead*, is he envisioning the boldest prophetic ministry the world has ever seen – Israel's future gift to the world? Perhaps God never intended for the predominantly Gentile church to complete the Great Commission alone. Israel's spiritual contribution just might be the decisive factor.

We Are The Army of God

Over 2,600 years ago Ezekiel was given the 'vision of the dry bones.'

> The hand of the Lord was upon me, and He brought me out by the Spirit of the Lord and set me in the middle of a valley; it was full of bones. He led me back and forth among them, and I saw a great many bones on the floor of the valley, bones that were very dry. He asked me, "Son of man, can these bones live?" I said, "O Sovereign Lord, You alone know"...Then He said to me, "Prophesy to the breath; prophesy, son of man, and say to it, "This is what the Sovereign Lord says: Come from the four winds, O breath, and breathe into these slain, that they may live.' So I prophesied as He commanded me, and breath entered them; they came to life and stood up on their feet – a vast army. Then He said to me: "Son of man, these bones are the whole house of Israel. They say, 'Our bones are dried up and our hope is gone; we are cut off.' Therefore prophesy and say to them: 'This is what the Sovereign Lord says: O my people, I am going to open your graves and bring you up from them; I will bring you back to the land of Israel. Then you, My people, will know that I am the Lord, when I open your graves and bring you up from them. I will put My Spirit in you and you will live, and I will settle you in your own land. Then you will know that I the Lord have spoken, and I have done it, declares the Lord.'"[20]

Ezekiel looked down through the ages and saw the nation of Israel scattered across the planet like dead bones strewn across a

---

20 Ezek. 37:1-3, 9-14

valley. Pogroms, gulags and death camps had nearly finished them off. Israel's voice is a hoarse whisper, "We are completely cut off!" God's heart of compassion is stirred, and He promises to open up the graves of His people, to restore them to the land of Israel and to bring them back from the dead.

In Ezekiel's vision the Jewish people are too traumatized to understand that God is restoring them. The text indicates that Israel becomes aware of her God only gradually, after life begins to course through her national veins. Then the Holy Spirit is placed within the Jewish people,[21] they are returned again to their homeland, they come to life and they stand on their feet, an exceedingly great army. Have you ever considered why God will raise up this great army? What exploits will it do? God has gone on record promising to transform the whole nation of Israel into a mighty army of believers. Will this army be created only to stand at attention and welcome Yeshua a few seconds before He returns to this earth? Could it be that God has greater plans than this?

In various passages the Scriptures describe a faith-filled Israeli army which defeats all its future enemies. The favor of God rests upon this army.[22] Could life from the dead also be related to the future activities of this born-again Jewish fighting force? Will world evangelism be one of the main objectives of these crack soldiers? Will this Jewish army be on the cutting edge of the body of Messiah as it fulfills the Great Commission in our generation?

End-Time Revival and Israel

The term *life from the dead* might refer to the physical resurrection of the dead.[23] If that is the preferred meaning of *life from the dead* in this context, then Romans 11:15 teaches that the Jewish people's salvation will trigger the first resurrection and the thousand-year reign of Messiah in a rebuilt Jerusalem.

---

21 Cf., Jer. 31:33-34; Ezek. 11:17-20

22 Eg., Isa.11:11-14; Isa. 41:12-16; Jer. 51:19-24; Joel 2:11; Oba. 17-21; Mic .4:11-13; 5:7-9; Zech. 12:4-6; 14:14; etc. The operating principle behind the concept of this victorious army is reflected in Psa. 118:10-12.

23 Cf., Dan. 12:2; Rev. 20:4-6

Another possible meaning is that the term *life from the dead* is describing Israel as a spiritually reborn nation, like Ezekiel's vision in chapter 37. It will certainly be exciting for the world to see Israel truly alive and totally in love with God for the first time in a long while! Yet it seems that the earth-shaking proportions of the term *life from the dead* would barely be touched were one to limit this verse to Israel's restoration alone.

Life from the dead can also describe physical resuscitation or spiritual revival. In 2 Kings13:21 an interrupted funeral ended up with a corpse being hastily thrown into Elisha the prophet's grave. When the dead body touched Elisha's bones, the man "revived' (NASB) and stood up on his feet. Another example of life from the dead is found in Yeshua's parable of the prodigal son. The prodigal had strayed from intimacy with his father. Upon his return, his father rejoiced and proclaimed that "this brother of yours was dead and is alive again..."[24]

Life from the dead could be describing a time nearly upon us, when the body of Messiah will be utterly captivated by the beauty and holiness of Yeshua; when the church will be given a revived spirit to love God with all her heart, soul and strength; when intimacy with God will be the believer's crown, and purity and power will be the jewels; when compassion and kindness, healing and humility will characterize Messianic believers. Will this end-time revival will be catalyzed by a mighty army of on-fire Jewish prophets and evangelists, spiritual shock-troops preaching the holiness and compassion of God to men and women across this planet?

As the God of Israel brings greater clarity to His body concerning the exact meaning of *life from the dead*, every believer should look forward to this event with barely contained excitement. The Jewish people are God's strategic key which will open the door to the most awesome events this planet has ever seen – the Second Coming, life from the dead, a world filled with fruit, and much greater riches! "But the plans of the Lord stand firm forever, the purposes of His

---

24 Lk. 15:32

heart through all generations. Blessed is the nation whose God is the Lord, the people He chose for His inheritance!"[25]

25 Psa. 33:11-12

Section Two:
ISRAEL
GOD'S THERMOMETER
FOR THE NATIONS

Chapter Five

The Priority of Israel: An Offense to the Gentiles

A s God begins to focus the spotlight of the Church's attention on the subject of Israel and the Jewish people, a paradigm shift of staggering proportions is occurring. God is changing the way His Church looks at the Jewish people. At present many believers see Israel as a fossil people who somehow have not become extinct. The Jewish people, it is said, were once on the fast track of God's racecourse, but now they are a nation of 'has beens', 'might have beens' or 'wannabees.' These believers are comfortable with a past role for Israel. Some even allow for a future role for the Jewish people as long as it is a minor one, hidden under the benign and sheltering Gentile wing of the Church.

The Bible declares that God gives top priority to Israel, and the nations of the world are called to do the same. This is a hard pill for many to swallow. Some may respond with a charge of *Galatianism* or *Judaizing.* So the question must be asked: Was the nation of Israel just an Old Testament priority? Or is the modern nation of Israel still a priority in the heart of God?

First Things First

The Scriptures say that God is a God of order.[1] All that He has created reflects order. The star systems and the galaxies move through space in divine order. God asks Job, "Can you bind the chains of the Pleiades or loose the cords of Orion? Can you lead forth a constellation in its season and guide the Bear with her satellites? Do you know the ordinances of the heavens or fix their rule over the earth?"[2] The tides, the seasons and the laws of physics all witness to the precision, wisdom and order of the Creator.

The Creator has also established social order, biblical guidelines for the preservation and betterment of human society. At the close of the twentieth century God's order is not greatly appreciated on this planet. The nuclear family which was fashioned in Eden is often mocked on television. Obedience to parents, the first Commandment with a blessing, is considered *passé.* Teenage rebellion, sexual promiscuity and widespread cynicism toward all authority express mankind's open revolt against God's design. Biblical teaching on the callings of men and women[3] are increasingly considered sexist, irrelevant and politically incorrect. This intellectual climate has chilled the courage of many.

God's order extends beyond physics and family to the affairs of nations. He has established guidelines for international relations which the nations of the world ignore at their peril. The core of God's international statecraft revolves around the nation of Israel. Much of the modern Church is distracted and dull of hearing concerning what the Bible teaches about Israel's priority, even though two thousand years ago Paul did his best to warn believers

---

1   1 Cor. 14:33

2   Job 38:31-33 (NASB)

3   Eg.,1 Cor.5:1-2, 13; 7; 11; 14:34-38; Eph. 5:2, 21-33; Col. 3:18-21; 1 Tim. 2:11-15 etc.

about the danger of ignoring the Jewish people.[4] These next three chapters present the Scriptures' teaching on the priority of Israel, analyze why some have difficulty receiving this, and offer some practical suggestions.

Who's on First?

The heart of Paul the Apostle's life-message is trumpeted in the first chapter of the Book of Romans. "I am not ashamed of the gospel, because it is the power of God for the salvation of everyone who believes: first for the Jew, then for the Gentile"[5] The gospel is God's powerful truth, and this good message of salvation is especially directed toward the Jewish people. The Greek word *prwton* ('first') in this context emphasizes degree: 'in the first place', 'above all', 'especially'.[6] There is a special connection between the Jewish people and the gospel. Paul affirms that the priority of Israel is not only an Old Testament teaching; it lies at the very heart of the gospel, and he announces it with apostolic authority.

This principle should not be surprising. The Jewish people were the first preachers of the gospel. Historically they were also the first to hear the good news. Acts 11:19 describes this time period very simply: Messianic Jews "who had been scattered by the persecution in connection with Stephen traveled as far as Phoenicia, Cyprus and Antioch, telling the message only to Jews." Actually, for the first eight years after the resurrection of Yeshua the gospel was preached to Jews alone. Only then did the Samaritans come to faith, and later still Cornelius the Italian. Within twenty years of the cross the message was freely being preached to Jew and Gentile alike. By Paul's day, it could be said that now "Gentiles are fellow heirs and fellow members of the body"[7] along with Messianic Jews. But even though Paul says that the gospel is to be preached to both groups

4 Rom.11:25

5 Rom. 1:16

6 A Greek-English Lexicon of the New Testament and Other Early Christian Literature, ed. W.Bauer, W.F.Arndt, F.W. Gingrich, Chicago, The University of Chicago Press 1979, p. 726, 2.c., 'pr Ω ton'

7 Eph. 3:6

without prejudice, at the same time the Apostle announces that the gospel is pre-eminently directed to the Jewish people. How can this be?

Some say that although the gospel <u>was</u> originally 'first to the Jew,' such a state of affairs wasn't meant to last. The Greek word order of Romans 1:16 offers help here. In translation it reads, "power for/ of God/ it is/ to the salvation of all the believing ones/ to the Jew especially and to the Greek." The verb *estin* ('it is') is the only verb in this sentence. *Estin* modifies two phrases, "power of God to the salvation of all the believing and "to the Jew especially (or 'in the first place') and to the Greek." If someone wants to suggest that the gospel <u>was</u> first to the Jew but is no longer, then the Greek construction and logic would force him to conclude that the gospel <u>was</u> the power of God for salvation but is no longer. Conversely, if the gospel still <u>is</u> the power of God for salvation, then the gospel still <u>is</u> to the Jew first. Paul links the present power of the gospel to the present priority of the Jewish people!

Added testimony on this point comes to us from Paul the missionary's own example in the Book of Acts. Though he was called by God to be an apostle to the Gentiles,[8] his habitual methodology was to go to the Jewish people first in every location.[9] Paul practiced what he preached. 'First to the Jew' is the apostolic gospel, both in teaching and in practice.

All's Well That Ends Well

The gospel age began with the principle 'first to the Jew.' It will end with the same principle in effect. On Judgment Day at the end of the gospel age, Jewish people will be the first ones to receive their due, whether it be wrath or blessing. Paul points this out in Romans 2, a passage written to both Jews and Gentiles.

But because of your stubbornness and your unrepentant

---

8   Gal. 2:8

9   Acts 9:20; 13:5, 14, 42-48; 14:1; 16:13, 20; 17:2, 10, 16-17; 18:1-8, 12-17, 18-21, 24-28; 19:8, 33-34; 20:6, 16; 21:11, 18-25; 28:17; 1 Cor. 9:19-23

heart, you are storing up wrath against yourself for the day of God's wrath, when His righteous judgment will be revealed. God will give to each person according to what he has done. To those who by persistence in doing good seek glory, honor and immortality, He will give eternal life. But for those who are self-seeking and who reject the truth and follow evil, there will be wrath and anger. There will be trouble and distress for every human being who does evil: first for the Jew, then for the Gentile; but glory, honor and peace for everyone who does good: first for the Jew, then for the Gentile. For God does not show favoritism.[10]

The gospel is to the Jew first at the beginning of the gospel age. Judgment and reward are to the Jew first at the end of the New Testament age. Whether for good or bad, apostolic teaching links the Jewish people to God's priority throughout the entire gospel age.

First the Good News

Cut into the Bible anywhere and it will bleed this principle of Israel's priority. Amos announces to Israel, "You only have I chosen of all the families of the earth; therefore I will punish you for all your sins."[11] Asaph asks God to "remember the people You purchased of old, the tribe of Your inheritance, whom You redeemed..."[12] Balaam pronounces a benediction over the Jewish people, "...I see (Israel) from the top of the rocks, and I look at him from the hills; Behold, a people who dwells apart, and shall not be reckoned among the nations."[13] Deuteronomy declares, "For the Lord's portion is His people, Jacob His allotted inheritance."[14] The psalmist proclaims, "He declares His words to Jacob, His statutes and His ordinances to

10   Rom. 2:5-11
11   Amos 3:2
12   Psa. 74:2
13   Num. 23:9 NASB
14   Deut. 32:9

Israel. He has not dealt thus with any nation."[15]

Paul affirms that the gifts God gave to Israel are irrevocable, and His divine calling on the Jewish people is unchanging.[16] That is why King David's declaration holds true in our day, "Blessed are the people of whom this is true; blessed are the people whose God is the Lord."[17]

Looking Out for Number One

Israel stands at the top of God's 'Christmas list' of nations. God calls the Jewish people 'God's firstborn among the nations,' His priority among the peoples. "This is what the Lord says: 'Israel is My firstborn son...'"[18] The status of the firstborn son is a biblical concept that needs some explaining in our modern age.

The firstborn son receives great honor in the Bible. When Jacob blessed his firstborn he said, "Reuben, you are my firstborn, my might, the first sign of my strength, excelling in honor, excelling in power."[19] The firstborn's life is dedicated to the Lord in a special way. God told Moses to teach this principle to the nation of Israel. "Consecrate to Me every firstborn male. The first offspring of every womb among the Israelites belongs to Me, whether man or animal."[20]

The firstborn son also receives a special inheritance. The Torah commands that he receive a double portion, twice as much, as what the other sons inherit. "... (A) man ... must acknowledge ... the firstborn by giving him a double share of all he has. That son is the first sign of his father's strength. The right of the firstborn belongs to him."[21] Isaiah prophesies that at the end of the ages the Jewish people will receive a double inheritance befitting a firstborn son. "Instead of their shame My people will receive a double portion, and instead of disgrace they will rejoice in their inheritance; and so

15   Psa. 147:19-20 NASB

16   Rom. 11:29

17   Psa. 144:15

18   Exod. 4:22-23

19   Gen. 49:3

20   Exod. 13:2

21   Deut. 21:15-17

they will inherit a double portion in their land, and everlasting joy will be theirs."[22]

To summarize, the Bible says that the Jewish people are 'firstborn' or first chosen among the nations. They are the only nation on earth that can be called *God's Priority People*, God's portion and His inheritance in some unique way. Their destiny needs to be considered separately from that of other nations. As God's firstborn, the Jewish people are the first sign of their Father's strength. They are set apart for the Lord's use in a special way and they receive a double portion of God's inheritance.

Double or Nothing

The good news is that the Jewish people receive a double blessing. The bad news is that they receive double of everything! Scripture says that Israel receives twice as much discipline as do the nations. "I will repay them double for their wickedness and their sin, because they have defiled My land with the lifeless forms of their vile images and have filled My inheritance with their detestable idols."[23] Isaiah prophesies, "Speak tenderly to Jerusalem, and proclaim to her that her hard service has been completed, that her sin has been paid for, that she has received from the Lord's hand double for all her sins."[24]

This is one of the main reasons why the Jewish people have suffered so much throughout history. Their unusual suffering proves that they remain God's firstborn son. "For the Lord has chosen Jacob to be His own, Israel to be His treasured possession."[25] Some Gentiles who have a secret desire to become Jews lose their appetite for such a step when they realize that double judgment is part of the deal!

The firstborn son is usually disciplined more severely, and history dispassionately recounts how God has used cruel Gentile

---

22   Isa. 61:7

23   Jer. 16:18

24   Isa. 40:2

25   Psa. 135:4

nations to discipline Israel.[26] Yet at the same time the Lord jealously guards the life of His firstborn and promises to ultimately redeem him from all harm. "Do not fear, O Jacob My servant, for I am with you, declares the Lord. Though I completely destroy all the nations among which I scatter you, I will not completely destroy you. I will discipline you but only with justice; I will not let you go entirely unpunished."[27] "Surely the eyes of the Sovereign Lord are on the sinful kingdom. I will destroy it from the face of the earth, yet I will not totally destroy the house of Jacob, declares the Lord. For I will give the command, and I will shake the house of Israel among all the nations as grain is shaken in a sieve, and not a pebble will reach the ground."[28]

Hath Not a Jew Honor?

As an adolescent I once went to hear the rock group Deep Purple perform at the Montreal Forum. During the concert a sallow Quebecois teenager leaned over to me and asked if I was Jewish. From his tone it was clear that he wasn't exactly excited about Jewish people. A momentary sense of panic, one that Diaspora Jews know only too well, flooded my soul. What if I told him yes? Would he try to beat me up, as forty kids had once done to me in high school? Should I respond boldly, ready for a rumble?

In the end I said, "Why do you want to know?" a diplomatic sidestep at best. Many Jewish people have learned that being Jewish can be an invitation to trouble, to dishonor and to humiliation. Most Jews really are not looking for an idyllic paradise where Israel enjoys a priority status – just the opportunity to live a quiet and peaceful life.

Nevertheless, Isaiah declared that one day Jewishness will not turn people into living targets, but will be universally recognized as a badge of honor. Jewish people will happily confess their racial roots, and all nations will humbly honor Israel as well.

26   Cf., Isa. 10:5-27, etc.

27   Jer. 46:28

28   Amos 9:8-9

But now listen, O Jacob, My servant, Israel, whom I
have chosen. This is what the Lord says – He who made
you, who formed you in the womb, and who will help
you: Do not be afraid, O Jacob, My servant, Jeshurun,
whom I have chosen. For I will pour water on the
thirsty land, and streams on the dry ground; I will
pour out My Spirit on your offspring, and My blessing
on your descendants. They will spring up like grass in
a meadow, like poplar trees by flowing streams. One
will say, "I belong to the Lord.; another will call himself
by the name of Jacob; still another will write on his
hand, "The Lord's," and will take the name Israel.[29]

"This is what the Lord Almighty says: 'In those days ten men
from all languages and nations will take firm hold of one Jew by
the hem of his robe and say, "Let us go with you, because we have
heard that God is with you."[30]

God's Entebbe Rescue

When hostages are seized on planes or in office buildings,
trained law enforcement specialists immediately swing into action.
They set up a command-and-communications center and begin to
negotiate with the terrorists. Professional psychologists and police
have developed guidelines over the years on how to conduct such
hostage negotiations.

It comes as a surprise to discover that God is an experienced
hostage negotiator, and that He is ready to bargain with hostage
takers. In the Book of Isaiah, God views Israel as so important to
His heart and His plans that He will willingly exchange other
peoples as a ransom in order to set the Jewish people free from
captivity and scorn. "For I am the Lord, your God, the Holy One
of Israel, your Savior; I give Egypt for your ransom, Cush and Seba
in your stead. Since you are precious and honored in My sight, and
because I love you, I will give men in exchange for you, and people

29   Isa. 44:1-5
30   Zech. 8:23

in exchange for your life."[31] Though the ramifications of these verses are radical, they are part of the counsel of God, and they shape God's foreign policy toward the nations.

On His Majesty's Secret Service

The nations are unaware of God's priority concerning Israel. But that doesn't bother God in the slightest. As Bob Dylan says, He's got plans of His own! God still operates according to His own guidelines and Israel's welfare is His top international priority. A good illustration of this dynamic concerns Cyrus King of Persia and world ruler.God declares that Cyrus' empire-destroying powers came from the Lord alone, yet Cyrus did not even know Him. God blessed Cyrus with success in order to capture this king's attention and turn his heart to the one true God. What is most fascinating here is that God raised Cyrus up to be dictator over the world just so that the Persian monarch would help the Jewish people! "I will give you the treasures of darkness, riches stored in secret places, so that you may know that I am the Lord, the God of Israel, who summons you by name. For the sake of Jacob My servant, of Israel My chosen, I summon you by name and bestow on you a title of honor, though you do not acknowledge Me."[32] Israel is God's hot button on the international scene, whether or not the Gentile nations acknowledge it.

Our God is a Sovereign God

God's choosing of Israel is a mighty stumbling block for some people. Though they think that they are stumbling over Israel, what ultimately offends them is the sovereignty of God. Does God have the right to choose one nation out of many and to do with it as He pleases? The witness of the Scriptures is resoundingly 'Yes!' Asaph, Daniel, Hannah and Mary agree with one voice: "But it is God who judges: He brings one down, He exalts another."[33] "He changes

---

31   Isa. 43:3-4

32   Isa. 45:3-4

33   Psa. 75:7

times and seasons; He sets up kings and deposes them."[34]

> The Lord brings death and makes alive; He brings
> down to the grave and raises up. The Lord sends
> poverty and wealth; He humbles and he exalts. He
> raises the poor from the dust and lifts the needy from
> the ash heap; He seats them with princes and has
> them inherit a throne of honor... He will guard the
> feet of His saints, but the wicked will be silenced in
> darkness. It is not by strength that one prevails...[35]

> He has performed mighty deeds with His arm; He
> has scattered those who are proud in their inmost
> thoughts. He has brought down rulers from their
> thrones but has lifted up the humble. He has filled
> the hungry with good things but has sent the rich
> away empty. He has helped His servant Israel,
> remembering to be merciful to Abraham and his
> descendants forever, even as He said to our fathers.[36]

God prioritizes the nations in accordance with His own wisdom, based on His covenant of love with Abraham and all of Jacob's children. His choice of Israel is not based on the Jewish people's ability or righteousness, their zeal or their industry. Paul points out,

> What then shall we say? Is God unjust? Not at all! For
> He says to Moses, "I will have mercy on whom I have
> mercy, and I will have compassion on whom I have
> compassion." It does not, therefore, depend on man's
> desire or effort, but on God's mercy... Does not the potter
> have the right to make out of the same lump of clay some
> pottery for noble purposes and some for common use?[37]

The conclusion is emphatic: since God has called the Jewish people noble, let no man call them *common*! Let God's priorities become our priorities as well!

---

34   Dan. 2:21

35   1 Sam. 2:6-9

36   Lk. 1:51-55

37   Rom. 9:14-16, 21

Chapter Six

Billboard To The Nations

Advertising! Any Fortune 500 company president will tell you that advertising pays. "Don't sell the steak! Sell the sizzle!" "Get the message out there where people live!" "Repetition is the key word! Get them to remember the product name!" These are the modern proverbs of profit, the bywords of business.

In His own way God is a master of public relations, a maven when it comes to getting His message out. His prime-time portfolio is Israel. The Jewish people are His billboard to the nations.

Sign Language

Israel is God's timepiece. If the nations of the world want to understand what God is up to, let them pay attention to what is happening with the Jewish people. The comings and goings of the nation of Israel have prophetic significance. "He will raise a banner for the nations and gather the exiles of Israel; He will assemble the scattered people of Judah from the four quarters of the earth"[1] Israel is called a *banner* in this verse, the closest thing to a billboard the ancient Near East knew. Isaiah says that when God begins to bring the scattered Jewish people back to the land of Israel, this will be a billboard, a warning sign, a shout to the nations saying "Pay attention!" From God's perspective the return to Zion is not a work of man but a divine wake-up call to the Gentiles. God is on the move!

In Ezra's day only 10,000 Jewish people returned from Babylon at first, and a total of approximately 50,000 immigrated as a result of ancient Persia's 'open doors' policy. This was such a momentous act of God that at least two biblical books (Ezra and Nehemiah) are dedicated to describing the return, while a handful of other books detail spiritual and physical aspects of that time (Haggai, Zechariah, Malachi). In comparison, between 1989 and 1998 over 750,000 Russian speaking Jews have returned to the land of Israel. This is an event fifteen to seventy five times larger than the initial return under Ezra. Yet for the most part the Church is unaware of the significance of this amazing *aliyah*.[2] God is lifting up His billboard to the nations in our day. Hello! Is anyone paying attention?

I've Got to Get a Message to You

When E.F. Hutton talks, people listen. When the God of the Bible talks, believers among the nations should also sit up and take notice. About 600 B.C. Jeremiah prophesied that God will one day bring all the Jewish people back to their ancestral homeland. In light of this future event God commands Gentile believers to 'announce tomorrow's news today' to the world. God Himself will soon end Israel's exile and restore her to full favor.

> Hear the word of the Lord, O nations; proclaim it in
> distant coastlands: "He who scattered Israel will gather

---

1   Isa. 11:12

2   *Aliyah* is a Hebrew word meaning 'ascent'. It can refer to an ascent to the synagogue platform to read from the Torah, an incline on a hill, or a pilgrimage/immigration to Jerusalem/the land of Israel. In modern usage it refers to the return of the Jewish people to the State of Israel, the Jewish homeland.

them and will watch over His flock like a shepherd." This is what the Lord says: "Sing with joy for Jacob; shout for the foremost of the nations. Make your praises heard, and say, 'O Lord, save Your people, the remnant of Israel.'"[3]

Since God has commanded believers everywhere to shout out this message across the globe, one would expect pulpits and prayer meetings to resound with this word. Jeremiah's message is a mandate that all believers need to proclaim. God's prioritized dealings with Israel are meant to be our priority as well – in our intercessory meetings, in our sermons and in our private meditations.

His Banner Over Them is Love

God is raising the profile of His 'product,' the people of Israel, on the world scene. He is calling His people back home and also calling on the nations of the world to recognize His hand in this return, to help wherever it is needed. Incrementally God is making the country of Israel impossible to ignore. Isaiah prophesied that the Lord will soon rouse world rulers from a deep spiritual slumber and impart understanding to them about Israel His *banner nation*. These presidents and princes will humbly recognize that God's gifts to Israel and His calling on that people are very much in force. Isaiah says that one day they will honor the Jewish people with a full heart, and will vie for the privilege of helping Israel return to her homeland.

> This is what the Sovereign Lord says: "See, I will
> beckon to the Gentiles, I will lift up My banner to
> the peoples; they will bring your sons in their arms
> and carry your daughters on their shoulders. Kings
> will be your foster fathers, and their queens your
> nursing mothers. They will bow down before you
> with their faces to the ground; they will lick the dust
> at your feet. Then you will know that I am the Lord;
> those who hope in Me will not be disappointed."[4]

3   Jer. 31:10, 7
4   Isa. 49:22-23

Blazing Spotlights on Zion

When a stage director wants the audience to focus on the most important actor, he uses theater spotlights. These blazing beams pick out the main character and cause him to shine brilliantly and clearly. All other actors are relegated to a supportive role as the audience leans forward with bated breath.

Toward the end of the Scroll of Isaiah, the prophet receives a vision of the future. He beholds not a thousand points of light, but one awesome blazing torch – Jerusalem, the shining home of the Jewish people, now following God with all their heart, mind and soul. When all the people of Israel accept Yeshua as Messiah, the world will actually see God's righteousness and glory reflecting off the Jewish people's faces. "For Zion's sake I will not keep silent, for Jerusalem's sake I will not remain quiet, till her righteousness shines out like the dawn, her salvation like a blazing torch. The nations will see your righteousness, and all kings your glory; you will be called by a new name that the mouth of the Lord will bestow."[5] The nations will behold Israel's glory and be amazed. Israel's exaltation will channel light and salvation to the whole earth.

Homecoming Queen

Zephaniah prophesied that all the peoples of the earth will recognize Israel's abiding calling when God brings Israel back to her homeland for the final time. In that day honor and praise will be showered on the Jewish people by a world no longer jealous of Israel's calling. The homecoming queen will be the hit of the party! "At that time I will gather you; at that time I will bring you home. I will give you honor and praise among all the peoples of the earth when I restore your fortunes before your very eyes, says the Lord."[6]

Arm and Hammer

A day of judgment is coming to this planet when the Lord will bare His holy arm in the sight of all nations. This day of vengeance

5   Isa. 62:1-2
6   Zeph. 3:20

is mentioned in many texts,[7] including Isaiah 61, the passage from which Yeshua drew His first recorded sermon. The phrase "arm of the Lord" usually describes how God defends His people Israel and zealously reinstates them to a priority position. The message to the nations is pure Clint Eastwood: "Remember that Israel is My firstborn son. Mess with him and you've just made My day!"

> Surely the arm of the Lord is not too short to save, nor his ear too dull to hear...The Lord looked and was displeased that there was no justice (for Israel).He saw that there was no one, He was appalled that there was no one to (intercede); so His own arm worked salvation for Him, and His own righteousness sustained Him. He put on righteousness as His breastplate, and the helmet of salvation on His head; He put on the garments of vengeance and wrapped Himself in zeal as in a cloak. According to what they have done, so will He repay wrath to His enemies and retribution to His foes; He will repay the islands their due. From the west, men will fear the name of the Lord, and from the rising of the sun, they will revere His glory. For He will come like a pent-up flood that the breath of the Lord drives along. The Redeemer will come to Zion, to those in Jacob who repent of their sins, declares the Lord.[8]

God's arm (His judgments) has an educational purpose. As He bares His holy arm and strikes the enemies of Israel with His hammer, the nations of the world begin to understand God's ways, His priorities and His love for Jacob's children.[9]

> O Lord God Almighty, the God of Israel, rouse Yourself to punish all the nations; show no mercy to wicked traitors... But You, O Lord...scoff at all those nations...For the sins of (the nations) mouths, for the words of their lips, let them be caught in their pride...Then it will be known

---

7   Isa. 30:30, 32; 40:10; 48:14; 52:9-10

8   Isa. 59:1, 15-20

9   *Cf.*,Isa. 26:9

to the ends of the earth that God rules over Jacob.[10]

God's judgment on Israel's enemies and the redemption of the Jewish people are Scripturally linked to world-wide salvation. Isaiah says it well: "Burst into songs of joy together, you ruins of Jerusalem, for the Lord has comforted His people, He has redeemed Jerusalem. The Lord will lay bare His holy arm in the sight of all the nations, and all the ends of the earth will see the salvation of our God."[11] Israel is God's billboard to the nations, and within a very short time all mankind will stop, look and listen!

The Glorified Apple

God is uniquely connected to the land of Israel, the city of Jerusalem and the Jewish people. These three are set apart in a special way for God's name, His rule, His glory, for His dwelling place, His plans and His ministry. A few aspects of this divine priority will now be considered.

God's glory is tied in a special way to the Jewish people. "...(The Jewish people) were given rest by the Spirit of the Lord. This is how You guided Your people to make for Yourself a glorious name."[12] Isaiah says that God led Israel out of Egypt and guided her through the Sinai wilderness in order to bring glory to His own name. Israel's past, present and future are being guided by the hand of God to bring great glory to His name.

One of the reasons for this intimate connection between the Jewish people and God's glory touches on the fact that Israel is the apple of God's eye.

> For I, declares the Lord, will be a wall of fire around
> her, and I will be the glory in her midst...For thus says
> the Lord of hosts, 'After glory He has sent Me against
> the nations which plunder you, for he who touches you,
> touches the apple of His eye...Sing for joy and be glad,

---

10   Psa. 59:5, 7-13

11   Isa. 52:9-10

12   Isa. 63:14

O Daughter of Zion; for behold I am coming, and I will dwell in your midst,' declares the Lord...And the Lord will possess Judah as His portion in the holy land and will again choose Jerusalem. Be silent, all flesh, before the Lord, for He is aroused from His holy habitation.[13]

This connection is found throughout the Scriptures. When Jeremiah intercedes for Israel, he points out that God's presence is Israel's portion, and that the Jewish people have an intimate connection to God's own name. "Why are You like a man taken by surprise, like a warrior powerless to save? You are among us, O Lord, and we bear Your name; do not forsake us!"[14] The nation of Israel actually bears the very name of God. The Hebrew name 'Israel' is composed of two Semitic words, *isra* (he has 'princed' or 'has become victorious' with) and *El* (the Hebrew word for God). The name 'Jew' comes from the word 'Judah' (*Heb. Yehuda*) which in turn is based on two Hebrew words, *hod* (thanks) and *Yah* (the shortened personal name for Jehovah or YHVH). Whether one uses the name 'Israel' or 'the Jewish people' to describe the sons of Jacob, that people bears the name of the Lord. God's imprint is on their flesh and His calling is upon their lives.

Localized Glory

Secular Western thought has difficulty comprehending the biblical view that holiness can be found in certain places. Ask modern people if they believe in holy places and they may start having flashback images of Indiana Jones, raiders of the lost ark and the bones of saints. Interestingly, the Bible teaches that there really are areas of relative holiness on earth. Israel is considered the Holy Land[15] and Jerusalem the most sanctified area on earth. This is due to the connection between the God of Israel and the city of Jerusalem, His past and future dwelling place. Ezekiel prophesies that when Yeshua sets up His kingdom in all its fullness in Jerusalem, "the

---

13 Zech. 2:5-13NASB

14 Jer. 14:9

15 *E.g.*, Psa. 78:54; Zech. 2:12

name of the city from that time on will be: The Lord Is There."[16]

Jeremiah speaks of a day when all nations will recognize the connection between God, Jerusalem and the Jewish people.

> In those days, when your numbers have increased greatly in the land: declares the Lord, men will no longer say, The ark of the covenant of the Lord. It will never enter their minds or be remembered; it will not be missed, nor will another one be made. At that time they will call Jerusalem "The Throne of the Lord," and all nations will gather in Jerusalem to honor the name of the Lord. No longer will they follow the stubbornness of their evil hearts.[17]

Isaiah commands his people to sing with great passion, for a day will dawn when God will again take up visible residence in Jerusalem. "Shout aloud and sing for joy, people of Zion, for great is the Holy One of Israel among you."[18] When Yeshua returns to reign in Jerusalem, all the Gentiles will see and appreciate God's special connection with the Jewish people. "Then the nations will know that I the Lord make Israel holy, when My sanctuary is among them forever."[19] God decided on this course of action a long time ago, before even the stars were formed, and won't be dissuaded from bringing it to pass. "For the Lord has chosen Zion, He has desired it for His dwelling: This is My resting place for ever and ever; here I will sit enthroned, for I have desired it."[20]

Israel My Glory

An unusual link exists between God's eternal holiness and Israel's future holiness. Isaiah says, "I am bringing My righteousness near, it is not far away; and My salvation will not be delayed. I will grant salvation to Zion, My splendor to Israel."[21] Though God does

---

16   Ezek. 48:35
17   Jer. 3:16-17
18   Isa. 12:6
19   Ezek. 37:28
20   Psa. 132:13-14
21   Isa. 46:13

not share His glory with any person,[22] He shines His splendor on believers and promises to enter into intimate fellowship with them in the glorious eternal state. Various Scriptures try to describe this indescribable experience.[23]

In a similar way, in days to come Israel will be endowed with an unusual splendor and holiness. "They will be called 'the Holy People', 'the Redeemed of the Lord'; and you will be called 'Sought After', 'the City No Longer Deserted'"[24] "Surely you will summon nations you know not, and nations that do not know you will hasten to you, because of the Lord your God, the Holy One of Israel, for He has endowed you with splendor."[25] "Those who are left in Zion, who remain in Jerusalem, will be called holy, all who are recorded among the living in Jerusalem...Then the Lord will create over all of Mount Zion and over those who assemble there a cloud of smoke by day and a glow of flaming fire by night; over all the glory will be a canopy."[26]

All creation is invited to join in the celestial song of joy that will burst forth across the universe when these Scriptures come to pass. "Sing for joy, O heavens, for the Lord has done this; shout aloud, O earth beneath. Burst into song, you mountains, you forests and all your trees, for the Lord has redeemed Jacob, He displays His glory in Israel."[27]

Journey to the Center of the Earth

Cartographers argue among themselves about how to design an accurate world map. Where should the center of the map be – North America, Europe or Australia? The Bible's perspective is that the land of Israel is the center of the earth. Israel is at the center of God's international priorities. This truth is taught in the Book of

---

22   Isa. 42:8; 48:11

23   Rom. 8:17; 1 Cor. 11:7; 2 Cor. 3:18; 2 Thess. 2:14; 1 Pet. 5:1; Rev. 21:26 *etc.*

24   Isa. 62:12

25   Isa. 55:5

26   Isa. 4:3,5; *cf.*, Zech. 14:16-21

27   Isa. 44:23

Ezekiel where Gog declares his intention to attack Israel: "I will go up against the land of unwalled villages...against the waste places which are now inhabited, and against the people who are gathered from the nations, who have acquired cattle and gold, who live at the center of the world."[28]

The center of the world is Israel. The Jewish people, God's first-born son, are the centerpiece of that land. To attack the son is to attack the father, and an assault against the people of Israel is considered an assault against the God of Israel. God has gone on record on this point, having established a defense pact between Himself and Israel in the prophetic Psalm 83. In that psalm various Arab countries draw up war plans against the Jewish state. The psalmist says that in doing so these countries are actually banding together against Israel's God. "They have said, 'Come and let us wipe them out as a nation, that the name of Israel be remembered no more.' For they have conspired together with one mind; against Thee do they make a covenant."[29] The wars of the Middle East are actually a concerted satanic attempt to overthrow the purposes and the people of the God of Jacob.

Witnessing on the West Bank

The priority of Israel has offended many people throughout time. It certainly offended the Samaritans of Yeshua's day, whose ethnic and religious origins are described in 2 Kings 17:24-41. This people proclaimed that they and not Israel were God's priority people, that Mount Gerizim and not Mount Moriah was the Mountain of the Lord, and that the Samaritan Pentateuch and not the Hebrew Bible was the inspired version.

When Yeshua met the Samaritan woman of John 4, she asserted Samaritan priority over Israel, claiming that Jacob was her physical/spiritual forefather and that Gerizim was God's holy mountain. "Are you greater than our father Jacob, who gave us the well and drank

28   Ezek. 38:11-12 NASB

29   Psa. 83:4-5 NASB

from it himself, as did also his sons and his flocks and herds?...Our fathers worshipped on this mountain, but you Jews claim that the place where we must worship is in Jerusalem."[30]

Yeshua responded graciously and with dry humor. But He did not budge an inch on the non-negotiables. "Yeshua declared, '... You Samaritans worship what you do not know; we worship what we do know, for salvation is from the Jews.'"[31] God has chosen the Jewish people and Jerusalem. Salvation is still part of the Jewish people's spiritual inheritance. And even Samaritans must bow the knee before the stumbling block of a Jewish Messiah to receive God's living waters.

The Skirts of a Jew

Can you imagine a day when an international body like the United Nations will consult with Israel before passing any resolution of international importance? Though this scenario sounds like something from *The X-Files*, Scripture says that this is the shape of things to come.

Universal recognition will one day be given to Israel's priority relationship with the God of Jacob. Some nations will joyfully accept this state of affairs. Others will not be so happy. "This is what the Lord says: ... Egypt and...Cush and those...Sabeans...will come over to you and will be yours; they will trudge behind you, coming over to you in chains. They will bow down before you and plead with you, saying, 'Surely God is with you, and there is no other; there is no other God.'"[32] "For the nation or kingdom that will not serve you will perish; it will be utterly ruined... The sons of your oppressors will come bowing before you; all who despise you will bow down at your feet and will call you the City of the Lord, Zion of the Holy One of Israel."[33]

The attitude of the nations to God's Jewish billboard is important

30   Jn. 4:12,20
31   Jn. 4:21-22
32   Isa. 45:14
33   Isa. 60:12, 14

to the Lord. He promises that the Gentiles will one day come under the full blessings of the Abrahamic covenant when they accept Israel's firstborn status and when they thank God for the favor poured out on the world through the Jewish people's obedience. "As you have been an object of cursing among the nations, O Judah and Israel, so will I save you, and you will be a blessing. Do not be afraid, but let your hands be strong."[34]

God has granted 'most favored nation status' to the Jewish people. When the Gentiles accept God and desire to follow after His heart, they will discover a wonderful spiritual side effect – Israel's priority will bring joy to their hearts, and they will be filled with a Spirit-breathed desire to follow after the Jewish people. "... (M)any peoples and powerful nations will come to Jerusalem to seek the Lord Almighty and to entreat Him. This is what the Lord Almighty says: In those days ten men from all languages and nations will take firm hold of one Jew by the hem of his robe and say, 'Let us go with you, because we have heard that God is with you.'"[35] What the King James Version calls 'the skirts of a Jew' is actually a reference to typical Jewish clothing in Yeshua's day, the fringed-border garment or *tzitzit*.[36] Zechariah is prophesying that recognition of Israel's unique covenant-based relationship with God will be widespread among the nations in the Messianic Age.[37] Today the priority of Israel may still be opposed by many believers, but a day will soon dawn upon us when argument will give way to amazement and appreciation.

---

34   Zech. 8:13

35   Zech. 8:22-23

36   *Cf.*, Num.15:37-40; 1 Sam. 24:4, 11 ; Lk. 8:44

37   *Cf.*, Isa. 11:10; 14:1; Psa. 72:8-11

Chapter Seven

Taking the Temperature of the Human Race

One Sign, Two Directions, Many Thoughts

Someone has coined the proverb, "God offends the mind to reveal the heart." This phrase captures one of the ways of God with mankind and has a biblical basis as well. The Christmas story underscores this proverb. When Joseph and Mary (*Hebrew* for Miriam) brought their firstborn baby Yeshua to the Temple, they met Simeon (*Shim'on*), a righteous man filled with the Holy Spirit. After Shim'on blessed Yeshua at the close of His *pidyon ha-ben* (ceremony marking the redemption of the firstborn son)[1], he said to Miriam His mother: "This child is destined to cause the falling and rising of many in Israel, and to be a sign that will be spoken against, so that the thoughts of many hearts will be revealed. And a sword will pierce your own soul too."[2]

Shim'on prophesied that Yeshua would be a banner sign for Israel,

1 *Cf.*, Exod. 13:11-15
2 Lk. 2:34-35

separating spiritual wheat from unspiritual chaff among the Jewish people. Today Messiah Yeshua is a sign which offends some Jews. He also causes other Jews to rise up into the presence and favor of God. Shim'on was right to declare that Yeshua is a spiritual polarizer for Israel. The way Jewish people respond to Yeshua decides their eternal spiritual direction. The thoughts of many Jewish hearts will be revealed to all creation based on their acceptance or rejection of Miriam's prophetic baby.

Yeshua's ministry of revealing hearts is not confined to the Jewish world alone. He empowers believers in Yeshua to reach out to the world with a similar ministry. "For we are to God the aroma of Messiah among those who are being saved and those who are perishing. To the one we are the smell of death; to the other, the fragrance of life. And who is equal to such a task?"[3]

Like Yeshua, the Jewish people are a banner to the nations, God's sign to reveal the hearts of many peoples. The Abrahamic Covenant promises that Gentile attitudes and actions toward Israel will bring divine blessing or curse. The nation of Israel is a sign which polarizes the nations, and the prophets make a connection between God's final judgment on Gentile nations and how those nations treat the Jewish people. "In those days and at that time, when I restore the fortunes of Judah and Jerusalem, I will gather all nations and bring them down to the Valley of Jehoshaphat. There I will enter into judgment against them concerning My inheritance, My people Israel, for they scattered My people among the nations and divided up My land."[4] The multitudes in the Valley of Decision will discover that real and healthy faith also creates a positive heart attitude in the believer toward the Jewish people and their land.

A Syrian in Whom There is no Guile

The Bible presents a montage of Gentile personalities who responded to the priority of Israel, each in his or her own way. King

---

3   2 Cor. 2:15-16

4   *Eg.*, Joel 3:2

Cyrus was ignorant of God's heart toward the Jewish people.[5] He was unaware of how God had raised him up to deliver Israel from Babylonian exile. Nevertheless Cyrus was moved by God to bless the Jewish people and to help those who wanted to return to the Promised Land.

Na'aman the Syrian five-star general is the very picture of haughtiness until he is driven to consult a Jewish prophet because of a humbling physical disease. His encounter with Jewish prophetic advice triggers deep anger in his soul and he responds politically, boasting of Syria's superiority over Israel. When he calms down and is willing to humble himself before the Jewish prophet by bathing in a muddy Jewish river, he receives his healing. As a result, Na'aman recognizes God's hand on Israel and God's connection with the Jewish people, declaring his faith in the Lord of the Hebrews. Israel is God's thermometer and she has just been used to take Na'aman's spiritual temperature.

> So Na'aman went with his horses and chariots and stopped at the door of Elisha's house. He sent a messenger to say to him, "Go, wash yourself seven times in the Jordan, and your flesh will be restored and you will be cleansed." But Na'aman went away angry and said, "I thought that he would surely come out to me and stand and call on the name of the Lord his God, wave his hand over the spot and cure me of my leprosy. Are not Abana and Pharpar, the rivers of Damascus, better than any of the waters of Israel? Couldn't I wash in them and be cleansed?" So he turned and went off in a rage. Na'aman's servants went to him and said, "My father, if the prophet had told you to do some great thing, would you not have done it? How much more, then, when he tells you, 'Wash and be cleansed!'" So he went down and dipped himself in the Jordan seven times, as the man of God had told him, and his flesh was restored and became clean like that of a young boy.Then Na'aman and all his attendants went back to the man of God. He stood before him and said,

---

5   *Cf.*, Isa.45:4

"Now I know that there is no God in all the world except in Israel. Please accept now a gift from your servant."[6]

Three other positive examples of godly Gentile response to the priority of Israel will be considered – Ruth the Moabite, Luke's anonymous Roman centurion and Cornelius of the Italian Regiment.

Ruth: Your People Will be My People

Ruth and her sister-in-law Orpah were born on the Plains of Moab (modern Jordan). Faced with the choice of remaining in her motherland or emigrating with Naomi her Hebrew mother-in-law, she humbly embraced the Jewish people and their God as her own personal priority.

> At this they wept again. Then Orpah kissed her mother-in-law good-by, but Ruth clung to her...But Ruth replied, "Don't urge me to leave you or to turn back from you. Where you go I will go, and where you stay I will stay. Your people will be my people and your God my God. Where you die I will die, and there I will be buried. May the Lord deal with me, be it ever so severely, if anything but death separates you and me."[7]

Ruth did not assume that God's grace was her due. She looked for refuge under the wings of the God of Israel and realized that, as a Gentile, divine mercies would come to her only through her relationship with and service to the Jewish people.

> (S)he bowed down with her face to the ground. She exclaimed, "Why have I found such favor in your eyes that you notice me – a foreigner? ... You have given me comfort and have spoken kindly to your servant – though I do not have the standing of one of your servant girls"... Boaz replied, "I've been told all about what you have done for your mother-in-law since the death of your husband – how you left your father and mother and your homeland and came to live with a people you did not know before.

6   2 Kgs. 5:9-15
7   Ru. 1:14, 16-17

> May the Lord repay you for what you have done. May
> you be richly rewarded by the Lord, the God of Israel,
> under whose wings you have come to take refuge."[8]

Ruth had blessed Naomi a daughter of Abraham, and now it was Naomi's turn to bless Ruth according to Genesis 12:3. God would pour out a mighty blessing on Ruth, the woman of noble character and humility of heart.[9] He would make a place for her in the very lineage of Messiah Yeshua. Ruth was welcomed into the commonwealth of Israel with great honor. Her very body was dedicated to building up and blessing the Jewish people. A Gentile who understood the priority of Israel in God's sight, became better to Naomi than seven Jewish sons!

> Then the elders and all those at the gate said, "We are
> witnesses. May the Lord make the woman who is coming
> into your home like Rachel and Leah, who together
> built up the House of Israel. May you have standing in
> Ephrathah and be famous in Bethlehem. Through the
> offspring the Lord gives you by this young woman, may
> your family be like that of Perez, whom Tamar bore to
> Judah ... He will renew your life and sustain you in your
> old age. For your daughter-in-law, who loves you and who
> is better to you than seven sons, has given him birth."[10]

The Roman Centurion: He Loves our Nation

The anonymous Roman centurion who requested that Yeshua heal his dying servant is another example of a Gentile who humbly accepted the priority of Israel and acted accordingly. The centurion did not presume on the grace of God. He felt small in his own eyes. He did not feel worthy to meet Yeshua face-to-face, and asked some Jewish elders to intercede with Yeshua. He had proved his love for God and for God's priority people by contributing to the building program of the local synagogue. It turns out that Yeshua not only

---

8   Ru. 2:10, 13, 11-12

9   Ru. 3:1, 10-11

10   Ru. 4:11-12, 15

granted this man's request, but also blessed him with one of the highest compliments ever given to a human being. All this was done for a Gentile who blessed Abraham's children and honored their calling.

> When Yeshua had finished saying all this in the hearing
> of the people, He entered Capernaum. There a centurion's
> servant, whom his master valued highly, was sick and
> about to die. The centurion heard of Yeshua and sent
> some elders of the Jews to Him, asking Him to come
> and heal his servant. When they came to Yeshua, they
> pleaded earnestly with Him, "This man deserves to have
> You do this, because he loves our nation and has built
> our synagogue." So Yeshua went with them. He was not
> far from the house when the centurion sent friends to
> say to Him: "Lord, don't trouble yourself, for I do not
> deserve to have You come under my roof. That is why
> I did not even consider myself worthy to come to You.
> But say the word, and my servant will be healed. For I
> myself am a man under authority, with soldiers under
> me. I tell this one, 'Go,' and he goes; and that one, 'Come,'
> and he comes. I say to my servant, 'Do this,' and he does
> it." When Yeshua heard this, He was amazed at him,
> and turning to the crowd following Him, He said, "I tell
> you, I have not found such great faith even in Israel."[11]

Cornelius: Respected by all the Jewish People

The first Gentile to receive the gospel 'just as he was' without undergoing circumcision was hand-picked by God for his heart attitude to the Jewish people. Cornelius was held in high regard by his Hebrew neighbors as a lover of Israel who blessed the Jewish people and gave to the Jewish poor. God always honors those who honor Him and tremble at His word.[12]

Now there was a certain man at Caesarea named

---

11   Lk. 7:1-9

12   *Cf.*, 1 Sam.2:30; Isa. 66:5

> Cornelius, a centurion of what was called the Italian cohort, a devout man, and one who feared God with all his household, and gave many alms to the Jewish people, and prayed to God continually...(The angel) said to him, "Your prayers and alms have ascended as a memorial before God"...And they said, "Cornelius, a centurion, a righteous and God-fearing man well spoken of by the entire nation of the Jews, was divinely directed by a holy angel to send for you to come to his house and hear a message from you."[13]

Na'aman, Ruth, the anonymous centurion and Cornelius are four positive examples of Gentiles who willingly worshipped the God of Israel and honored His priorities concerning the Jewish people. Considering the other side of the coin, the Bible also describes the heart attitudes of other non-Jews who rejected Israel's calling and as a result experienced God's blazing anger.

I Don't Get No Respect!

In the Book of Jeremiah the Lord explains part of His reasoning for restoring the Jewish people to a priority position. Some Gentile nations have concluded in the secret place of their own hearts that God doesn't care about Israel like He once did, and that God has bumped the Jewish people off the stage of world events. Responding to those heart attitudes God promises that He will restore and heal the Jewish people. God's glory is maligned whenever the nations disregard His everlasting promises to Israel. "For I will restore you to health and I will heal you of your wounds, declares the Lord, because they have called you an outcast, saying, 'It is Zion; no one cares for her.'"[14] To paraphrase Rodney Dangerfield, when God's people 'don't get no respect,' ultimately God 'don't get no respect'!

All Quiet on the Gentile Front

At the close of the fifth century B.C. Zechariah received a night

13   Acts 10:1-2, 4, 22 (NASB)

14   Jer. 30:17 (NASB)

vision of angelic patrols returning from an international sortie. As the angels report in, they announce, "We have patrolled the earth, and behold, all the earth is peaceful and quiet." Though the situation sounds idyllic, in fact it is not. While the Gentile nations are at rest and sleeping peacefully, the nation of Israel is still languishing in Babylon. Though this state of affairs does not even cause a ripple of concern among the peoples of the Middle East, God's response is different.

> Then the Angel of the Lord answered and said, "O Lord of hosts, how long wilt Thou have no compassion for Jerusalem and the cities of Judah, with which Thou hast been indignant these seventy years?" And the Lord answered the Angel who was speaking with me with gracious words, comforting words. So the Angel who was speaking to me said to me, "Proclaim, saying, 'Thus says the Lord of hosts, I am exceedingly jealous for Jerusalem and Zion. But I am very angry with the nations who are at ease; for while I was only a little angry, they furthered the disaster... Be silent, all flesh, before the Lord; for He is aroused from His holy habitation.'"[15]

God's burning anger flares up because the nations just don't care about Israel. Not only that – God Almighty says that the political plans of the Gentile superpowers weaken the Jewish people, while the Machiavellian machinations of the peoples wreak disaster on Israel. Though the nations scorn Israel's priority, God promises that He will restore Jerusalem to a choice position as the head of the nations and not the tail. The nations are warned to bow down very low as God's flaming fury approaches. Even the mountains are about to quake at this visitation of the Lord's wrath.[16]

Joseph and His Brothers: a New Typology

Some Bible teachers have noted a typological similarity between the lives of Joseph and Yeshua. Another helpful parallel can be

---

15   Zech. 1:11-17; 2:13 (NASB)

16   *Cf.*, Isa.63:17-64:12

drawn between the life of Joseph and his brothers on the one hand, and the relationship between the Jewish people and the Gentiles on the other hand. When Joseph symbolically represents the Jewish people, and when his brothers represent the nations, some sobering lessons from history present themselves for consideration. The watershed events in Joseph's life – his brothers' mockery, betrayal, their guilty conscience and ultimately their bowing down before the offended party – these have present and future parallels for Jewish/Gentile relations.

Joseph was born with a silver spoon in his mouth. At that point in time he was the only child of his father's only true love, Rachel. The favor that his father lavished on him sparked jealousy in the hearts of his brothers. Every time they saw him they were reminded that Joseph was their father's priority child. His hated coat of many colors was proof that they would never inherit the double portion. "Now Israel loved Joseph more than any of his other sons, because he had been born to him in his old age; and he made a richly ornamented robe for him. When his brothers saw that their father loved him more than any of them, they hated him and could not speak a kind word to him."[17]

To make matters worse, Joseph aggravated his brothers' jealousy by bragging about revelation he had received from God. If that revelation were true it would destroy his brothers' ambitious dreams of glory.

> Joseph had a dream, and when he told it to his brothers, they hated him all the more. He said to them, "Listen to this dream I had: We were binding sheaves of grain out in the field when suddenly my sheaf rose and stood upright, while your sheaves gathered around mine and bowed down to it." His brothers said to him, "Do you intend to reign over us? Will you actually rule us?" And they hated him all the more because of his dream and what he had said...His brothers were jealous

---

17   Gen. 37:3-4

of him, but his father kept the matter in mind.[18]

When ungodly desires come to full term they give birth to sin. When sin becomes fully grown, it brings forth death.[19] Joseph's brothers had secretly nursed their hatred of Joseph for years. The murderous fruit it was about to bear would rule over their lives for years to come.

> So Joseph went after his brothers and found them near Dothan. But they saw him in the distance, and before he reached them, they plotted to kill him. "Here comes that dreamer!" they said to each other. "Come now, let's kill him and throw him into one of these cisterns and say that a ferocious animal devoured him. Then we'll see what comes of his dreams."[20]

Jealousy over how their father preferred Joseph led to attempted murder. Genesis 50:20 is clear about the motives of his brothers: they intended to kill Joseph. It was God's hand that spared his life and preserved him for a higher purpose. Later on in Egypt, the land of Joseph's exile and his affliction, "the Lord was with Joseph and he prospered...(T)he Lord gave him success in everything he did..."[21]

Many years later, after Joseph had endured long years of suffering, false accusation, imprisonment and broken promises, God decreed that the time had come for the fulfillment of Joseph's dream. Joseph's brothers "arrived (and) they bowed down to him with their faces to the ground. As soon as Joseph saw his brothers, he recognized them... Although Joseph recognized his brothers, they did not recognize him. Then he remembered his dreams about them."[22] Joseph took advantage of this unexpected situation, threatening his brothers with collective punishment to see what was in their hearts. A gray fog of guilt hung over the brothers' collective conscience for

---

18   Gen. 37:5-8, 11
19   *Cf.*, Ja.1:13-16
20   Gen. 37:17-20
21   Gen. 39:2-3
22   Gen. 42:6-7, 9

what they had done to Joseph. Each one heard his own hidden voice thundering 'Guilty! Guilty!'

> They said to one another, "Surely we are being punished because of our brother. We saw how distressed he was when he pleaded with us for his life, but we would not listen; that's why this distress has come upon us." Reuben replied, "Didn't I tell you not to sin against the boy? But you wouldn't listen! Now we must give an accounting for his blood."[23]

The next time his brothers came to Egypt to seek grain, Joseph decided to reveal himself to them. Before doing this, he sent all the Egyptian servants out of the hall. It was in the privacy of this setting that he and his brothers witnessed the fulfillment of Joseph's dreams. "Joseph said to his brothers, 'I am Joseph! Is my father still living?' But his brothers were not able to answer him, because they were terrified at his presence."[24] They were overwhelmed by their guilty consciences, terrified that the one they had abused was now their judge. They rightly expected to be executed, tortured or receive life imprisonment at hard labor.

> Then Joseph said to his brothers, "Come close to me." When they had done so, he said, "I am your brother Joseph, the one you sold into Egypt! And now, do not be distressed and do not be angry with yourselves for selling me here, because it was to save lives that God sent me ahead of you. For two years now there has been famine in the land, and for the next five years there will not be plowing and reaping. But God sent me ahead of you to preserve for you a remnant on earth and to save your lives by a great deliverance. So then, it was not you who sent me here, but God. He made me father to Pharaoh, lord of his entire household and ruler of all Egypt."[25]

When Jacob's sons told him that Joseph was alive and living in

---

23   Gen. 42:21-22

24   Gen. 45:3

25   Gen. 45:4-8

Egypt as Pharaoh's grand vizier, the patriarch of Israel's twelve tribes was stunned.[26] At first he did not believe that such good news was possible. Years later, after Jacob had died, Joseph's brothers were also not sure that such good news was possible. They hatched a plot, fabricating a secret deathbed testament of Jacob, and came into Joseph's presence bowing and scraping again, just like in Joseph's original dream.

> When Joseph's brothers saw that their father was dead, they said, "What if Joseph holds a grudge against us and pays us back for all the wrongs we did to him?" So they sent word to Joseph, saying, "Your father left these instructions before he died: 'This is what you are to say to Joseph: I ask you to forgive your brothers the sins and the wrongs they committed in treating you so badly.' Now please forgive the sins of the servants of the God of your father." When their message came to him, Joseph wept. His brothers then came and threw themselves down before him. "We are your slaves," they said. But Joseph said to them, "Don't be afraid. Am I in the place of God? You intended to harm me, but God intended it for good to accomplish what is now being done, the saving of many lives."[27]

There are many parallels in this story which can be applied to the history of Jewish/Gentile relations. Like Joseph, the Jewish people were born into a place of favor, as God's most favored nation, the apple of His eye. This divine choice sparked burning jealousy among the Gentile nations. History reveals that this jealousy manifested itself in Egyptian attempts at genocide, in Assyrian attempts at assimilation through transfer of populations, in Persian attempts at state-sponsored pogroms, in the murderous cries of St. John Chrysostom and in the furious diatribes of Martin Luther.[28] Today this jealousy still smolders in the coals of Replacement Theology,

---

26 *Cf.*, Gen. 45:26

27 Gen. 50:15-20

28 A helpful list of books on the history of anti-Semitism can be found in chapter 10, footnote 1.

which are discussed in chapter nine. The limitations of this book do not permit a serious consideration of Islamic beliefs on the rejection of the Jewish people and of the murderous calls for *jihad* against Israel – all based on jealousy toward Isaac and Jacob the chosen seed.

Like Joseph, the Jewish people have boasted in their chosenness. "Blessed are You O Lord our God King of the universe, Who has not made me a Gentile!" are the words of a synagogue prayer from the late Second Temple period. While some Jews have boasted like Joseph did, the Church has grievously behaved like Joseph's brothers, throwing Israel into European pits called ghettos while mocking the Jewish people's calling, "Let's see what will come of their dreams of priority!"

Throughout the long years of Israel's exile God prospered the Jewish people and gave them success,[29] as He had done with Joseph in Pharaoh's dungeons. But Joseph still remained in an Egyptian prison while his brothers raised families and 'looked out for number one.' Similarly, while the Church went about its business enjoying its new self-proclaimed status as the 'true Spiritual Israel' and as 'God's Jerusalem That Is Above,' the Jewish people had to contend with Talmud burnings, murderous Crusades, forced baptisms, ghettos, special 'Jewish' clothing and headgear, pogroms and lynchings – all in the name of the Gentiles' Christ and at the hands of Eastern and Western Churches.

The time will soon be upon the Church when Israel will be revealed as God's priority people. On that day many Christians will fall down in terror like Joseph's brothers did, asking the Jewish people to forgive the sins and the wrongs Christians have committed over the centuries in treating Israel so badly. Like Joseph, the Jewish people will weep and gently explain, "Don't be afraid. Are we in the place of God? You intended to harm us, but God intended it for good to accomplish what is now being done, the saving of many lives." As God had saved Joseph's life many times, God has preserved the

---

29 *Cf.,* Jer. 29:7

lives of the Jewish people down through history, saving them also from the murderous jealousy of many Christians. In the near future Yeshua will bring the Jewish nation to Himself and use them as He once used Joseph, to preserve a remnant on earth – to save many Gentile lives by a great deliverance. "For if their rejection is the reconciliation of the world, what will their acceptance be but life from the dead?"[30]

The International House of Prayer

How do Gentiles feel in their gut about the priority of Israel? To speak frankly, supernatural revelation and a gift of humility are needed for any non-Jew to rejoice in the Jewish people's calling. Just as many Jews stumbled over God turning to the Gentiles with the gospel, so many Gentiles find it painfully difficult to swallow the issue of Jewish priority. Green hues of jealousy tend to shade the clarity of their theological vision.

The prophet Isaiah offers the nations some much needed words of comfort. In a prophecy describing the End of Days, Isaiah gently turns to those Gentiles who might be feeling left out of the process.

> Let no foreigner who has bound himself to the Lord
> say, "The Lord will surely exclude me from His people."
> For this is what the Lord says…"(F)oreigners who bind
> themselves to the Lord to serve Him, to love the name
> of the Lord, and to worship Him, all who keep the
> Sabbath without desecrating it and who hold fast to
> My covenant – these I will bring to My holy mountain
> and give them joy in My house of prayer. Their burnt
> offerings and sacrifices will be accepted on My altar;
> for My house will be called 'A House Of Prayer For
> All Nations.'" The Sovereign Lord declares – He
> who gathers the exiles of Israel: "I will gather still
> others to them besides those already gathered."[31]

Gentiles whose hearts are given over to the Lord and who

---

30 Rom. 11:15
31 Isa. 56:3-8

honor the people of Israel will receive four special gifts. They will be brought to the land of Israel to worship the Lord. They will be drawn by God Himself onto the Temple Mount in Jerusalem. Their offerings and sacrifices to the Lord will be accepted with favor, and a special gift of joy will be their portion when they meet in God's Temple, His House of Prayer.

Nursing on the Blessed Bosom

In the last chapter of the Scroll of Isaiah the prophet specifically addresses those from among the nations who love the Jewish people and intercede for Israel's salvation. God promises some special benefits to these special intercessors. Comfort and delight will flow in abundance to all who love Jerusalem and have mourned for her. When Yeshua returns to His city and covers Israel with His peace, and when He causes the wealth of the world's empires to come coursing into Israel, these intercessors will be especially comforted over what God will have accomplished for the Jewish people. The image is that of a cute little baby who has nursed so much that he has nodded off to sleep still clinging to his mother's breast, a half-smile playing about his tiny mouth. He has drunk deeply with delight, and now he is satisfied with an overflowing sense of peace. Such is the portion for those who embrace the priority of the Jewish people.

> Rejoice with Jerusalem and be glad for her, all you who love her; rejoice greatly with her, all you who mourn over her. For you will nurse and be satisfied at her comforting breasts; you will drink deeply and delight in her overflowing abundance. For this is what the Lord says: "I will extend peace to her like a river, and the wealth of nations like a flooding stream; you will nurse and be carried on her arm and dandled on her knees. As a mother comforts her child, so will I comfort you; and you will be comforted over Jerusalem."[32]

---

32   Isa. 66:10-13

Things Go Better with Jewish Olive Oil

Before auto manufacturers start to produce new automobile models, they have their engineers design a prototype of the car. This model is the original. All other cars are copies of this prototype. This same process is true regarding the origins of the nation of Israel. She is the prototype, lovingly designed and developed by God.[33] The cars which later come off the production line are the believers from the Gentile nations.

Because Israel is the original prototype, Paul the Apostle says that she actually fits better in 'the natural olive tree' described in Romans 11. When the Jewish people will be grafted back into the natural olive tree again, when they as a nation come to faith in Messiah Yeshua, their graft will 'take better' and they will fit into the tree more naturally. The spiritual DNA of this reborn Jewish nation matches most closely the spiritual DNA of the original natural olive tree. "(Y)ou, though a wild olive shoot, have been grafted in among the others and now share in the nourishing sap from the olive root...(I)f you were cut out of an olive tree that is wild by nature, and contrary to nature were grafted into a cultivated olive tree, how much more readily will these, the natural branches, be grafted into their own olive tree!"[34]

The very genes of God's Jewish olive tree are encoded with a divine priority. And when the original Jewish sap – the prophetic promises of God – starts running again, when these Jewish juices flow freely through the ingrafted natural olive branches to the rest of God's olive tree, great blessing will overtake the entire world.

---

33   *Cf.*, Isa. 5:1-7; Ja.1:18

34   Rom. 11:17, 24

Section Three:
MURDERING
THE DAUGHTER OF ZION

Chapter Eight

Dragon Theology:
The Spiritual Roots Of Anti-Semitism

E ver wonder why humanity is in such a mess? Take into consideration Satan's role in history. In the same way, to understand why the Jewish people have suffered so much anti-Semitism, one needs to take into consideration the satanic origins of *Judenfeind*, hatred of the Jewish people.

The origins of anti-Semitism are described in Revelation 12, in John's apocalyptic vision. That chapter deals with Israel's calling, the birth of Messiah, and spiritual warfare. These verses will now be examined in some detail, since they offer unparalleled insight into Satan's *modus operandi* with regard to Israel.

The Mother of All Dreams

Revelation chapter twelve begins with John receiving a vision of two powerful heavenly signs. The first of these two signs reminds us of Joseph's dream in Genesis. where the same symbols of sun, moon and twelve stars are found.

> Then (Joseph) had another dream, and he told it to
> his brothers. "Listen," he said, "I had another dream,
> and this time the sun and moon and eleven stars
> were bowing down to me." When he told his father as
> well as his brothers, his father rebuked him and said,
> "What is this dream you had? Will your mother and
> I and your brothers actually come and bow down to
> the ground before you?" His brothers were jealous
> of him, but his father kept the matter in mind.[1]

Jacob interpreted his son Joseph's dream to mean that these heavenly bodies represent the Jewish people. The sun represented Jacob the Patriarch, the moon was the Matriarch and the twelve stars were their twelve sons from whom the people of Israel are descended. Jacob the Patriarch's interpretation of this dream is also the interpretive guideline for John's vision in Revelation 12.

> A great and wondrous sign appeared in heaven: a woman
> clothed with the sun, with the moon under her feet and
> a crown of twelve stars on her head. She was pregnant
> and cried out in pain as she was about to give birth.
> Then another sign appeared in heaven: an enormous
> red dragon with seven heads and ten horns and seven
> crowns on his heads. His tail swept a third of the stars
> out of the sky and flung them to the earth. The dragon
> stood in front of the woman who was about to give
> birth, so that he might devour her child the moment
> it was born. She gave birth to a son, a male child, who
> will rule all the nations with an iron scepter. And her
> child was snatched up to God and to His throne. The
> woman fled into the desert to a place prepared for her by
> God, where she might be taken care of for 1,260 days.[2]

The woman clothed with the sun, standing on the moon and having a crown of twelve stars is the Jewish people, those same

---

1 Gen. 37:9-11

2 Rev. 12:1-6. Due to the limited focus of this book, verse six (which has reference to another future event concerning the Jewish people) will not be dealt with here.

twelve tribes which are Jacob's descendants. In this vision the Jewish people are pregnant with a special seed and are about to give birth to a special child. The concept of a special seed of a woman hearkens back to Genesis 3:15. In that verse it was prophesied that a deliverer known as "the seed of the woman" would conquer the Serpent. As if struck by that same thought, John sees a horrific vision rising up in front of him. Satan himself appears, the great red dragon, who in verse 9 is described as "that ancient serpent called the devil, or Satan, who leads the whole world astray." Revelation 12 is unwrapping the great promise of the seed given to Adam and Eve in the Garden of Eden. The flowering of that promise is the birth of Messiah Yeshua.

Kingdoms in Conflict

John turns to look at the dragon, the second sign in this chapter. He notices that this beast has seven heads, ten horns and seven crowns. This description reminds us of Daniel 7:7, 20, 24. In Daniel, three anti-Messianic kingdoms rise up out of the sea of the nations, followed by a fourth and final superpower. That kingdom is described as a beast having large iron teeth and being dreadful, terrifying and extremely strong. This beast originally had ten horns, but then three horns fall away and only seven remain. This beast is the final earthly expression of anti-God power.

In John's vision the dragon had already swept one third of the stars out of the sky and flung them to earth. Based on similar language in Job 1:6 and 38:7, many Bible students understand that this verse is describing the original rebellion of Lucifer. At one time Lucifer seduced one third of all the angels to rebel against God's authority. These angels became demons, soldiers of the kingdom of darkness, and their initial punishment was to be cut off from the presence of God.

Coming back to John's vision, we see two kingdoms in conflict. One kingdom is represented by the Jewish people who gives birth to the seed of the woman. The opposing kingdom is represented by the beast who is remarkably similar to the fourth beast in the Book of Daniel. This beast symbolizes the anti-Messiah forces of the kingdom of Rome[3] and he is empowered in a special way by Satan. The dragon is snarling at the birthstool, waiting to devour the baby even as his head begins to crown.

Miraculously the Jewish people give birth to a healthy male child in spite of the dragon's destructive presence. This baby is described as the one "who will rule all the nations with an iron scepter." This term iron scepter is taken from Psalm 2, a Messianic psalm which looks past the crowning of King David to the coronation of David's Greater Son the Messiah.[4]

> Why do the nations conspire and the peoples plot in vain? The kings of the earth take their stand and the rulers gather together against the Lord and against His Anointed One. "Let us break their chains," they say, "and throw off their fetters." The One enthroned in heaven laughs; the Lord scoffs at them. Then He rebukes them in His anger and terrifies them in His wrath, saying, "I have installed My King on Zion, My holy hill." I will proclaim the decree of the Lord: He said to me, "You are my Son; today I have become your Father. Ask of Me, and I will make the nations your inheritance, the ends of the earth your possession. You will rule them with an iron scepter; you will dash them to pieces like pottery."[5]

Yeshua, God's Anointed One, will one day rule all nations from His chosen city of Jerusalem. In that day rebellion or sullenness will not be tolerated from any people. Disobedient subjects will feel the iron power of Yeshua's hand. Psalm 2 paints a prophetic picture of Messiah Yeshua's thousand year future reign over this planet.

---

3   *Cf.*, Dan. 8:20-22 which calls the third kingdom "Greece," and Dan. 7:2-8,16-24, which says that the fourth kingdom comes after the third kingdom, having conquered it in battle. Alexander the Great's empire was conquered by Rome after the Hellenistic Empire had been weakened in the Diadochine wars.

4   *Cf.*, Psa. 110; Matt. 22:41-46

5   Psa. 2:1-9. *Cf.*, Rev. 2:27 where the same quote applies to believers as co-rulers with Messiah, and Rev. 19:15 where the quote applies to Yeshua alone.

Looking again at Revelation 12:1-6, the following sentence gives the shortest Bible description of the life, ministry, death and resurrection of Messiah Yeshua: "And her child was snatched up to God and to His throne." John does not retell the gospel story in this chapter. Instead he focuses on the climax of spiritual warfare and how that battle especially concerns the Jewish people.

So far John's first vision describes how the Jewish people brought Messiah into the world. Though Satan personally opposed the birth of the promised seed of the woman, the Child was born and God's purposes came to pass through Him. This passage also pulls back the curtain on the Christmas story. Satan was pulling Herod the Great's strings, causing the king to order the murder of Bethlehem's Jewish babies. A broader application of this passage would touch on other such attempts to murder the Daughter of Zion, like Pharaoh's decree to annihilate all Jewish male babies in the first chapter of Exodus, and Haman's decree to destroy all Jews in Esther 3. Secular history contributes other lists of bloody but failed satanic attempts to destroy Israel.

Jewish Strategic-Level Spiritual Warfare

And there was war in heaven. Michael and his angels fought against the dragon, and the dragon and his angels fought back. But he was not strong enough, and they lost their place in heaven. The great dragon was hurled down – that ancient serpent called the devil, or Satan, who leads the whole world astray. He was hurled to the earth, and his angels with him. Then I heard a loud voice in heaven say: "Now have come the salvation and the power and the kingdom of our God, and the authority of His Christ. For the accuser of our brothers, who accuses them before our God day and night, has been hurled down. They overcame him by the blood of the Lamb and by the word of their testimony; they did not love their lives so much as to shrink from death. Therefore rejoice, you heavens and you who dwell in them! But woe to the earth and the sea, because the devil has gone down to you! He is filled with fury, because he knows that his time is short."[6]

Revelation 12:7-12 kicks into high gear at this point. A battle royal is in progress, and John is watching in awe. An angelic being known as Michael is surrounded by his angelic warriors and they are in hand-to-hand combat with Satan and his minions. Michael's presence is significant here, because it establishes that the focus of this chapter is indeed on the Jewish people.

Michael is first mentioned in Daniel 10:13 where an angel tells Daniel: "Michael, one of the chief princes, came to help me, because I was detained there with the king of Persia." Michael is a high-ranking angel who comes to the aid of a lower angel as they fight together against a demonic principality who oversees the Persian Empire. That powerful demon was violently opposing God's purposes in freeing the Jewish people and returning them to the land of Israel. God's reinforcements were called in and directed by Michael. In the end, history tells us that the Jewish people were not destroyed by Haman but were preserved.

The next reference to Michael is in Daniel 10:20. Here he is described as the angelic prince who is assigned to the Jewish people. "So (the angel) said, 'Do you know why I have come to you? Soon I will return to fight against the prince of Persia, and when I go, the prince of Greece will come...No one supports me against them except Michael, your prince.'"[7] The angel talking with Daniel says that as soon as he finishes conveying the divine message, he must leave and rejoin the battle against Persia. After the demonic overlord of Persia is defeated, another demonic prince called the prince of Greece would arise. World history and Daniel 11:21-35 reveal that the next superpower to take the stage after the decline of Persia was Greece, and that Greek forces in the days of Antiochus IV Epiphanes would eventually attempt to destroy Israel.[8] When Daniel received this prophecy, all these events were yet future

---

6   Rev. 12:7-12

7   Dan. 10:20

8   *Cf.*, Dan. 11:28-35

and they would have great importance for the survival of Israel. So Michael the angelic prince of Israel would be called to join that battle as well.

Michael is mentioned again in Daniel 12:1. The same angel who had been speaking with Daniel prophesies about the very end of time. In this passage Michael is described as "the great prince who protects the Jewish people." "At that time Michael, the great prince who protects your people, will arise. There will be a time of distress such as has not happened from the beginning of nations until then. But at that time your people – everyone whose name is found written in the book – will be delivered." Michael's activities and presence will become boldly known in the Latter Days as he arises to protect and preserve the remnant of Israel.

The last biblical reference to Michael is in Jude 9, where he is referred to as the archangel Michael. The only other mention of an archangel is in 1 Thessalonians 4:16: "For the Lord Himself will come down from heaven, with a loud command, with the voice of the archangel and with the trumpet call of God, and the dead in Messiah will rise first."

The biblical perspective is clear. Michael is a high angel, an archangel, one of the chief angelic princes. What is of paramount importance here is that Michael is the princely protector of the Jewish people. Whenever Michael's name appears, the reader knows immediately that the safety and calling of the Jewish people are under attack.

The accuser among us

If there is any passage in the Scriptures that describes strategic-level spiritual warfare, Revelation 12:7-12 takes the prize. This prophecy states that war in the heavenlies will break out and Michael, the archangel who holds the Jewish portfolio, will battle Satan over an Israel-related event. Satan and his demons will be thrown out of heaven and hurled down to the earth. A synthesis of Job 1:6-7, 2:1-7, Zechariah 3:1 and 1 John 2:1 indicates that Satan is still permitted occasional access to the very presence of God in His throne room. Satan is a Hebrew word meaning he who accuses, and the accuser of our brethren still accuses believers before our God day and night. When Satan will be thrown down to the earth, his freedom of access to heaven will be finally revoked. In that hour all heaven will rejoice, for the enemy's sulfurous smell will no longer pollute the courts of the Most High.[9]

But when Michael revokes Satan's access to the very presence of God (Revelation 12:8-9), spiritual warfare will jump to another level. Total warfare will break out on earth. The enemy will attack the most strategic of all targets with great fury, knowing that his campaign will only triumph by a decisive blow. At the same time an angel proclaims that the kingdom of God has just taken a powerful step forward. God's royal standards are now firmly planted in the soil and His unfurled banners flap powerfully in the wind.

John hears a loud voice reminding him that in the coming conflict believers on earth will defeat Satan, but at a high cost. The weapons in the hands of the saints at that time will be the charismatic power of the blood of Messiah, the evangelistic testimony of the gospel, and the spiritual power released through the blood of the martyrs. Both the cross and the resurrection power of Yeshua will be clearly seen in all the world, through the miracles and the martyrdom of Yeshua's followers.

Satan's Final Solution

Satan and his hordes hit the ground running. They immediately begin to carpet bomb the quadrant where it will hurt most. Withering fire is trained on the Jewish people, directed at the woman who gave birth to the male child. Satan has activated his own 'final solution of the Jewish problem' for the last time. "When the dragon saw that he had been hurled to the earth, he pursued the woman who had given birth to the male child...Then the dragon was enraged at the woman and went off to make war against the

---

9   *Cf.*, Rev. 12:12

rest of her offspring - those who obey God's commandments and hold to the testimony of Yeshua."[10]

Anti-Semitism has always been a central plank in hell's platform. It is one of Lucifer's major mandates. The enemy knows that the Jewish people are God's key to many end-time events – life from the dead,[11] the times of refreshing,[12] the return of Messiah Yeshua[13] and the restoration of all things.[14] Satan's persecution of the apple of God's eye reveals his desire to deal a death-blow to God Most High Himself, to frustrate His plans, to violate His priorities and to rob His glory. To annihilate the Jewish people is to destroy the linchpin of God's prophetic plan, to hijack the nuclear core of Yeshua's kingdom.

It comes as no surprise to the reader that modern anti-Semitic movements are satanically influenced. The neo-Nazi skinhead, the anti-Semitic Militiaman, the Iranian Hizbullah terrorist, the Islamic Jihad or Hamas suicide bomber, the black-jacketed thug of Pamyat or Zhirinovsky, the 'Christian Identity' preacher – each one's hatred of the Jewish people is fueled by the same hellish source. Unless these people turn from their rebellious ways and kiss the King of Zion, they will one day feel the cold metal of God's iron scepter on their backs.

---

10   Rev. 12:13, 17

11   Cf., Rom. 11:15

12   Cf., Acts 3:19

13   Cf., Matt. 23:39; Acts 3:20

14   Cf., Acts 3:21

Chapter Nine

How Have We Robbed God?
Replacement Theology and You

In the days of Tsar Nicholas I, an old Jewish gentleman, Shmulik Kaganovitch by name, was walking along the palace-lined embankments of St. Petersburg, Russia. Slipping on a patch of ice, he fell from a bridge into the dark waters of the Neva River and began to drown. He thrashed about in the water, yelling for help at the top of his lungs. Two Cossack officers heard his screams and ran over to the railing. When they saw that the dying man was a Jew, they began to guffaw. Kaganovitch shouted, "Help! Save me! I'm drowning!" The soldiers laughed, "It's your problem, *Zhid*!" As Shmulik felt himself sinking into the cold black waters, he suddenly had an inspired thought: "Down with Tsar Nicholas!" he roared. Immediately the officers jumped into the water, dragged Kaganovitch out and arrested him for sedition.

Proverbs says that "the kindest acts of the wicked are cruel."[1] The two officers in this apocryphal story saved Kaganovitch not because they were concerned for the life of a Jew, but because they hated anarchists. Cossacks have tended to be indifferent to the fate of the Jews. The Nobel Prize-winning author Elie Wiesel once said, "The opposite of love is not hate, it's indifference."[2] George Bernard Shaw added, "The worst sin toward our fellow creatures is not to hate them, but to be indifferent to them; that's the essence of inhumanity."[3] Indifference to the fate of the Jewish people has characterized Gentile Christianity. Though the Scriptures ooze God's love for Israel, these passions of God have been plugged up in the Church by a dominating theological stronghold. This theology is known today as Replacement Theology. Its historical origins are wrapped around the gnarled and ancient roots of the Church's anti-Semitic past.

An Apostolic Warning

In Malachi 3:7-13 God accused many in Israel of spiritual robbery. The Lord declared that the majority of the nation were "cursed with a curse, for you are robbing Me, the whole nation of you."[4] As well, God said that many Jewish people were guilty of arrogance toward God: "Your words have been arrogant against Me, says the Lord."[5]

Four hundred year later the Apostle Paul warned Gentile believers in Messiah to avoid these same sins (spiritual robbery and spiritual arrogance) towards Israel. Gentiles, watch your attitude towards the Jewish people, he warned. Don't be ignorant of God's calling on them![6] Don't be wise in your own estimation towards Israel![7] Don't be conceited or puffed up, thinking that Gentiles are

---

1   Prov. 12:10

2   *U.S. News and World Report* (New York, 27 Oct. 1986)

3   George Bernard Shaw, in *The Devil's Disciple*, Act 2, spoken by Anderson.

4   Mal. 3:9 NASB

5   Mal. 3:13 NASB

6   Rom. 11:25a

7   Rom. 11:25b

now better than Jews.[8] Don't be arrogant towards the Jewish people, assuming that God has changed His plan or His word regarding Israel's priority status.[9]

For the most part Paul's warnings have been ignored. Within three hundred years of this clear apostolic caution, the Church jumped with both feet into a theological position known today as Replacement Theology.[10] This position is also called Supercession or Displacement or Transfer Theology. Simply put, this theology says that the Jewish people have forever lost their covenantal priority status, and that God has now irrevocably transferred that priority status to the Church which is predominantly Gentile. The Jewish people are no longer a chosen people according to Replacement Theology. Replacement theologians see no spiritual difference today between Jerusalem and Paris, though some believe that other spiritual centers have replaced Jerusalem. Roman Catholics favor Rome while the Eastern Orthodox recognize Istanbul/ Constantinople. The Russian Orthodox insists on Moscow, while some Reformation buffs cast a longing eye toward Geneva.

Replacement Theology can be described as an expression of Gentile triumphalism in the Church. Its distorted shadow has fallen on Systematic Theology, leaving confusion in the areas of hamartiology, bibliology, ecclesiology and eschatology, as well as in apologetics and ethics. This chapter will consider a biblical perspective on Replacement Theology.

The Samaritan Factor

One of the first to espouse Replacement Theology was a Samaritan believer ca. 150 A.D. named Justin Martyr.[11] Justin probably inherited

---

8   Rom. 11:20

9   Rom. 11:18

10   A helpful documentation of early church history on this subject is Peter Richardson's *Israel in the Apostolic Church* (Cambridge: Cambridge University Press, 1969)

11   Justin Martyr, "Dialogue With Trypho, A Jew," in *The Ante-Nicene Fathers* (Grand Rapids: Wm. B. Eerdmans, 1975) *ed.* Alexander Roberts & James Donaldson, Vol. I, ch. 120.

a predisposition to anti-Semitism from the Samaritan community,[12] and this predisposition influenced his theologizing about the Jewish people. His book *Dialogue With Trypho* is the first written account of a polemical discussion between himself (a Samaritan Christian) and a learned Jewish man (possibly Rabbi Tarphon of the Tannaitic period). One of Justin's contentions is that Gentile Christians and not Jews are the real Israel, and that the Jewish people are now excluded from God's purposes. The following are selected quotes from this work.

[1] Jews have forfeited the title "Israel" but Gentile Christians have received it.

> Since then God blesses (the Gentiles), and calls them Israel, and declares them to be His inheritance, how is it that you repent not of the deception you practice on yourselves, as if you alone were the Israel, and of execrating the people whom God has blessed?... "What, then?" says Trypho, "are you Israel? And speaks He such things of you?"...I continued: "...(W)e from Christ, who begat us unto God, like Jacob, and Israel, and Judah, and Joseph, and David, are called and are the true sons of God, and keep the commandments of Christ." And...I saw that they were perturbed because I said that we are the sons of God...[13]

[2] Jewish physical circumcision is a sign of judgment.

> For the circumcision according to the flesh, which is from Abraham, was given for a sign; that you may be separated from other nations, and from us; and that you alone may suffer that which you now justly suffer; and that your land may be desolate, and your cities burned with fire; and that strangers may eat your fruit in your presence, and not one of you may go up to Jerusalem.[14]

[3] God likes Gentile worship better than Jewish worship.

12   *Cf.*, John 4:9
13   *ibid.*, ch. 123-124
14   *ibid.*, ch. 16

> Let us glorify God, all nations gathered together;
> for He has also visited us ... For He has been
> gracious towards the Gentiles also; and our
> sacrifices He esteems more grateful than yours.[15]

[4] Jews have forfeited the Bible and it now belongs to Gentile Christians.

> What need, then, have I of circumcision, who have
> been witnessed to by God? ...For (regarding) these
> words...David sung them, Isaiah preached them,
> Zechariah proclaimed them, and Moses wrote them.
> Are you acquainted with them, Trypho? They are
> contained in your Scriptures, or rather not yours,
> but ours. For we believe them; but you, though you
> read them, do not catch the spirit that is in them.[16]

[5] Gentile Christians are now the 'true Israel.'

> As, therefore, Christ is the Israel and the Jacob, even
> so we, who have been quarried out from the bowels
> of Christ, are the true Israelitic race... Such are the
> words of Scripture; understand, therefore, that the
> seed of Jacob now referred to is something else, and
> not, as may be supposed, spoken of your people.[17] God
> has shown that those who were selected out of every
> nation have obeyed His will through Christ – whom
> He calls also Jacob, and names Israel – and these, then,
> as I mentioned fully previously, must be Jacob and
> Israel.[18] For the true spiritual Israel, and descendants
> of Judah, Jacob, Isaac, and Abraham...are we who
> have been led to God through this crucified Christ, as
> shall be demonstrated while we proceed.[19] But Israel
> was (Christ's) name from the beginning, to which He
> altered the name of the blessed Jacob when He blessed
> him with His own name, proclaiming thereby that all

---

15   *ibid.*, ch. 29
16   *ibid.*
17   *ibid.*, ch. 135
18   *ibid.*, ch. 130
19   *ibid.*, ch. 11

who through Him have fled for refuge to the Father, constitute the blessed Israel. But you, having understood none of this, and not being prepared to understand, ... you are the children of Jacob after the fleshly seed...[20]

Variations on a Theme

Modern Replacement Theology builds its interpretation of Scripture, its hermeneutical grid, on Justin Martyr's foundations. With him it believes that three watershed events occurred when the Jewish people's spiritual leadership rejected Yeshua's Messiahship. These three events are repeated in the following quotes from "Jesus And Israel" by David Holwerda, a recently published book promoting Replacement Theology, and "Jesus and the Old Testament" by R.T. France.

[1] Israel has forever lost her priority status by rejecting Yeshua's Messiahship. Her sins are worse than those of the nations.

...(T)he majority view within the Church has been...that the Jews have lost title to (the) claim (to being the True Israel). Historical Israel had failed, and the promises had not come to fulfillment through the Israelites. Judgment falls on those who do not believe...(Israel') privileged position as the heirs of the kingdom would be taken from them... Because of this failure to comprehend, Israel loses what it had and continues to manifest the judgment that Isaiah had pronounced on his own unbelieving generation... (U)nbelieving Israel... will lose its privileged position as "heirs of the kingdom"...(and will lose the God-given) task of Old Testament Israel.[21]

...(S)ince Jesus is superior to the Old Testament types, the Jewish refusal to accept him as God's messenger must carry a greater condemnation. Their punishment, in the destruction of Jerusalem and the final rejection

---

20   ibid., ch. 125

21   David E. Holwerda, *Jesus And Israel: one covenant or two?* (Grand Rapids, Wm. B. Eerdmans; 1995), pp. 4, 33, 55-56

116

of the nation from their privileged status as the people
of God, will be on a scale higher than even the most
terrible disasters known to the Old Testament.[22]

[2] The title 'Israel' now means 'Yeshua' and not the Jewish people.
Replacement Theology believes that the term 'Israel' has had its
original meaning changed or 'transferred.' In the Hebrew Scriptures
the term 'Israel' meant 'the Jewish people.'[23] The Replacement
position is that, after the majority of Israel failed to accept was
now taken away from the Jewish people and transferred to Yeshua.
Now it would refer only to Christ. Replacement Theology is now
metamorphosing or changing the meaning of the term 'Israel' in the
first part of a two-step process.

> Jesus, then is true Israel, the one who does everything
> that Israel was supposed to do and who is everything
> that Israel was supposed to be...Jesus...is the Israel
> who is the object of God's love. He is chosen by
> God and responds in perfect obedience...Jesus is the
> corporate representative of Israel...As God's anointed
> servant, Jesus fulfills that task of Israel... Jesus is
> Israel, and Israel is Jesus...Jesus has been identified
> as Israe l... and the one who takes Israel's place.[24]

[3] The title 'Israel' and all formerly Jewish privileges are now
transferred to the Christian Church — now called 'the New Israel,'

---

22   R.T. France, *Jesus and the Old Testament* (Downer's Grove: InterVarsity, 1971), pp. 79-80

23   The term 'Israel' was used by the prophets to refer only to Jews. Three different categories of Jews
are described by the term "Israel." The broadest use of the term refers to the whole nation which has
been called by God to be His servant-people (*e.g.*, Isa. 41:8-14; 44:1-5; *etc.*). The second and narrower
use refers to the Jewish remnant, that portion of Israel which is circumcised in heart (*cf.*, Deut. 30:1-6;
Isa. 10:20-23; 65:8-13, 20; Ezek. 20:33-38; Amos 9:7-10; Zech. 13:8-9; Lk. 2:34; 3:8-9, 16-17; Rom. 9:6, 27-29;
11: 4-7; Gal. 6:16, *etc.*). The third use of the term "Israel" refers to the Messiah, the only Jew who never
sinned (*E.g.*, Isa. 42:1-4; 49:1-7; 52:13-53:12; Acts 4:27; Rom. 15:8, *etc.*). Yeshua the Jew is God's faithful
sign to the whole Jewish people that all of God's promises to the nation will be fulfilled. Yeshua is
not only the Second Adam; He is the Second Abraham (*cf.*, Rom. 5:12-21). For more information on
the threefold use of 'Israel' *cf.*, Herbert M. Wolf, *Interpreting Isaiah* (Grand Rapids: Zondervan, 1985)
pp. 190-191; Franz Delitzsch, *Biblical Commentary on the Prophecies of Isaiah*, transl. James Martin, 3d
ed., 2 vols. (1877; reprint, Grand Rapids: Wm. B. Eerdmans, 1967), 2:174.

24   Holwerda, *op. cit.*, pp. 33, 57, 44-45

'the True Israel' or 'the Israel of God'

This is the third step: the Gentile Church now replaces the Jewish people as God's priority people. They only are called 'Israel' by God. All the formerly Jewish promises have been transferred to the predominantly Gentile Church.

> Since Jesus is the corporate representative of Israel, God now recognizes as Israel all who respond in faith and obedience to the presence and will of God revealed in Jesus That was and continues to be the only question that decides the identity of Israel: Not ancestry but faith, not human achievement but God's gift, calling and election, acknowledged in Jesus, son of Abraham, son of David, Son of God. If the church is Israel, then the church is not just an interim arrangement but a people standing in continuity with Old Testament Israel and carrying out Israel's mission in the world...God's promises are for Israel, but Israel is not established simply by birthright...(T)he definition of Israel cannot be restricted to physical descendants of Abraham forming a political nation requiring armies for its maintenance. From a New Testament perspective it was Jewish nationalism...that led to (Jesus') rejection as Messiah... As the people of God, Israel was always intended to be and to become a universal people, not limited by racial purity...God decides who belongs to Israel... Because Israel's disobedience...thwarted God's intention... God will create on earth his true people...The task of all the disciples as those who confess faith in Jesus... will be to gather the church, the people of God, who are seen here as the remnant of Israel or as true Israel... (T)hose who believe in Jesus...are the recipients of the privileged status and task of Old Testament Israel.[25]

> The true Israel of this eschatological age is no longer the nation of the old covenant, but the Christian community, inaugurated by a new covenant through

---

25 *ibid*.,, pp. 57, 34, 183, 35, 40, 51, 56

a mediator greater than the Israelite priesthood...[26]

Replacement theologians believe that the Apostles initially had difficulty grasping these abovementioned truths. It seems that the Apostles had been led into error by their own hopes for a national Jewish restoration. The theological understanding of the Apostles therefore had to be shattered and altered (though, of course, no Scripture ever teaches this).

> (Paul's) previous Jewish focus on a particularistic fulfillment has been transferred onto Christian universalism focused on a new creation...The people of God, Israel, is still a flesh and blood historical reality, although now a universal people and no longer a single, particular people as in the Old Testament... Such is the inexorable unfolding of God's promises from particularism to universalism, a movement that necessarily shatters the particularistic limits that were originally in the disciples' minds when they asked about the restoration of the kingdom to Israel... (The apostles) were in error in their expectations and had to have their understanding altered.[27]

Setting Limits on the Patience of God

The foundation stone of Replacement Theology is a belief that God has rejected the Jewish people. Replacement Theology says that something traumatic happened which caused God to alter or change His 'business as usual' relationship with Israel. According to this perspective Israel's rejection of Yeshua's Messiahship was the straw that broke the camel's back, the perfidious act that exhausted God's patience with the Jewish people. As a result, they say, God transferred or expanded the title 'Israel' so that Gentiles could now be called 'Israel.' But has God lost patience with the Jewish people? Have Israel's sins disqualified her from reaping the final blessing of her own covenants? Has the priority of Israel been altered to a

---

26 France, *op. cit.*, p. 80
27 Holwerda, *op. cit.*, pp. 104, 179, 181, 180

priority of the predominantly Gentile church?

History helps answer this question. In the days of the Babylonian scourge the people of Israel were surrounded by scoffing and evilhearted enemies like the Edomites of TransJordan. These anti-Jewish neighbors crowed with delight to see Israel and Judah bite the dust. In derision they shouted out that God had abandoned His people and would dispense with the Jewish people's priority national status. The Lord's answer to these mockers came through the mouth of Jeremiah.

> The word of the Lord came to Jeremiah: "Have you not noticed that these people are saying, 'The Lord has rejected the two kingdoms He chose?' So they despise My people and no longer regard them as a nation. This is what the Lord says: If I have not established My covenant with day and night and the fixed laws of heaven and earth, then I will reject the descendants of Jacob and David My servant and will not choose one of his sons to rule over the descendants of Abraham, Isaac and Jacob. For I will restore their fortunes and have compassion on them."[28]

God takes exception to Gentile nations who proclaim that He has rejected the Jewish people. In the above context to *not regard Israel as a nation* is to say that Israel has lost its status as the chosen ethnic nation of God. God wants the world to know that Israel in exile will never be rejected but rather will be restored to full favor. As the Apostle Paul said, "I say then, God has not rejected His people, has He? May it never be! For I too am an Israelite, a descendant of Abraham, of the tribe of Benjamin. God has not rejected His people, whom He foreknew."[29]

But haven't Israel's great sins exhausted the patience of God? Hasn't their rejection of Yeshua radically changed the rules of the game? Jeremiah prophesies the heart of God in answer to this

---

28   Jer. 33:23-26

29   Rom. 11:1-2 NASB. *Cf.,* John R. Wilch, "Did God Reject the Jews?" in *Lutheran Theological Review* II:1 (Fall/Winter 1989-90) reprinted in *MISHKAN: A Forum On The Gospel And The Jewish People* (Jerusalem: U.C.C.I., 1992) issue 16, pp. 30-35.

question.

> This is what the Lord says, He who appoints the sun to
> shine by day, who decrees the moon and stars to shine
> by night, who stirs up the sea so that its waves roar – the
> Lord Almighty is His name – Only if these decrees vanish
> from My sight, declares the Lord, will the descendants
> of Israel ever cease to be a nation before Me. This is
> what the Lord says: Only if the heavens above can be
> measured and the foundations of the earth below be
> searched out will I reject all the descendants of Israel
> because of all they have done, declares the Lord.[30]

God does not appreciate statements that He no longer cares for the Jewish people. The Lord gets upset by those who claim that Israel has been cast away by her God. "For I will restore you to health and I will heal your wounds, declares the Lord, because they have called you an outcast, saying: 'It is Zion; no one cares for her.'"[31] The more that unfriendly nations challenge the continuing nature of the Jewish people's priority status, the more God is committed to restoring Israel to her privileged position.

Missing the Mark of God's Heart

God is not afraid to rebuke His own people and to judge them severely. Yet the Scriptures also declare that behind God's judgments lies a heart still lovesick for Israel. Though God at times brings a double portion of judgment on the Jewish people, the rejection of Israel is the farthest thing from His mind. "Is not Ephraim My dear son, the child in whom I delight? Though I often speak against him, I still remember him. Therefore My heart yearns for him; I have great compassion for him, declares theLord."[32]

There is a great difference between destruction and judgment. Destruction results in annihilation, while judgment can be a divine discipline fashioned for correction and restoration. Some believers

---

30   Jer. 31:35-37 (emphases mine, *ed.*)

31   Jer. 30:17 NASB

32   Jer. 31:20

find it difficult to distinguish between these two concepts, and they conclude that God's judgment on Israel means that God's promises to the Jewish people are now pre-empted. King Solomon once said, "For love is as strong as death, jealousy is as severe as Sheol. Its flashes are flashes of fire, the very flame of the Lord."[33] God's covenant love for Israel is unchanging. His affections for the Jewish people are stronger than the powers of death. The Lord's commitment to purify the Jewish people is more powerful than all the wages of sin.

It seems that a spiritual blindness exists in the hearts of Replacement theologians concerning God's passionate love for the Jewish people. Though Replacement adherents delight in Jesus' great passion for the Church, they seem unable to simultaneously recognize Messiah's great passion for His own Jewish people. Kay Arthur's recent best seller "Israel My Beloved"[34] may be therapeutic for Replacement theologians. Her book paints a glowing picture of God's hot pursuit of His Jewish bride down through the ages.

Yet Replacement Theology averts its gaze from the many avowals of divine love for Israel that are found throughout the Scriptures. Instead it focuses on how Israel's sins have removed the Jewish people from God's unconditional love. By giving an unbalanced and determinative place to judgment on Israel, while not focusing on God's undying commitment to rescue the Jewish people, Replacement Theology has missed the heart of God in this matter.

One Step over the Line

Some Bible commentators do an 'end run' on the Scriptures. Without consulting God they take the text just a little bit farther than it should go. This behavior has also characterized many nations' treatment of the Jewish people. When God called certain empires to be the rod of His judgment against Israel, those nations independently decided that they had been given *carte blanche* to

---

33 Song 8:6 NASB

34 Kay Arthur, *Israel, My Beloved* (Eugene: Harvest House, 1996). Kay Arthur is the founder and director of Precept Ministries.

finish Israel off. In their arrogance these Gentile powers arrogated authority to themselves that they had not been given by God. They decided that Israel was worse off than God had declared. "Then the angel who was speaking to me said, 'Proclaim this word: This is what the Lord Almighty says: I am very jealous for Jerusalem and Zion, but I am very angry with the nations that feel secure. I was only a little angry, but they added to the calamity.'"[35]

Assyria had an overly critical attitude towards Israel. This nation saw her victory over Israel as proof of Assyria's priority status. God reproves Sennacherib for his arrogance and promises to consume Assyria's forces in the fires of His wrath.

> Woe to the Assyrian, the rod of My anger, in whose hand is the club of My wrath! I send him against a godless nation, I dispatch him against a people who anger Me, to seize loot and snatch plunder, and to trample them down like mud in the streets. But this is not what he intends, this is not what he has in mind; his purpose is to destroy, to put an end to many nations... (Assyria says), "As my hand seized the kingdoms of the idols, kingdoms whose images excelled those of Jerusalem and Samaria – shall I not deal with Jerusalem and her images as I dealt with Samaria and her idols?" When the Lord has finished all His work against Mount Zion and Jerusalem, He will say, "I will punish the king of Assyria for the willful pride of his heart and the haughty look in his eyes. For he says: 'y the strength of my hand I have done this, and by my wisdom, because I have understanding. I removed the boundaries of nations, I plundered their treasures; like a mighty one I subdued their kings'...Does the ax raise itself above him who swings it, or the saw boast against him who uses it? As if a rod were to wield him who lifts it up, or a club brandish him who is not wood! Therefore, the Lord, the Lord Almighty, will send a wasting disease upon his sturdy warriors; under his pomp a fire will be kindled like a blazing flame. The Light of Israel will become a fire, their Holy One a flame; in a single day

35   Zech. 1:14-15

it will burn and consume his thorns and his briers."[36]

Down on the Threshing Floor

The Scroll of the Prophet Micah reflects this same reality. As the nations of the world gather around the country of Israel with destruction in their eyes, they gloat over the fact (so it seems to them) that God is finished with the Jewish people. "The fate of Israel will be just like the fate of all the other peoples we have destroyed," they think. Yet God has purposed that Israel's judgment will be reversed and that the Jewish people will bring glory to God through their own restoration.

> But now many nations are gathered against you. They say, "Let her be defiled, let our eyes gloat over Zion!" But they do not know the thoughts of the Lord; they do not understand His plan, He who gathers them like sheaves to the threshing floor. Rise and thresh, O Daughter of Zion, for I will give you horns of iron; I will give you hoofs of bronze and you will break to pieces many nations. You will devote their ill-gotten gains to the Lord, their wealth to the Lord of all the earth.[37]

Like these nations, Replacement Theology has drawn conclusions about Israel without consulting the heart of the Lord of Hosts. Influenced by centuries of anti-Semitism, these theologians have happily administered the theological coup de grace to Israel's priority status without feeling the tiniest pangs of conscience. For the most part Replacement theologians do not know the thoughts of the Lord for His people Israel. They do not understand God's plan for His priority nation. They are out of touch with the passions of God's heart.

A Promise is Forever

Replacement Theology believes that the term 'Israel' can be fairly applied to the Church because all the promises are now taken from

---

36   Isa. 10:5-7, 10-13, 15-17

37   Micah 4:11-13

the Jewish people.This position disagrees with Romans 9:4-5 where Paul affirms that the Jewish people still possess "the covenants... and the promises." Though Justin Martyr said that the Bible is now "ours, not yours," the Book of Romans says that the Scriptures still belongs to the Jewish people: "What advantage, then, is there in being a Jew, or what value is there in circumcision? Much in every way! First of all, they have been entrusted with the very words of God."[38]

The Apostle Paul disagrees with a central tenet of Replacement Theology when he teaches that all the spiritual blessings of the New Covenant still belong to the Jewish people. "(The Gentile believers of Macedonia)… indeed...owe it to (the saints in Jerusalem). For if the Gentiles have shared in the Jews' spiritual blessings, they owe it to the Jews to share with them their material blessings."[39]

Perhaps the clearest of all Scriptures is Romans 11:28-29: "As far as the gospel is concerned, (*ed., the unbelieving Jewish people*) are enemies on your (*ed., Gentile*) account; but as far as election is concerned, they are loved on account of the patriarchs, for God's gifts and His call are irrevocable."

All Are Not Israel Who Call Themselves 'The True Israel'

A consideration of the biblical use of the term "Israel" helps to unravel another theological knot. The word 'Israel' is used 69 times in the New Testament. In five cases it refers to the land of Israel.[40] In 63 cases it refers to the nation of Israel. The 69th time the word 'Israel' is used is in Galatians 6:16 where the expression 'the Israel of God' is found. Replacement theologians interpret this phrase as meaning 'the Church.' S. Lewis Johnson Jr.'s *festschrift* article "Paul and the 'Israel of God'"[41] examines the exegesis of this phrase and

---

38 Rom. 3:1-2

39 Rom. 15:26-27

40 *I.e.*, Matt. 2:20-21; 10:23; Lk. 4:25, 27

41 S. Lewis Johnson Jr., "Paul and the 'Israel of God': An Exegetical and Eschatological Case-Study," ed. Stanley D. Toussaint and Charles H. Dyer, *Essays in Honor of J. Dwight Pentecost* (Chicago: Moody Press, 1986).

concludes that the overwhelming evidence favors interpreting this term as a reference to Jewish believers in Yeshua.To argue for calling Gentiles 'Israel' based on Gal.6:16 is special pleading. New Testament usage offers no convincing reason for applying the term 'Israel' to the Gentiles.

Unity Not Uniformity

Throughout the Bible God consistently uses different terms to distinguish between the Jewish people and the Gentiles. The Scriptures are not afraid to appreciate the differences between Jews and Gentiles. It is God who has created this diversity and it is the Lord who rejoices as He brings unity out of this diversity. This is the case in Isaiah 49:5-6 where Yeshua's ministry is described as touching Israel/Jacob on the one hand, and the Gentiles on the other. It holds true in Ephesians 2:11-3:6 where unity is created between circumcised Israel, and uncircumcised Gentiles on the other. New Testament distinctions between Jews and Gentiles are described in Romans 1:16, where modern missiological priorities are established. Jews and Gentiles are also distinguished from one another in Romans 2:9-11, a passage which describes the return of the Lord and the day of final judgment.

There are no biblical texts commanding that the name 'Israel' be used to describe Gentile believers. So why is this an issue in the Church today? Why are some Gentiles intent on calling themselves 'Israel'? Who would get hurt if this were done?

These three questions cut to the heart of the matter. The reason why many Christians believe that they are spiritual Israel is because they have been taught so from the pulpit. This is because Replacement Theology is still a theological stronghold in much of the Church today. Israel-related subjects are becoming an issue in our day because God is beginning to restore the Jewish people physically and spiritually. That restoration of the real Israel makes some grafted-in branches uncomfortable. Some Christians might be saying in their hearts, "What if the original owners of the property come back and find out that we are not only living in their apartments, but that we are laying exclusive claim to the title for the whole house? We just might get evicted!"

Perhaps a hidden motivation undergirds the 'spiritual Israel' debate – a form of reverse Galatianism.In Paul's day some Messianic Jews told new Gentile converts that being Gentile was a defect that could be rectified by physical circumcision and conversion to Pharisaic Judaism. Today Replacement Theology teaches that God has removed the 'defect' of being Gentile by turning Gentile converts into a new form of Israel. Both systems are in error on this point, since there is nothing wrong in being Gentile. God does not turn women into 'spiritual men' when they come to Messiah. Neither does He turn Gentiles into 'spiritual Israel.' "Then Peter began to speak: 'I now realize how true it is that God does not show favoritism but accepts men from every nation who fear Him and do what is right.'"[42] Paul adds, "Is God the God of Jews only? Is He not the God of Gentiles too? Yes, of Gentiles too, since there is only one God, who will justify the circumcised by faith and the uncircumcised through that same faith."[43]

God is not looking for uniformity among His children. He doesn't want to turn us all into 'spiritual Israel.' He is looking to create unity between the diverse children of His kingdom, between Israel and the Gentiles.

Names and Stones Will Break My Bones!

One question is rarely considered when discussing Replacement Theology. Who gets hurt when Gentiles call themselves 'Israel'? First of all, the Jewish community is offended. They see Christian use of the term 'New Israel' as an expression of Christian anti-Semitism. In light of Justin Martyr's abovementioned comments, they have ample cause for concern. The term 'spiritual Israel' sets off alarm bells in the Jewish community. It offends. At the very least, it is an

---

42   Acts 10:34-35

43   Rom. 3:29-30

impediment to the gospel.

Second, most Messianic Jews are offended. They have struggled to love their Gentile brothers and sisters in Messiah with a pure heart. At the same time they have struggled to maintain their own Jewish identity while paddling about in an ocean of Gentile Christianity. They cannot be expected to rejoice when Gentile Christians boast of having taken away Israel's priority status and trademark name. The use of the term 'spiritual Israel' or 'new Israel' runs roughshod over their already strained sensibilities.

Third, Gentile Christians who pride themselves in the title 'the New Israel' tend to show precious little Christian compassion for the Jewish people. They are so busy enjoying their own spiritual inheritance that they have no time to hear the cries of all the drowning Shmuel Kaganovitchs, deserted in their hour of need.

Fourth, the historical evidence (which is considered in chapter 10 is clear. The process began by believing that God rejected the Jewish people spiritually. It ended up not caring when the Jewish people were being physically decimated, and actually justified their persecution. Centuries of Replacement Theology added fuel to the flames of anti-Semitism and provided an encouragement in Europe for the spiritual forces that gave birth to the Crusades, the Inquisition, the pogroms and the Nazi genocide of the Jewish people in the Holocaust. The pen is mightier than the sword, and clear lines can be drawn from Justin Martyr's and Martin Luther's words to Adolf Hitler's actions.

The Apostle Paul once said, "Do not cause anyone to stumble, whether Jews, Greeks or the church of God..."[44] Using the term 'the Israel of God' to describe the Church offends both the Jews who are not believers and the Jews in the body of Messiah. These terms should be dropped from popular Christian usage.

Justice and Only Justice

Replacement Theology seriously undermines a healthy trust in

---

44   1 Cor. 10:32

the justice of God and in the reliability of His promises. History shows that the Jewish people have certainly experienced judgment, but they have not yet experienced the fullness of national restoration. According to Replacement Theology, that's simply 'tough luck.' The Jewish people will never receive those blessings promised to ethnic Israel, since the promised blessings have now been transferred to the predominantly Gentile Church. These blessings are now to be realized spiritually for the Church but never again physically for the Jews as God's priority people.

This scenario, if it were true, would shatter the promise that many prophetic Scriptures hold out to the Jewish people. If Replacement Theology were true, every time a Jew reads his Bible he would be reminded that God's tender promises to his nation have now been transferred to Gentile Christians. What an unappetizing scenario – the Jewish Scriptures have now become an eternal reminder to the Jewish people that they have been displaced, that they no longer are the 'People of the Book'!

One can only be thankful that the same God who said "He who scattered Israel" also promised in the same verse "will gather him and keep him as a shepherd keeps his flock."[45] The God who said, "And it will come about that as I have watched over them to pluck up, to break down, to overthrow, to destroy, and to bring disaster" also promised in the same verse "so I will watch over them to build and to plant."[46] The same Shepherd who said "My flock was scattered over all the surface of the earth; and there was no one to search or seek for them" also prophesied in the same passage,

> And I will bring them out from the peoples and gather
> them from the countries and bring them to their own
> land; and I will feed them on the mountains of Israel, by
> the streams, and in all the inhabited places of the land...
> And they will no longer be a prey to the nations, and the
> beasts of the earth will not devour them; but they will
> live securely, and no one will make them afraid... and

45   Jer. 31:10 NASB
46   Jer. 31:28 NASB

they will not endure the insults of the nations anymore.[47]

The heart of God is reflected in Yeshua's words in Luke 18. He declares that He will do justly with Israel. God will not only judge Israel; He will also bring to them all His promised blessings. "And will not God bring about justice for His chosen ones, who cry out to Him day and night? Will He keep putting them off?"[48]

Robbing the Israel of God

To rob the Jewish people is to rob the Jewish God. To appropriate Israel's priority status without Scriptural warrant is to steal the Jewish people's God-given promises. When many Gentile Christian theologians arrogate to the Church those callings that primarily or exclusively belong to the people of Israel, these men and their followers become arrogant and are guilty of violating the Eighth Commandment, "Thou shalt not steal!" Like all sins, theft needs to be confessed and, according to 1 John 1:9, God will forgive theft when it is confessed. But along with confession comes the need for restitution, or what John the Baptist called "fruits in keeping with repentance."[49]

Fruits of Repentance

Zacchaeus may have been a wee little man, as the children's song goes, but he was a giant in demonstrating what true biblical repentance looks like. When the Jewish population of Jericho was offended by Yeshua lunching with Zacchaeus (the town tax collector and embezzler), the little man "stood up and said to the Lord, 'Look, Lord! Here and now I give half of my possessions to the poor, and if I have cheated anybody out of anything, I will pay back four times the amount.' Yeshua said to him, 'Today salvation has come to this house, because this man, too, is a son of Abraham. For the Son of Man came to seek and to save what was lost.'"[50]

---

47   Ezek. 34:6, 13, 28-29 NASB

48   Lk. 18:7

49   Lk. 3:7-9

50   Lk. 19:8-10

According to the Mosaic Covenant a man who has robbed or extorted his fellow Jew needs to present a guilt offering at the Temple altar. He also needs to make restitution in full for the original sum and then add one fifth of the value as a penalty.[51] Zacchaeus demonstrated such a heartfelt repentance that he was willing to return not 120% but 400%, far beyond the requirement of the Torah. Christians who confess to the sin of robbing the Jewish people know that they already have an offering for sin. Yeshua's offering of His own sinless life has been accepted as a complete and eternal atonement by the Father. But one thing is still lacking. Christians who desire real reconciliation to Israel should join heartfelt repentance to concrete, Spirit-motivated acts of restitution.

Transplant versus Transfer

Replacement Theology has offered a false title of honor and a false hope to the Gentile stream of the Church. But is there true hope? How are Jewish and Gentile branches supposed to enjoy the company of the other? Paul offers a helpful paradigm here. In Romans 11 he says that some (though not all) of the Jewish branches have been broken off of their own Jewish olive tree. Some Jews (perhaps even a majority) rejected the Messiahship of Yeshua, and as a result they were individually separated from salvation. At the same time many Gentiles (who are described as *wild olive shoots*) were grafted into the Jewish olive tree among the other Jewish branches.

Today both Jewish and Gentile branches share in the nourishing sap from the olive root. As Paul says in Ephesians 2:19 and 3:6, Gentiles are now "fellow citizens with God's people and members of God's household...heirs together with Israel, members together of one body, and sharers together in the promise in Messiah Yeshua." In Paul's understanding Gentiles have been transplanted into a Jewish olive tree or commonwealth without losing their God-given ethnic identity as Gentiles. Israel's blessings are not

---

51   *Cf.*, Lev. 6:1-7; Num. 5:6-7

transferred, they are joyfully shared. Though some Jewish branches were broken off because of individual unbelief, the whole tree and many other branches are still Jewish. The Gentile branches should therefore approach the whole matter in humility and awe, knowing that the Jewish nation is soon coming to faith in Yeshua and will be grafted back into their own olive tree again.

> If some of the branches have been broken off, and you, though a wild olive shoot, have been grafted in among the others and now share in the nourishing sap from the olive root, do not boast over those branches. If you do, consider this: You do not support the root, but the root supports you. You will say then, "Branches were broken off so that I could be grafted in." Granted. But they were broken off because of unbelief, and you stand by faith. Do not be arrogant, but be afraid. For if God did not spare the natural branches, he will not spare you either. Consider therefore the kindness and sternness of God: sternness to those who fell, but kindness to you, provided that you continue in his kindness. Otherwise, you also will be cut off.And if they do not persist in unbelief, they will be grafted in, for God is able to graft them in again. After all, if you were cut out of an olive tree that is wild by nature, and contrary to nature were grafted into a cultivated olive tree, how much more readily will these, the natural branches, be grafted into their own olive tree![52]

---

52   Rom. 11:17-24

Chapter Ten

In All Their Afflictions: Anti-Semitism and the Tears of God

Examining anti-Semitism is like trying to defuse a ticking terrorist bomb. One needs a clear focus, extreme accuracy and cool-headedness. Two main pitfalls should also be avoided when considering anti-Semitism – letting readers get sucked into the horror of what has happened, or of manipulating readers into a fleshly response.

A balanced examination of anti-Semitism also needs to consider Christianity's contribution to this sad chronicle. Whereas in Puritan America the scarlet letter 'A' was a crimson badge of shame which branded the wearer an adulterer, history reveals that another scarlet letter is still firmly fastened to the breast of the Church. The 'A' in this case stands for *anti-Semitism*. This chapter focuses on some important aspects of the broad historical picture. Many books are available which delve into greater detail on this subject, and a list of these is found in this footnote.[1]

Pagan Anti-Semitism

Anti-Semitism actually began long before Christianity. The Bible teaches that Satan has always been the spiritual catalyst behind anti-Semitism. Pharaoh, Haman and Antiochus Epiphanes knew nothing of Christianity, yet their intentions were none the less murderous. Menachem Stern's *Greek and Latin Authors on Jews and Judaism* catalogues the writings of pagan anti-Semitism, most of which predate the rise of Gentile Christianity.[2]

The earliest documented expressions of anti-Semitism revolve around the Jewish people's refusal to assimilate into their host cultures or worship the gods of the nations. The Jewish people's belief that the one true God had chosen Israel and had given them inerrant revelation was an offense to a pantheistic and ecumenical ancient world. Jewish circumcision was seen as a barbaric, bloody and primitive practice by the Greeks. The Jewish emphasis on purity of body, food and social relationships caused pagans to conclude that Jews saw all non-Jews as unclean. The Sabbath, a day of rest, was another alien and offensive concept to the Hellenistic world.

> To the proud heirs of Pericles, Aristotle and Homer, this aloofness was an insufferable arrogance. Convinced that all that was not Greek was barbarian, they naturally resented rival claims to superiority or privilege on the part of a people they considered politically and culturally undistinguished. A collision between these two proud and

1   Brown, Michael L., *Our Hands Are Stained With Blood* (Shippensburg: Destiny Image, 1992); Flannery, Edward H., *The Anguish of the Jews* (New York/Mahwah: Paulist Press, 1985); Hay, Malcolm, *The Roots of Christian Anti-Semitism* (New York: Library Press, 1981); Parkes, James, *The Conflict of the Church and the Synagogue: A Study in the Origins of Antisemitism* (New York: Atheneum, 1985); Rausch, David A., *A Legacy of Hatred: Why Christians Must Not Forget the Holocaust* (Grand Rapids: Baker, 1990); Talmage, Frank E. ed., *Disputation and Dialogue: Readings in the Jewish-Christian Encounter* (New York: Ktav, 1975); Wilson, Marvin R., *Our Father Abraham: Jewish Roots of the Christian Faith* (Grand Rapids: Eerdmans, 1989).

2   *Cf.*, Stern, Menachem (ed.), *Greek and Latin Authors on Jews and Judaism* (Jerusalem: Israel Academy of Sciences and Humanities, 1974-1980). *Cf.*, Sevenster, J.N., *The Roots of Pagan Anti-Semitism in the Ancient World* (Leiden: E.J. Brill, 1975).

dissimilar mentalities could only be a matter of time.[3]

Jean-Paul Sartre, the famous French existentialist, touches the heart of Hellenism in describing how modern anti-Semites feel about Jews: "Thus the Jew remains the stranger, the intruder, the unassimilated at the very heart of our society."[4]

The Egyptians of Alexandria were a strongly Hellenized population who resented the presence of a large number of non-assimilating Jewish foreigners. "The old Egyptian xenophobia, moreover, was still alive and Egyptians, discontent under Greek and Roman rule, took offense at the tolerance shown Jews... Alexandria was manifestly predestined to become the chief center of anti-Semitism in the ancient world."[5] Manetho, an Egyptian writer ca. 270 BC, declared that the Jews had originally been Egyptians but had been driven out of that country because of leprosy. According to Manetho, they were led out of Egypt by an apostate priest named Moses who had been expelled by Pharaoh Amenophis. Moses supposedly taught the Jewish people not to worship the gods, to eat sacred animals and to have nothing to do with Gentiles. The Jews refused to eat pork, Manetho said, because they believed that leprosy could be contracted from touchingham.[6]

Democritus, a pagan writer, stated that Jews secretly worshipped the golden head of a donkey. As well, "every seven years they capture

3   Flannery, *op. cit.*, pp. 6-7

4   Sartre, Jean-Paul, *Anti-Semite and Jew* (New York: Schocken Books, 1962), p. 83

5   *ibid.*, p. 7. Alexandria was not only an ancient center of pagan anti-Semitism. This city would later become the Christian center for the use of the allegorical method of Scripture interpretation. This method of Bible interpretation forsakes the literal meaning of the text in favor of a deeper and different meaning, a 'more spiritual' one. Allegorical methodology was developed in the rhetorical schools of Greece during the lifetime of Homer. This method is often called *isogetical* (reading a meaning into the text) rather than *exegetical* (leading a meaning out from the text). Christian allegory was used to find typologies of Christ where none existed, and to turn prophecies about the Jewish people into prophecies about the Gentile Church. Jerome, Hillary, Ambrose, Augustine and Bernard of Clairvaux made extensive use of allegory. The Reformers generally rejected allegory as a valid principle of Scripture interpretation. Luther called allegory "the scum on Scripture" "a monkey game," and a "nose of wax"(*cf.*, Wilson, *op. cit.*, p. 97).

6   *ibid.*

a stranger, lead him to their Temple, and immolate *(ed. burn)* him by cutting his flesh into small pieces." About 90 AD Flavius Josephus answered such charges in his work *Against Apion*, defending his own people against an anti-Semitic Alexandrian author. Josephus quoted from Apion's *History of Egypt* where Antiochus Epiphanes supposedly breaks into the Holy of Holies and discovers a poor Greek fellow being fattened up for sacrifice.

> Finally...he heard of the unutterable law of the Jews,
> for the sake of which he was being fed. The practice
> was repeated annually at a fixed season. They would
> kidnap a Greek foreigner, fatten him up for a year,
> and then convey him to a wood, where they slew
> him, sacrificed his body with their customary ritual,
> partook of his flesh, and while immolating the Greek,
> swore an oath of hostility to the Greeks. The remains
> of their victim were then thrown into a pit.[7]

Haters of the Gentiles, guardians of strange and suspicious rituals, bearers of disease, ritualistic murderers – by 100 AD the pagan origins of Christian anti-Semitism were already in place. Salo Baron has said: "Almost every note in the cacophony of medieval and modern anti-Semitism is sounded by the chorus of ancient writers."[8]

The Conflict of the Church and the Synagogue

Two events now occurred in Judea which would lay the groundwork for anti-Semitism's growth within the new Christian movement. The first was a decisive break between Rabbinic Jews and Messianic Jews.[9] In approximately 80 AD the Pharisee Samuel the Lesser codified a new version of *Birkat Ha-Minim*, the

---

7   Flavius Josephus, *Against Apion*, II, 8 (H. Thackeray, *Josephus* [9 vol.; Cambridge: Harvard University Press, 1956]), I, pp. 329-330

8   Baron, Salo W., *A Social and Religious History of the Jews* (8 vols.: New York: Columbia University Press, 1951), I, p. 194. The charges of cannibalism, donkey worship, impiety, orgies and ritual murder were later leveled by pagans against the first Jewish and Gentile Christians.

9   *Cf.*, Katz, Stephen T., "Issues in the Separation of Judaism and Christianity after 70 C.E.: A Reconsideration," *Journal of Biblical Literature* 103, no.1 (1984): pp. 63-76.

'benediction against heretics.' This new synagogal prayer was meant to weed out and excommunicate all non-Pharisaic expressions of Judaism, especially Messianic Judaism.[10] Rabbinic Judaism was on the warpath to destroy the Messianic faith. Memories of this persecution would influence and shape Christianity for centuries to come.

Fifty years later the second decisive event took place – the second Jewish revolt of 132-135 AD led by Shimon Bar Kokhba, a self-styled messiah. During that revolt Messianic Jews refused to fight under the banner of a false messiah. As a result they were tortured and murdered by Bar Kokhba's forces and ultimately were rejected as 'traitors' by the larger community. Both the *Birkat Ha-Minim* and Bar-Kokhba's persecutions helped form a decidedly negative picture of Rabbinic Judaism among followers of Yeshua.

In the middle of the second century AD Justin Martyr's attacks on the Jewish people (as presented in chapter nine) formed theological foundations for what would become Replacement theology. Unfortunately, Justin's attacks were not spoken into a vacuum but into a pagan world already hostile to Israel.

But a new dilemma was to further complicated relationships between Synagogue and Church. During Justin's lifetime both Rabbinic Judaism and Messianic Judaism (or Jewish Christianity) were acknowledged by Rome as being legally recognized expressions of the same Jewish religion. Nevertheless the Church and the Synagogue saw themselves locked in mortal combat. "The Church's debate with Judaism...was by no means purely academic, but rather the fruit of an intense and perilous rivalry."[11] As the Gentile percentage of the body of Messiah exploded, Messianic Judaism stood in danger of being considered a Gentile religious movement. This would result in it losing its legal Roman umbrella

---

10   Cf., Justin Martyr, *op. cit.*, ch.137; also *cf.*, the Cairo Genizah text of *Birkat Ha-Minim* originally published by Solomon Schechter in *Jewish Quarterly Review* 10 (1898): 197-206, 654-59. The complete text of the prayer is republished in Emil Schuerer, *The History of the Jewish People in the Age of Jesus Christ* (175 BC-AD 135) rev. ed., ed. G. Vermes, et al. (Edinburgh: T. & T. Clark, 1979), 2: 256-59

11   Flannery, *op.cit.*, p. 39

of protection, since that right had been granted only to a primarily Jewish movement.

In the first three centuries AD the struggle between the established Rabbinic Synagogue and growing Gentile Christianity exploded into documented cases of sporadic but intense Jewish violence against the fledgling Christian movement. The deaths of James the Just and Bishop St. Simeon (both in Jerusalem), St. Polycarp and St. Pionius (in Smyrna, Asia Minor) and St. Philip of Heraclea (to name only a few) can be attributed to some Jewish communities' active support or even direct participation.[12] Marcel Simon stresses that "the few sure cases of active hostility do not, it seems, go beyond the realm of individual and local actions. It cannot be a question of a general conspiracy of Judaism…but merely of actions of certain Jews who abetted or stimulated popular hatred."[13]

Until 325 AD a political victor was not clearly defined. Justin's strident statements had occurred in the context of festering conflict between the predominantly Gentile Church and the anti-Messianic Jewish Synagogue. But these clashes of the second through fourth centuries AD would profoundly poison relations between the Jewish people and the Christian Church for the next eighteen hundred years.[14]

When Christianity became the official religion of the Roman Empire ca. 325 AD, it simultaneously became the most powerful religious force on the planet. At the same time Jews became second-class citizens subject to government sponsored humiliations and religious persecutions. Whereas paganism had once been Judaism's chief antagonist, now Christianity willingly took that role upon itself.

---

12 Flannery, op.cit., p. 32-34

13 Simon, Marcel, Verus Israel (Paris: De Boccard, 1948), p. 152

14 Two helpful books which discuss this process in greater depth are Marcel Simon's Verus Israel (Paris: De Boccard, 1948) and James Parkes' The Conflict of the Church and the Synagogue (op.cit) which offer a documentary history of these events.

Golden Tongued Bigotry

Origen (*ca.* 185-254 AD) was an Alexandrian theologian whose Christian father was martyred when Origen was 17 years old. He was one of the first textual critics of the Bible, one of the first Bible commentators and one of the first to author a systematic statement of Christian faith. He is considered one of the Greek Fathers of the Church. Origen's comments on the Jewish people are primarily drawn from his book Against Celsus.

Speaking of the destruction of the Second Temple and the scattering of the Jewish people, Origen remarked that "they will never be restored to their former condition. For they committed a crime of the most unhallowed kind, in conspiring against the Savior of the human race..."[15] Origen taught that the Jewish people were guilty of committing deicide (they had 'killed God') and as a result would be forever punished by God Himself. These ominous seeds would sprout in the fourth century and bear bitter fruit.

Saint John Chrysostom (ca. 344-407 AD) was born in Antioch and served as patriarch of Constantinople (398-404 AD). "John's writings, in an attractive Attic style, have nearly all survived... For his straightforward, if artless, integrity and his lively and earnest inculcation of Christian mores, John has enjoyed a wider esteem than any other Father. After Augustine, none was so popular with the Reformers."[16] John was known as chrysostomos, Greek for 'golden-mouthed.' In his eight Homilies Against The Jews[17] John tried to create so much fear and disgust among his own parishioners towards the Jewish people, that they would keep away from any contact with Antioch's Jewish population. John was afraid that if his congregants fraternized with Jews, that would lead them

---

15   Origen, *Against Celsus*, 4:22 in *Ante-Nicene Christian Literature* (New York: Scribner, 1905), IV, p. 506

16   'Chrysostom, John' by D.F. Wright in *The New International Dictionary of the Christian Church*, [passim *NIDCC*] ed. J.D. Douglas (Grand Rapids: Zondervan, 1978) pp. 225-226. No mention is made in Wright's article of Chrysostom's virulent anti-Semitic attacks (which were also written, it is assumed, in an attractive Attic Greek style).

17   John Chrysostom, *Adversus Iudaeos* in *The Fathers of the Church: Saint John Chrysostom*, vol.68 (Washington, D.C.: The Catholic University of America Press, 1979).

to abandon Christianity. If his church members ate meals together with Jewish people, soon they might want to convert to Judaism. Chrysostom's sermons unleashed a torrent of hatred against the Jewish people, proving that all that glitters is not gold. Here is a compendium of some of his scathing remarks.

> The Jews are most miserable of all men... lustful, rapacious, greedy, perfidious bandits...inverterate murderers, destroyers, men possessed by the devil... Debauchery and drunkenness have given them the manners of the pig and the lusty goat. They know only one thing, to satisfy their gullets, get drunk, to kill and maim one another...They have surpassed the ferocity of wild beasts, for they murder their offspring and immolate them to the devil...They are impure and impious...(Their Synagogue) is a theater...a house of prostitution...a den of thieves...a repair of wild beasts...an abyss of perdition...the domicile of the devil...Indeed Jews worship the devil... their rites are criminal and impure... their religion is a disease...[18]

> (Concerning the Jews' "assassination of Christ" there is) no expiation possible, no indulgence, no pardon...(The destruction of Jerusalem) was done by the wrath of God and His absolute abandon of you...(Jews will live) under the yoke of servitude without end...He who can never love Christ enough will never have done fighting against those (Jews) who hate Him...Flee, then, their assemblies, flee their houses, and far from venerating the synagogue because of the book it contains, hold it in hatred and aversion for the same reason...I hate the synagogue precisely because it has the law and the prophets...I hate the Jews also because they have the law ...[19]

Flannery states that these sermons "represent a grave lapse from Christian charity that cannot be condoned...In the eyes of the historian, Chrysostom cannot be spared his niche in the pantheon

---

18   Flannery *op. cit.*, pp. 48-49, quoting from *Adversus Iudaeos* chapters 1:2, 4, 6 ; 3:1 ; 4:1 ; 6: 5-6.

19   *ibid.*, 6:2, 4 ; 7:1; 6:4; 1:7; 1:5 ; 6:6.

of anti-Semitism....A generalized popular hatred of the Jew was now rapidly under way; and among the literati the tone of Chrysostom's diatribe found an echo in and out of the Church for centuries."[20]

The City of God in Disrepair

The sack of Rome by the Visigoths in 410 AD caused some Roman pagans to charge that Christianity was responsible for Rome's defeat. Augustine, bishop of Hippo Regius in Roman North Africa, responded to these charges in his *The City of God* (ca. 413-427 AD). Augustine interpreted Rome's Christian history in eschatological terms, proclaiming that the contemporary Byzantine Church was, allegorically speaking, the millennial reign of Christ on earth. In spite of temporal setbacks Christ's kingdom was glorious and unstoppable.

Since Augustine believed that there was no longer room for a physical and Jewish Messianic kingdom headquartered in Jerusalem, what possible role could the Jewish people now fulfill? His answer was that the Jewish people are now a witness-people. Israel exists to testify both to its own wickedness and to the truth of Christianity's message. The Jewish people's sufferings are God-ordained. Like Cain, they carry the sign of judgment on their national body and, like Cain, they are not to be destroyed.[21] Augustine perverted the chosenness of Israel, standing it on its head. The Jewish people's irrevocable calling is to punishment, not to preeminence.

> No one can fail to see that in every land where the Jews are scattered they mourn for the loss of their kingdom, and are in terrified subjection to the immensely superior number of Christians. Not by bodily death shall the ungodly race of carnal Jews perish. For whoever destroys them in this way shall suffer sevenfold vengeance, that is, shall bring upon himself the sevenfold penalty under which the Jews lie for the crucifixion of Christ. So to the

---

20   Flannery, *op. cit.*, p. 49

21   Augustine, *Commentary on Psalm 50* in *Nicene and Post-Nicene Christian Literature* (New York: Scribner, 1905), 8:177

end of the seven days of time, the continued preservation of the Jews will be a proof to believing Christians of the subjection merited by those who...put the Lord to death .[22]

In other literature Augustine also called upon Gentile Christians to "preach to the Jews, whenever we can, with a spirit of love... It is not for us to boast over them as branches broken off... We shall be able to say to them without exulting over them –

though we exult in God – 'Come, let us walk in the light of the Lord.'"[23] Flannery notes:

It is a misfortune of Christian history that Augustine's admirable reassertion of Paul did not receive the same hearing as his theory of the witness-people, which was destined for theological fame and for uses never intended by its author. History was to produce many who took their inspiration from this theory, and felt justified in assisting the Almighty in His supposed plan for the Jews by aggravating their miseries.[24]

N.R.M. deLange notes the fatal difference between pagan and Christian anti-Semitism:

Whereas pre-Christian anti-Judaism was sporadic, limited locally, unofficial and had no ideological foundation (apart from the Egyptian species and its offshoots), at least from around the time of Constantine the Christian kind was permanent, universal, officially stirred up, a matter of principle, and supported by an ideological system. It does not have its roots in historical events and conditions, but even occurs where there are no Jews.[25]

22   Schaff, Philip, ed., *St. Augustine* in *A Selection of the Nicene and Post-Nicene Fathers of the Christian Church* (8 vol., Grand Rapids: Eerdmans, 1983), 4:187-188

23   Augustine, *Treatise Against The Jews*, 15 in *Patrologia Latina* ed. P.L. Migne (217 vol., Paris: Garnier, 1878-1890), 42:63

24   Flannery, *op. cit.*, p. 51

25   Kueng, Hans, *Judaism: Between Yesterday and Tomorrow*, transl. John Bowden (New York: The Crossroad Publishing Company, 1992), p.151 quoting from N.R.M. deLange, "Antisemitismus IV", in *Theologische Realenzyklopaedie* ed. G. Krause and G. Mueller (17 vol., Berlin: W. De Gruyter, 1976), vol. 3, pp.128-137

The famous Orthodox Christian theologian F. Lovsky concludes:

> In final analysis there can be no debate. There are
> too many signs that stake out the permanence, the
> importance, and the gravity of Christian anti-Semitism:
> contempt, calumnies, animosity, segregation, forced
> baptisms, appropriation of children, unjust trials,
> pogroms, exiles, systematic persecutions, thefts and
> rapine, hatred, open or concealed, social degradation.[26]

Medieval Art and Architecture

In his informative book Our Father Abraham, Marvin R. Wilson describes how theology concerning the Jews even influenced art.

> During the twelfth and thirteenth centuries, especially in
> France, Germany and England, Christian art and sculpture
> represents the Jews as humbled and downcast rather
> than proud and upright. Of particular note is the artwork
> depicting two female figures, Ecclesia and Synagoga,
> symbolizing the triumphant Church and the defeated
> Synagogue. Ecclesia is often portrayed as graceful and
> crowned, with staff in hand. Synagoga, however, is
> often represented as blindfolded, with broken staff, and
> sometimes decorated with broken tablets of the Law.
> Ecclesia and Synagoga are often located on the exterior
> of cathedrals as stone figures or statues, and elsewhere
> are depicted on such items as medieval manuscripts,
> missals, stained-glass windows, and baptismal fonts.[27]

In Medieval painting and illuminated manuscripts the Jew was often portrayed laughing with demonic delight, having horns on his head and a devilish tail between his legs. Surrounding him were an assortment of demons, pigs and scorpions.[28]

---

26   in Flannery, *op. cit.*, p. 60

27   Wilson, *op. cit.*, p. 99. *Cf.*, Heinz Schreckenberg, *The Jews in Christian Art: An Illustrated History*
(London: SCM Press,1998); Binyamin Eliav, "Anti-Semitism" in *Encyclopedia Judaica* [passim *EJ*]
(Jerusalem: Keter, 1971) Vol.3, cols. 91-94; also Helen Rosenau, "Ecclesia et Synagoga," *EJ*, Vol. 6, cols.
346-349

28   Trachtenburg, Joshua, *The Devil and the Jews: The Medieval Conception of the Jew and its Relation to*

The Crusader Contribution

The destruction of the Church of the Holy Sepulchre in Jerusalem by Caliph al-Hakim (1009 AD) officially sparked the beginning of the Crusades. As the Crusaders set off from the town of Rouen, Guibert of Nogent reported their declaration: "We desire to combat the enemies of God in the East; but we have under our eyes the Jews, a race more inimical to God than all the others. We are doing this whole thing backwards."[29] The Crusaders then massacred all Jews in Rouen and Lorraine who refused to be baptized. Across the Rhine Valley in Speyer, Worms, Mainz, Cologne, Ratisbon, Treves, Neuss, along the Danube and in Bohemia the murders and forced baptisms multiplied.

Between January and July 1096 it is estimated that up to 10,000 Jewish men, women and children were massacred, at least one quarter of all Jews residing in Northern France and Germany.[30] After the Crusaders finally breached the walls of Jerusalem near the Tower of the Stork in 1099, soldiers belonging to Godfrey de Bouillon found the city's Jewish population hiding in the sanctuary of a wooden synagogue. They immediately set the synagogue ablaze, burning to death all who were inside it.

The Second Crusade of 1147 was similar in quality:

> But the damage was done. Massacres and brutalities occurred in Cologne, Speyer, Mainz, and Wüzburg in Germany, and in Carenton, Sully, and Rameru in France. In Rameru the famous Jewish scholar Jacob Tam had five wounds inflicted upon his head in vengeance for the five wounds of Christ. Though the Second Crusade was much milder than the first, the fatalities reached many hundreds.[31]

Modern Antisemitism (New York: Meridian Books, 1961), pp. 11-31

29   Guibert of Nogent, *De Vita Sua*, III, 5 in *Patrologia Latina, op. cit.*, 156:903

30   *Cf.*, Baron, *op. cit.*, IV, 104

31   Flannery, *op. cit.*, p.93; *cf.*, Payne, Robert, *The Dream and the Tomb: A History of the Crusades* (New York: Dorset Press, 1984).

The Spanish Inquisition

The Spanish Inquisition began in 1478, ostensibly to ferret out and burn *marranos* (Spanish for 'pigs'), those Catholic Jews who secretly practiced Judaism. Under Tomàs de Torquemada who was appointed Grand Inquisitor in 1483, the Inquisition would become "a gigantic operation that would spread to all major Spanish cities, condemn thousands of *marranos* to the stake and many times more to imprisonment, public humiliation, and confiscation of property."[32] Though a few of his victims included Moors and Moriscos (converts to Islam), the majority of his 12,000 victims were Jews. Though some victims were Orthodox Jews, most were *marranos* and some of these were genuine Jewish believers in Yeshua. (De Torquemada's) "ruthless efficiency...has left him with a reputation of cruelty and intolerance even for the times in which he lived."[33]

On January 2 1492 Ferdinand and Isabella of Spain issued a decree stating that any Jew remaining in Spain after July 30 1492 would be subject to the death penalty. Only baptized Jews would be allowed to remain in Spain, and these in turn would have to face the tender mercies of the Inquisition. Between 100,000 and 300,000 Jewish people fled the country, experiencing starvation, shipwreck, piracy and enslavement on the way.[34] "The traumatic experience of these years left its mark on the Jews...To their persecutors Jews reacted with a cold fury, recoiling still further into themselves from an 'adversary no longer considered human.'"[35]

Concerning Luther and His Diatribes

In the earlier part of his ministry the great Reformer Martin Luther spoke well of the Jewish people. In his pamphlet *That Jesus Christ Was Born A Jew* Luther said, "And though we vaunt ourselves equally highly, we are nevertheless Gentiles, and the Jews are of the

32   *ibid.*, p. 138. *Cf.*, Roth, Cecil, *A History of the Marranos* (New York: Schocken, 1974), and *The Spanish Inquisition* (New York: W.W. Norton, 1964).

33   "Torquemada" by Robert G. Clouse in *NIDCC, op. cit.*, p. 980

34   *Cf.*, Kung, *op. cit.*, pp. 165-166

35   Flannery, *op. cit.*, p.144

blood of Christ; we are kinsfolk and aliens, and they are the blood-friends, cousins and brothers of our Lord."[36] "If we are to help (the Jews), we must exercise on them the law of Christian love, not that of the Pope, accept them in a friendly fashion, attempt to win them over, and work so that they have a cause and a place to be with us and around us, to hear and see our Christian teaching and life."[37]

Luther's friendly attitude to the Jews did not bear desired fruit in two important areas. It did not enlist Jewish political support for his struggle to reform the Catholic Church, since the Jewish people did not want to get trapped into defending one side of a purely Christian conflict. Luther had also hoped that Jewish people would be attracted to the gospel through the testimony of a reformed Christian Church. When neither of these events took place, an embittered Luther authored two virulently anti-Semitic tracts in his later years, On The Jews and their Lies and On The Tetragrammaton and the Genealogy of Christ. In the former work Luther advocated the following:

> What then shall we Christians do with this damned, rejected race of Jews? Since they live among us and we know about their lying and blaspheming and cursing, we cannot tolerate them if we do not wish to share in their lies, curses, and blasphemy...We must prayerfully and reverentially practice a merciful severity...Let me give you my honest advice: First, to set fire to their synagogues or schools and to bury and cover with dirt whatever will not burn, so that no man will ever again see a stone or cinder of them. This is to be done in honor of our Lord and of Christendom...Second, I advise that their houses also be razed and destroyed... Third, I advise that all their prayer books and Talmudic writings, in which such idolatry, lies, cursing, and blasphemy are taught, be taken from them. Fourth, I advise that their rabbis be forbidden to

---

36   Martin Luther, *That Jesus Christ Was Born A Jew* (1523), in *Luther's Works*, ed. Jaroslav Pelikan and Helmut T. Lehmann 55 vol. (Philadelphia: Fortress Press and Saint Louis: Concordia Publishing House, 1962-1974) vol.45: 195-230

37   *ibid.*, p. 201

teach henceforth on pain of loss of life and limb... Fifth, I advise that safe-conduct on the highways be abolished completely for the Jews. For they have no business in the countryside, since they are not lords, officials, tradesmen, or the like. Let them stay at home ...Sixth, I advise that usury be prohibited to them, and that all cash and treasure of silver and gold be taken from them, and put aside for safe keeping... Seventh, I recommend putting a flail, an ax, a hoe, a spade, a distaff, or a spindle into the hand of young, strong Jews and Jewesses and letting them earn their bread in the sweat of their brow.[38]

Haim Hillel Ben-Sasson the doyen of Israeli historians comments, "Short of the Auschwitz oven and extermination, the whole Nazi Holocaust is pre-outlined here."[39] Hitler would often quote from Luther's On The Jews And Their Lies in his public rallies. Flannery wryly notes, "The devil the reformer would have exorcised from the Church seemed to have taken full possession of him."[40]

The 'Gift Of God' in Poland

For centuries Catholic Poland had oppressed the Ukraine and its Eastern Orthodox Cossacks, often using the Jews as vicarious landlords and tavern lessees. In 1648 AD Bogdan (Slavic for 'gift of God') Chmielnicki rose up as the hetman (leader) of the Eastern Orthodox Ukrainians and joined in with the Tartars and Zaporozhi Cossacks to destroy the Jewish communities of Poland. The following is a description of these atrocities.

Estates were devastated, manor-houses reduced to ashes, and human beings barbarously done to death. The victims were flayed and burned alive, mutilated and left to the agony of a lingering death. Infants were slit like fish or slaughtered at the breasts of their mothers or cast alive into wells. Women were ripped

---

38   from Luther's *On The Jews And Their Lies*, (1543), trans. Martin H. Bertram, in *Luther's Works*, 47:268-72

39   Ben-Sasson, Haim Hillel, "History" in *EJ*, Vol.8, col. 693

40   Flannery, *op. cit.*, p. 152-153

open and then sewed up again with live cats thrust into their bowels; many, unmarried or married, were violated before the eyes of their menfolk, and those that were comely were carried away. Thousands of Jews perished in the towns east of the Dnieper.[41]

"Some Jews were given the option of baptism …The toll of the decade was staggering. Estimates of Jewish deaths range from 100,000 to 500,000; and 700 Jewish communities were destroyed."[42]

The Colors of Modern Anti-Semitism: Red, Black and Green

The twentieth century has witnessed a cresting of anti-Semitic activity unparalleled in all of history. Virulent new strains of anti-Semitism have appeared in our day. The Communist strain can be called *red anti-Semitism*, the fascist/Nazi variety can be described as *black anti-Semitism*, while *green anti-Semitism* refers to fundamentalist Islam's anti-Israel strain.[43]

Between 1903 and 1906 over 670 Czarist pogroms caused the streets of Russia and Ukraine to run red with Jewish blood. Though tens of thousands were made homeless, thousands were maimed and hundreds were killed, within twenty years these atrocities would be outdone by the Communist regime in Russia. In the civil war between the White and Red Russian armies (1918-1920) at least 60,000 Jews were killed.[44] After the Revolution was consolidated, the Communist Party's *Yevsektzia* (Russian for 'Jewish Section') systematically destroyed Jewish culture and knowledge, outlawed Hebrew instruction, closed synagogues, shut down Yiddish newspapers and theaters, and sent instructors of Judaism into exile to Siberia. The leaders of Russia's Jewish communities were jailed, tortured, shot or exiled, while famous actors and writers

41   Margolis, L. and Marx, A., *History of the Jewish People* (New York: Meridian, 1956), p. 552

42   Flannery, *op. cit.*, p. 158

43   Green is the color which Islam has chosen to represent itself. Examples of these can be seen on many Islamic flags, notably that of Saudi Arabia. Moammar Khaddafi's 'The Green Book' is another example.

44   Flannery, *op. cit.*, p. 198

were mysteriously killed in hit-and-run accidents. In 1926 a Jewish ghetto-region was established in Birobidzhan, Manchuria near the Chinese border with the hope that Russia's Jews could be transferred away from population centers. In 1953 Stalin planned to unleash a decisive wave of persecution in the aftermath of the infamous 'Doctors' Plot,' and only his sudden death froze these plans.

There are no accurate statistics on the exact number of Jewish fatalities among the 25 to 50 million Russian citizens murdered in Stalin's gulags, prisons and state-sponsored famines. A joke still current in Russia reveals that anti-Semitism is far from dead. Jewish people are described as being 'invalids of the fifth point', a biting reference to the fifth line on all Russian identity cards which describes the nationality of the bearer. Even today one's Jewish identity is an impediment to advancement in many areas of Russian society.

Mass Murder and Indifference

The color black symbolizes European fascist anti-Semitism which attained horrific proportions in World War II. The systematic destruction of European Jewry by Europe's most advanced nation has shattered forever the myth that man is evolving upwards. Over 6,000,000 Jewish people (including over 1,000,000 children) were starved or worked to death, machine gunned and buried in huge open pits, or asphyxiated by poison gas and then burned in ovens.

Walter Laquer a scholar and expert on international affairs comments on contemporary German national indifference to the destruction of European Jewry.

> Millions of Germans knew by late 1942 that the Jews had disappeared. Rumours about their fate reached Germany through officers and soldiers returning from the eastern front but also through other channels. There were clear indications in the wartime speeches of Nazi leaders that something more drastic than resettlement had happened. Knowledge about the exact manner in which they had been killed was restricted to very few. It is, in fact, quite

likely that while many Germans thought that the Jews were no longer alive, they did not necessarily believe that they were dead... Very few people had an interest in the fate of the Jews. Most individuals faced a great many more important problems. It was an unpleasant topic, speculations were unprofitable, discussions of the fate of Jews were discouraged. Consideration of this question was pushed aside, blotted out for the duration.[45]

In Raul Hilberg's *The Destruction of the European Jews*[46] a chart compares Christian anti-Jewish measures in Medieval canon law with parallel Nazi anti-Jewish measures enacted in Germany between 1933 and 1941. Hans Kueng the noted Swiss Catholic theologian comments:

Bitter though this recognition may be, it cannot be passed over in silence. The racist antisemitism which reached its climax of terrorism in the Holocaust would not have been possible without the prehistory of the religious anti-Judaism of the Christian church extending over almost two thousand years. And is not the case of the Austrian Adolf Hitler the most abysmal example of this? Even now many people do not recognize the religious roots of his antisemitism.[47]

Jihad Against The Jewish State

The latest and potentially most virulent form of anti-Semitism spreading across the face of this planet is *green anti-Semitism*, that is to say, Islamic hatred of the Jewish state and the Jewish people. Anti-Judaism and hatred of the Jews are not considered socially acceptable (at least openly) in the West, and fundamentalist Islamic movements most attuned to Western sensibilities have shaped their strategies accordingly.

A petrodollar-funded public relations push has influenced the

---

45   Laquer, Walter, *The Terrible Secret* (Boston: Little Brown, 1981), p. 201

46   Hilberg, Raul, *The Destruction of the European Jews* (New York: Holmes & Meier, 1985), vol. 1, pp. 10-12

47   Kueng, *op. cit.*, p. 236

world's media for the most part to present Islamic terrorist attacks on Israeli targets as guerrilla warfare carried out by freedom fighters. The Islamic strategy of shrinking the State of Israel to the point where it could wiped out by a coordinated armed attack of several Arab nations is internationally described as 'the peace process.' Iran's ayatollahs, Hezbollah's sheikhs and Syria's warlords all insist that they are not anti-Semitic – only anti-Israeli. A live nuclear option is being actively pursued by Iran, Iraq, Libya, Pakistan and some of the formerly Soviet Moslem republics. The Islamic dream of a final destructive nuclear *jihad* against the 'perfidious' Jews (which may be described in Ezekiel 38-39) is quickly becoming a reality. This subject is considered in more detail in chapter sixteen.

Jewish Conspiracy Theories

One of the most common manifestations of modern anti-Semitism is the belief that an international Jewish conspiracy exists which has as its goal the enslavement of the world. The most infamous of these theories was created by Russia's *Okhrana* secret police at the end of the nineteenth century. Their Paris branch forged a book called *The Protocols of the Learned Elders of Zion* which was first published by the Russian government press office in 1905. The book purports to be secret minutes of the First Zionist Congress held in Basel, Switzerland in 1897. These counterfeit documents declare that Jews have been trying to take over the world since King Solomon's reign in 929 BC. Twenty-four 'secret lectures' detail how a world Jewish state will be established. These tactics include controlling the world's media, governments and economies. According to adherents of this book, the Jews have created both Communism and Capitalism as smokescreens to hide their real agenda.

This book was first published in German in 1919 and it strongly influenced the Nazi movement. In 1920 Henry Ford began a seven-year American anti-Semitic campaign in the pages of his newspaper *The Dearborn Independent*. His series *The International Jew, The World's Foremost Problem* was published in four volumes totaling 746 pages and was later reprinted and widely circulated in Nazi Germany. Carey McWilliams says, "In one sense, Hitler began where Ford left off."[48]

The *Protocols* were exposed as a forgery in 1921 by a correspondent for the London *Times*. Fifty percent of the *Protocols* were directly plagiarized from a French satirical play about the life of Napoleon III written by Maurice Joly. Other parts of the Protocols were lifted from an adventure story by Hermann Goedsche, where twelve Jewish princes meet in a Prague cemetery to discuss world domination.[49] The fact that the *Protocols* has been conclusively proven to be a forgery does not dissuade those who want to believe its dark tales. "When otherwise brilliant minds are so deceived and when some, even after irrefragable disproof, persist in believing, we are at grips with a collective psychosis, with a will to hate and destroy well beyond the pale of human rationality. We have in the Protocols...a sort of diabolism in a new form, a secularized diabolism."[50] The *Protocols* have been freely available to all foreign visitors who deplane at Saudi Arabia's main airport. White Supremacist newspapers and neo-Nazi publications still make the *Protocols* available to their readership.

It has been said that Satan uses a lake of truth to disguise a pint of poison. Sometimes he even uses a lake of poison to disguise a pint of truth. The 'fearful international Jewish conspiracy' described in the *Protocols* has a pint of truth concealed in its pages. The Scriptures proclaim that God is setting up an international kingdom based in Jerusalem. Yeshua the Messiah will rule all nations with a rod of iron. This thought terrifies Satan and motivated him to create the *Protocols*. The *Protocols* distort the biblical picture of Yeshua's Messianic kingdom and twist its beauty, spawning fear and hatred towards the Jewish people as the result.

---

48   McWilliams, Carey, *A Mask for Privilege: Anti-Semitism in America* (Boston: Little, Brown, 1948), p. 35.

49   *Cf.*, Flannery, *op. cit.*, pp. 192-193

50   *ibid.*, p. 193; *cf.*, Cohn, Norman, *Warrant for Genocide: The Jewish World Conspiracy and the Protocols of the Elders of Zion* (New York: Harper and Row, 1966).

Anti-Semitism: Satan's Gospel Vaccine

The sordid history of Christian anti-Semitism reveals another aspect of Satan's strategy. He has attempted to keep two powerful forces (the gospel and the Jewish people) from uniting. Satan has experienced a large measure of success in holding to this goal by fanning the flames of anti-Semitism within the Christian Church. This had led to a deep alienation between the Church and the Synagogue, between individual Christians and Jews, and between the Jewish people and their Messiah.

Christianity's behavior toward the Jews throughout history has beaten many new paths, but most of them have only led to a dead-end. An attitude of competition or fear towards Judaism led to hatred, slander and rabble-rousing attacks. An effort to explain Jewish suffering apart from a solid biblical understanding of God's irrevocable calling on the Jewish nation led to Gentile Christian triumphalism and Replacement theology. An attempt to create a Christian theocracy apart from accepting that the Jewish people are beloved for the sake of the Patriarchs led to anti-Semitic and racist legislation. An impatient attitude toward Jewish unbelief led to anger and bitterness against the Jewish people. Christian political attempts to bring peace between Jew and Arab while ignoring God's choosing of Isaac and God's establishing of Israel's borders,[51] result in political sanctions against the Jewish state. The above actions bring the curses of the Abrahamic covenant upon both the Christian Church and the governments involved.

What can believers do? Some answers are given in this book's conclusion, but a few brief comments might be helpful here. Christians must first recognize how deeply pagan anti-Semitism has infected the Church, and what a shameful stain it has left on Christian history. Individual repentance and corporate repentance are probably the next step. Prayer regarding how to make restitution is also in order: what can believers do educationally, financially, and in the pulpit ministry of the Church? Intercession might come

---

51 An example of this is former President Jimmy Carter's memoirs *Keeping Faith* (Bantam, 1982).

after that, prayer asking the God of Israel to tear down satanic stratagems and open the hearts of Christians to the Jewish people, and the hearts of Jewish people to the gospel. Last of all, practical measures need to be taken in all the above arenas.

Franklin Littell notes that theological strongholds need to be exposed and pulled down: "The cornerstone of Christian anti-Semitism is the superseding or displacement myth that old Israel is written off in favor of New Israel."[52] Rudolph Pfisterer adds,

> ... (M)any theologians and Christians are implicitly antisemitic when in principle they deny the reality and the meaning of Israel's election. For example, to say that the cross ended all the promises made to Israel is implicit antisemitism; or to say that the church simply displaces Israel is likewise implicit antisemitism. To claim that the Jews have forfeited all their claims because they have been disloyal to the Lord is yet another example.[53]

Jean-Paul Sartre points out that a passionate response is required if Christians are going to further God's purposes for the Jews. "Anti-Semitism...is first of all a *passion*... The cause of the Jews would be half won if only their friends brought to their defense a little of the passion and the perseverance their enemies use to bring them down."[54]

Finally it bears repeating that in Hitler's Germany, although initial attacks may have been directed against the Jews, in the end they were directed against all Christians of conscience. The Gentile secular philosopher Jean-Paul Sartre comments, "Richard Wright, the (African-American) writer, said recently, 'there is no (Black) problem in the United States, there is only a White problem.' In the same way, we must say that anti-Semitism is not a Jewish problem,

52   Littell, Franklin, *The Crucifixion of the Jews* (New York: Harper, 1975), p. 2

53   Bernard Ramm's paraphrase in "A Review of 'Antisemitismus und Eschatologie' by Rudolph Pfisterer" by Bernard Ramm in *Bibliotheca Sacra* (Dallas TX), vol. 118, #469, Jan.1961, pp. 22-24. The German article was originally published in the June 1959 issue of *Evangelische Theologie*, pp. 266-288.

54   Sartre, *op. cit.*, pp. 10, 153

it is our problem."[55] The Catholic theologian Edward Flannery confesses, "The sin of anti-Semitism is many things, but, in the end it is a denial of the Christian faith, a failure of Christian hope and a malady of Christian love."[56]

Surely Our Griefs He Bears

The Bible sheds helpful light on the subject of anti-Semitism. The Scriptures tell us that when the Jewish people are persecuted, God Himself actually feels their pain. When they are cut, He bleeds. When they are stabbed, He also feels the wrenching agony. God's heart-connection to the Jewish people goes far beyond sympathy into the realm of palpable empathy. Isaiah says: "In all their afflictions He was afflicted."[57] In Isaiah 53 the prophet tells us that on the cross Yeshua the Messiah actually experienced all the sorrows and griefs of the Jewish people – past, present and future. "Surely our griefs He Himself bore, and our sorrows He carried."[58] Anti-Semites are not aware that their bullets and bombs, their hatred and mockery, wound the very heart of God.

The Lord's heart is raw when it comes to His people's suffering. In the days of Samson and Jephthah, the writer of the Book of Judges commented: "(T)he Philistines and the Ammonites...shattered and crushed (the Jewish people)...And (the Lord) could bear Israel's misery no longer."[59] If God's heart was deeply pained by Israel's misery in the days of Jephthah the Judge, how much more anguish did He feel during the Shoah, the Holocaust, when Israel was starved, shot, gassed and burned!

The Jewish people have been tempted to feel that God has abandoned them in their affliction, that He either doesn't see, doesn't care, or perhaps is unable to do anything to stop Jewish suffering. The Father of Israel understands that pain, and speaks

---

55   *ibid*, p. 152

56   Flannery, *op. cit.*, p. 277

57   Isa. 63:8 NASB

58   Isa. 53:4 NASB

59   Judg. 10: 7, 16

tenderly to the heart of His people: "But Zion said, 'The Lord has forsaken me, the Lord has forgotten me.' Can a mother forget the baby at her breast and have no compassion on the child she has borne? Though she may forget, I will not forget you! See, I have engraved My people on the palms of My hands; your walls are ever before Me."[60] "The Lord will...have compassion on His servants when He sees their strength is gone and no one is left, slave or free."[61]

Wiping Away Every Tear

The pain of Israel's agony resounds in the chambers of God's heart, and Yeshua promises to personally wipe away every tear from the eyes of all those who turn to Him for help. He will dry their cheeks with His own handkerchief, and will remove all shame and disgrace from the Jewish people forever. Speaking of the Messianic Banquet at the End of Days, Isaiah prophesies: "On this mountain He will destroy the shroud that enfolds all peoples, the sheet that covers all nations; He will swallow up death forever. The Sovereign Lord will wipe away the tears from all faces; He will remove the disgrace of His people from all the earth. The Lord has spoken."[62]

---

60   Isa. 49:14-16; *cf.*, Exod. 2:23-25

61   Deut. 32:36

62   Isa. 25:7- 8

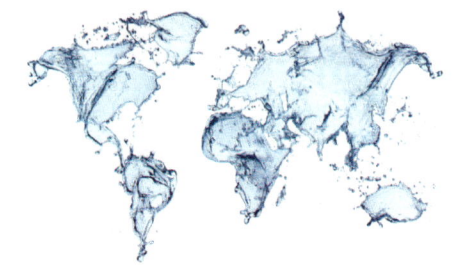

SECTION FOUR:
COMFORT,
COMFORT MY PEOPLE!

Chapter Eleven

The Bear and the Bunny

When I was barely five months old in the faith I asked a Bible teacher what being Jewish meant for me now that I was a believer. His answer was simple and to the point: "In Christ there is no Jew or Gentile." Therefore, he explained, I was no longer a Jew.

This brother believed that when Messiah had come into my heart, God had also severed my connection with my own people. The spiritual circumcision I had undergone had removed my own Jewishness from me! This man's teaching raised questions which took me years to properly answer. What does happen to the ethnic identity and calling of Jewish people who turn to Messiah? Is it obliterated? Is it rendered irrelevant?

Other important questions also arise. How should Jew and Gentile relate to each other in the body of Messiah? Are Jewish culture, music and ways superior to Gentile culture, music and ways? What did Paul mean by the term *one new man*, and what should that look like at the turn of the third millennium AD?

The Pig and the Chicken

An old barnyard tale tells the story of two farm animals who wanted to express their appreciation for their owner. "I know what to do," said the chicken. "Let's make a special meal of bacon and eggs for Farmer Jones!" The pig chewed slowly and carefully as he thought about that one. Then he grunted and replied, "That's not a fair deal! For you that's a one-time contribution, but for me it involves total commitment!"

There are parallels between the hog s wisdom and the state of Jewish-Gentile relationships in the body of Messiah today. Today the lion's share of interaction between Jewish and Gentile believers take place outside of the land of Israel, since that is where the majority of Jewish and Gentile believers live. For many Jewish people, the thought of attending church can be a frightening or disquieting experience. The danger of assimilation is high, and faithful Jews are not convinced that such a price tag is a necessary expression of biblical faith. The demographic challenge is daunting: the average church is 99% Gentile and many Jews feel culturally out of place. The chances of finding a Jewish spouse are slim, and most of one's Jewish culture (e.g., music, food, Hebrew, social customs) needs to be left at the door. Assimilation within one generation is a strong likelihood in most cases. Indeed, some Messianic Jews prefer churches for precisely that reason. But most Jewish believers are not interested in that solution.

Most other ethnic streams are not as skittish about attending the church of one's choice. African-Americans who don t feel at home in predominantly White churches can opt for Black churches, while Chinese and Asian-Americans often gather in their own mono-ethnic congregations. Yet when some Messianic Jews opt for Messianic congregations, accusations of Judaizing or being separationist have been raised. At the same time the larger Jewish community accuses Messianic Jews either of being assimilationist and traitorous by fellowshipping with Gentiles, or of being deceptive and sinister by expressing their faith in a Jewish way in

Messianic congregations. Who can win in such a situation!

While many Jewish believers feel immediately at home in a Messianic congregation, others are overwhelmed by the stronger Jewish emphasis. Occasionally they discern Jewish racial pride, a parochial attitude towards the predominantly non-Jewish body of Messiah or even anti-Gentile feeling, and are uncomfortable with this. Is the Jewish believer in the Diaspora doomed never to fit in, to be caught in a Catch-22 situation?

Of Bears and Bunnies

The mental snapshot of a bear and a bunny might help in crystallizing the nature of this present problem in the body of Messiah. Imagine a Gentile bear who wants to dance with a Jewish bunny. In his exuberance he may step on her by accident. If he gets overly affectionate he may hug the bunny to death. On the other hand if he does not appreciate the strong-minded little hare, the bear might lose his temper and his manners, roughly jerking the bunny by the arm and dislocating a shoulder at the very least. If he feels that the Jewish bunny doesn't treasure his Gentile attentions or even that the bunny may feel distant and cold, he may get really grumpy and swat the little rabbit away with his powerful paw. A Jewish bunny takes her life into her hands when she dances with a Gentile bear!

Most Jewish believers who attend predominantly Gentile churches are personally acquainted with two common Christian responses to their own Jewishness. On the one hand some Gentile believers who are genuinely thrilled with meeting Jewish people may idealize Jewish believers, putting them on spiritual pedestals. The Gentile may assume that the Jew has a deep knowledge of Hebrew, Rabbinic Judaism and Jewish social customs at the time of Jesus. However, since the average Jewish believer usually does not excel in these areas, like most other Jews, he or she may be tempted to pride as a result of this unbalanced attention.

On the other hand, many churches pass over the existence of the

Jewish people in stony silence. Some discourage discussion about the Jewish people today and relegate anything Jewish to Bible times. When the Scriptures are publicly taught, the promises of God for the Jewish people are interpreted as applying only to the Church. There is no mention or teaching about Israel from the pulpit on Sunday mornings. The Gentile bear has either put the Jewish bunny in the spotlight on center stage or has told the bunny never to get within one hundred feet of the platform!

One New Person

The *one new man* paradigm is becoming a focus of renewed interest in the Church today. The central biblical passage for the *one new man* comes from Paul's discussion in Ephesians 2-3.

> Therefore, remember that formerly you who are Gentiles by birth and called "uncircumcised" by those who call themselves "the circumcision" (that done in the body by the hands of men) – remember that at that time you were separate from Messiah, excluded from citizenship in Israel and foreigners to the covenants of the promise, without hope and without God in the world. But now in Messiah Yeshua you who once were far away have been brought near through the blood of Messiah. For He Himself is our peace, who has made the two one and has destroyed the barrier, the dividing wall of hostility, by abolishing in His flesh the law with its commandments and regulations. His purpose was to create in Himself one new man out of the two, thus making peace, and in this one body to reconcile both of them to God through the cross, by which He put to death their hostility. He came and preached peace to you who were far away and peace to those who were near. For through Him we both have access to the Father by one Spirit. Consequently, you are no longer foreigners and aliens, but fellow citizens with God's people and members of God's household, built on the foundation of the apostles and prophets, with Messiah Yeshua Himself as the chief cornerstone. In Him the whole building is joined together and rises to become a holy

temple in the Lord. And in Him you too are being built together to become a dwelling in which God lives by His Spirit. For this reason I, Paul, the prisoner of Messiah Yeshua for the sake of you Gentiles – surely you have heard about the administration of God's grace that was given to me for you, that is, the mystery made known to me by revelation, as I have already written briefly. In reading this, then, you will be able to understand my insight into the mystery of Messiah, which was not made known to men in other generations as it has now been revealed by the Spirit to God's holy apostles and prophets. This mystery is that through the gospel the Gentiles are heirs together with Israel, members together of one body, and sharers together in the promise in Messiah Yeshua.[1]

In this lengthy passage Paul contrasts what was before the cross with what is now, after the resurrection of Yeshua. Prior to the coming of the gospel the Gentiles were looked down upon by many Jews as uncircumcised savages. They had no privileged or covenantal access to the Jewish covenants, no revelation of God in the Scriptures, no relationship with God and no revealed hope for the End of Days. They were far from the promises of God and far from the people of God.

The incredible good news is that in Yeshua God has broken down the barriers and hedges which would keep Gentiles away from sharing in sweet spiritual fellowship with Jewish believers. God's intention was to remove the mutual hatred and hostility that can exist between both Jews and Gentiles, and to replace it with peace, love and hearty camaraderie. From Paul's perspective, the cross has made possible a change of reality, socially and spiritually. Gentiles who appropriate these benefits can step over the broken stones of a spiritual Berlin Wall to stand with Jews as free people on the soil of the Jewish spiritual commonwealth.

---

1 Eph. 2:11 - 3:6

Together on Jewish Soil

God brings unity between Jew and Gentile through a mechanism called *the one new man* or better still the *one new person*. Let's first understand what is not meant by the term the *one new man*. It is not the main or only Bible term used to describe Jewish and Gentile believers. Scripture also calls believers 'the bride of Messiah', the 'brothers of Yeshua', the 'slaves of Messiah' and the 'living stones'. Each one of these terms reveals another aspect of our spiritual identity. But because there are so many expressions used, it should be clear that no one term should override all the others. Believers are not only to be visualized as 'a virile male'; they also need to picture themselves corporately as 'a fetching bride'! These diverse terms are not meant to cause spiritual schizophrenia! They are Hebraic figures of speech meant to point toward spiritual realities.

Paul uses the term *one new man* in a very specific way. He is describing a new entity composed of Jews and Gentiles, not a raceless or sexless being, a colorless neuter entity. God is not envisioning racial or cultural assimilation here. Yeshua is not all of a sudden steamrolling the wonderful cultural and ethnic diversities He Himself has fashioned into a sludgy kind of spiritual asphalt. The different races of humanity were originally God s idea, His human sculptures. God has ordained that the time has come for Jew and Gentile to live together in peace and friendship, as one happy family. *One new person* means that Jew and Gentile are now able to have spiritual fellowship as equals within the body of Messiah. They are now able to worship the same God together, and they are being shaped by God's hand into one spiritual skyscraper.

This *one new man* community is a composite unity where Jew and Gentile co-exist in mutual delight and appreciation – the bear and the bunny finally at peace in 'Jewish Bunny-land,' in the Commonwealth of Israel! Ephesians is crystal-clear is stating that this unity takes place on Jewish soil, on the commonwealth territory of Israel (2:12). Gentiles become naturalized citizens of the Jewish spiritual commonwealth without losing their diverse ethnic inheritances – that endearing 'wild olive complexion' of Romans 11:17 and 24. The meeting ground for Jew and Gentile is in the one splendid Jewish olive tree[2] which is now made up of Jewish and Gentile branches.

The vision that Paul received from God was not Jewish assimilation into a Gentile body, a common practice today. Nor did Paul understand the *one new person* to mean Gentile assimilation into a Jewish body, a suggestion espoused by some on the fringes of Messianic Judaism. What Paul saw was a new and dynamic spiritual relationship occurring between Jews and Gentiles *in* the body of Messiah. Jews remain Jews and Gentiles remain Gentiles. What has changed is that now mutual respect and appreciation characterize their family relationship. In Paul s vision Jews and Gentiles actually praise God for each other. *Vive la différence*!

One Flock and One Shepherd

In Ephesians 3 the Apostle Paul said that this above description of the body of Messiah was not clearly understood prior to the cross. It was a mystery revealed to Yeshua's Apostles by God. A mystery is a New Covenant teaching that had previously been communicated as a 'dark saying' or in a hidden or veiled form in the Hebrew Scriptures. The mystery in this case is that Jews and Gentiles now have a communal spiritual fellowship in the Messiah, without either one giving up his own identity.

The concept of Jews and Gentiles worshipping together is described in Isaiah 56:3-8 and 66:18-21. Yeshua also obliquely referred to this mystery in John 10:"I have other sheep that are not of this sheep pen. I must bring them also. They too will listen to My voice, and there shall be one flock and one shepherd."[3] Amazingly, Caiaphas the High Priest also prophesied about this mystery, his words overshadowed and directed by the Holy Spirit, even as he was planning Yeshua's crucifixion.

---

2   *Cf.*, Rom. 11:24, "their own tree: indicates that God sees the olive tree as Jewish

3   Jn. 10:16

Then one of them, named Caiaphas, who was high priest
that year, spoke up, "You know nothing at all! You do not
realize that it is better for you that one man die for the
people than that the whole nation perish." He did not say
this on his own, but as high priest that year he prophesied
that Yeshua would die for the Jewish nation, and not
only for that nation but also for the scattered children
of God, to bring them together and make them one.[4]

Another hint regarding the *one new person* is found in Isaiah 25:6-
8 where the Messianic Banquet will host Jews and Gentiles together.
Yeshua was keenly aware of this reality when He prophesied,

I tell you the truth, I have not found anyone in Israel with
such great faith. I say to you that many will come from the
east and the west, and will take their places at the feast
with Abraham, Isaac and Jacob in the kingdom of heaven.[5]

If It's a Block Party, Who Brings the Music?

The wonderful plan described above may feel like an architect s
dream house – it looks fantastic on paper, but will it ever be built?
Certainly an incredulous response is not entirely out of place, given
the history of relations between Jews and Gentiles! What would
such a faith community look like? If the kingdom of God were
described as a feast, a party where Jewish and Gentile members
of the *one new person* get together for a spiritual celebration, who
gets to choose the music? Would Messianic CDs be played at such
a party or would high-powered Gentile praise music win the day?

What does a *one new man* congregation look like? Should it be
50-50 Jewish-Gentile? Paul nowhere legislates that only integrated
congregations of equal numbers of Jews and Gentiles can be
established, just to prove that the *one new person* concept is valid.
For the most part it is true that Paul's new congregations were a
mix of Jews and Gentiles, given the fact that Paul preached first in

4   Jn. 11:51-52
5   Matt. 8:10-11

Diaspora synagogues and then in public markets. But congregations composed primarily of Jews or primarily of Gentiles also existed in Paul's day, and today they are also kosher alternatives. A lot depends on the demography of the geographical area being considered and on the focus of evangelistic outreach in that area. One basic foundation stone must be that Jews and Gentiles are equally welcomed into any gathered congregation. Anything less than this is a violation of New Covenant teaching.

Another point to be weighed here is God's calling. Peter and Paul had different callings though both preached the gospel 'to the Jew first.' Peter s ministry was to the Jewish people, while Paul was called to the Gentiles.[6] In the same way some congregations have a specific calling to the Jewish people and a specific emphasis on Jewish expressions of faith, while most others are directed toward Gentiles. This is not only acceptable, it is highly commendable! In both cases each congregation should be encouraged to fulfill its own calling in humility and without legalism. Spiritual health and relational maturity should lead believers to openness to other cultural expressions and also to appreciation for God's diversity.

At the close of the twentieth century there is a renewed emphasis on discovering one's ethnic background. Alex Haley's television series *Roots* has created a user-friendly environment for all elements of the American melting pot, encouraging people to brush the dust off their own ethnic heirlooms and to reflect on the riches of their own family trees. God is speaking to the world through this trend, saying, "Look to the rock from which you were cut and to the quarry from which you were hewn."[7]

God is also speaking *through* the world to the body of Messiah. The Christian church has known the poison of racism at first hand. Believers are being challenged by God to learn new ways of affirming diversity, of accepting gloriously different people and of blessing them. Yeshua doesn't want us to condescendingly and

6   Gal. 2:8-9
7   Isa. 51:1

grudgingly toleratestrangers. A heart of thankfulness and respect for all of our brothers and sisters is the need of the hour!

Taking Over the Neighborhood

Jewish believers are often alarmed at the thought of being engulfed by the huge number of Gentile believers in a local congregation. Similarly some Gentiles are confused and caught off-balance by the thought of having to learn Jewish ways, eat Jewish food or learn Hebraic dances. Though believers are called to accept one another for Messiah's sake, it needs to be remembered that many churches have at times functioned as agents of assimilation and anti-Semitism. On the other hand some Messianic Jews have treated curious Gentiles visitors at Messianic congregations like second-class citizens and have fostered a reverence for Jewish cultural expressions that borders on auto-ethnolatry (the worship of a people by itself). Paul again offers some helpful guidelines in 1 Corinthians 9:

> For though I am free from all men, I have made myself
> a slave to all, that I might win the more. And to the
> Jews I became as a Jew, that I might win the Jews; to
> those who are under the Torah, as under the Torah,
> though not being myself under the Torah, that I might
> win those who are under the Torah; to those who are
> without Torah, as without Torah, though not being
> without the Torah of God but under the Torah of Messiah,
> that I might win those who are without Torah.[8]

One good motive for Gentiles to be open to embracing aspects of Jewish culture is because some Gentiles are called to live and minister among the Jewish people. They want to learn about the Jewish people s culture out of love for Israel, and they consider it a great privilege to do so. In this case the motivation to embrace Jewish cultural riches stems from God's calling.

Another reason why some Gentiles are interested in learning

---

8   1 Cor. 9:19-21

about Jewish culture, biblical traditions, feasts and music is because they appreciate the Jewish people's spiritual heritage. Romans 15:27 teaches that Gentiles now share in the Jewish people's spiritualthings.It is not surprising that some Gentiles may want to learn more about their new Jewish spiritual heritage. In Romans 11:17 Paul points out that now Gentiles partake of the sap which flows from the rich root of the Jewish olive tree. At the close of the twentieth century, Gentiles are rediscovering that the spiritual sap of this cultivated tree tastes Jewish! "Things go better with" Jewish olive sap, to paraphrase a popular American commercial.

Over the centuries Jews who embraced the Jewish Messiah were forced by the overwhelmingly Gentile Church to divest themselves of their Jewish cultural heritage. One typical example is the Father of Protestant Church History, a Jew named Johann August Wilhelm Neander. Prior to his 1806 baptism he was known as David Mendel. Neander, his baptismal name, means 'new man' in Greek. David Mendel clearly understood the rules of the game in Christian Europe: to become a new man in Christ meant that one had to put the old Jewish man to death. Jewish names and ways were'out,' and Greek or German names were 'in.' Such cultural imperialism has often characterized Gentile attitudes to Jewish believers in the body of Messiah. Messianic Jews and Christian Gentiles can together learn from history and avoid the pitfalls of cultural colonialism.

Honey versus Vinegar

There is an old Yiddish proverb, "You can attract more flies with honey than with vinegar." Messianic expressions of Jewish tradition and faith are sweet. They contain elements of great richness. Provided that these traditions focus on the Lord Yeshua and remain true to New Covenant teaching, they can bring much blessing and encouragement to believing Gentiles as well as to Messianic Jews. Jewish believers who are sufficiently equipped can offer helpful guidance to Gentile Christians on ways of enriching church worship and community through our common Jewish heritage.

The Talmud says, "More than the calf likes to suck, does the cow like to suckle." In other words, more than the student likes to learn, does the teacher like to teach! Some may be tempted to force Jewish delicacies down the throats of uninterested bystanders, much like geese are force-fed to produce a higher yield of *paté de foie gras*. A more excellent way would be to first identify those who already have an appetite for the Jewish people s spiritual heritage. The best way to serve Jewish spiritual delicacies is to lay them out attractively, to call people to the table with great respect, and to humbly offer these Semitic sweetmeats to those who are genuinely interested.

Jew/Gentile is Beautiful!

The beauty of the Jewish people's spiritual heritage in no way means that Gentile spiritual expressions are inferior. "Any view of the election of Israel which implies that Israel is superior in any regard to other peoples is wrong. Israel's election was an election of the pure grace of God... (A philosophy) which converts the election of Israel into an election of worth or superiority ... is contrary to Scripture."[9]

Back at our imaginary block party, Jews and Gentiles are dancing and having a great time. They are outdoing each other in preferring each other, each one sampling the other's desserts and making sure that the other's favorite CD gets airtime. In the end Jews and Gentiles go home marveling at God's wisdom in creating such strikingly beautiful diversities in food, music and people.

---

9   Pfister in Ramm, *op.cit.*, p. 22

Chapter Twelve

Bringing Kosher Comfort to Zion

Many Gentile Christians desire to bless and comfort Israel. Though they do not always know the subtleties of Jewish culture and religion, the purity of their motives and the openness of their heart is strong. Various ministries have placed themselves at the disposal' of Christians who want to bless and comfort Israel. Most of these are led by Gentile believers, like the International Christian Embassy Jerusalem, Christian Friends of Israel, Bridges For Peace, and others. Some are directed by Orthodox Jews, like the International Fellowship of Christians and Jews. It is important that followers of Yeshua everywhere understand what options and strategies these varying groups offer. Believers need to weigh these strategies in light of Scripture, discerning which elements are good and which are less than pure.

An Orthodox Jewish Agenda

Rabbi Yechiel Eckstein is founder and president of the Holyland

Fellowship of Christians and Jews, now known as the International Fellowship of Christians and Jews. He is a former national codirector of Interreligious Affairs for the Anti-Defamation League of B'nai Brith and the author of *What Christians should know about Jews and Judaism*.[1] Eckstein's *Wings of Eagles* program has brought hundreds of Russian-speaking Jews to Israel, and the lion's share of that money has been raised from Evangelical Christians. Rabbi Eckstein has been lecturer at Northern Baptist Seminary and Chicago Theological Seminary. Eckstein claims that "his face is almost as well known in the Bible Belt and other Evangelical strongholds as Pat Boone's"[2] and sees himself as a bridge between the Orthodox Jewish community and Evangelicals.

One of Rabbi Eckstein's goals is to raise financial and political support among Christians for the Jewish people and the State of Israel. The biblical teaching that Bible believers should bless Israel is a strong plank in Rabbi Eckstein's messages, and he gives Christians the opportunity to do just that. Rabbi Eckstein also wants to shape Christians' understanding about Jewish people and Judaism. Eckstein has both opposed Jewish evangelism, and directed fiery verbal arrows against both Evangelical support for Jewish missions and Messianic Jewish expressions of the New Covenant faith. His guiding principle is: "Cooperate (*ed., with Evangelical Christians*) wherever possible, oppose wherever necessary, and teach and sensitize at all times."[3] The noted Jewish scholar Geoffrey Wigoder sums up Eckstein's philosophy:

> Eckstein ... recognizes that the relationship (ed., between Jews and Evangelical Christians) is based on a basic conflict - the determination to evangelize versus the Jewish determination to survive - but feels that a modus vivendi can be built up, involving give and take on

1   Rabbi Yechiel Eckstein, *What Christians should know about Jews and Judaism*, Word, Incorporated, Waco, 1984.

2   Aryeh Dean Cohen, "Close encounters of the Evangelical kind," *The Jerusalem Post*, Tuesday, January 13, 1998, p. 11.

3   *ibid.*

both sides. Jews, he suggests, will have to recognize the centrality of mission for many Christians but in turn will demand the cessation of crude frontal activities in this direction and its restriction to frameworks of dialogue, model and example, without insistence on conversion.[4]

Rabbi Eckstein makes one thing perfectly clear: "'(I) make a distinction in my life and work between those who believe that will happen (ed., *that all Jews will believe in Jesus*), and those who actively try to bring it about.' (Eckstein) refuses to work with those who target Jews for conversion."[5] According to Eckstein, Evangelical efforts to evangelize the Jewish people "taints"[6] their contributions to the Jewish people and the State of Israel. Purity of motives, according to Rabbi Eckstein, means that Evangelical Christians need to stop sharing Jesus with their Jewish friends, stop bringing the gospel to the Jew first, and stop supporting Jewish evangelism. Only then will their money and their friendship be accepted.

You're Gentiles! You Can't Sing Jewish Songs!

Eckstein has another point to make in his teaching ministry to the Evangelical community:

> The fact that Christianity severed virtually all of its links with its Jewish origins also has important, irreversible theological implications. In truth, attempts to "Judaize" the church, as the Hebrew Christian movement essentially tries to do, are not new. Already in the second century C.E. Ignatius wrote that it was inconsistent to talk of Jesus Christ and to practice Judaism at the same time. The church, in short, made certain decisions that effectively brought about its severance with the Jewish people and faith. It must now live by those decisions.[7]

Rabbi Eckstein is not happy when Christians try to rediscover

---

4 Geoffrey Wigoder, "Evangelical Challenge," *JP*. Sunday Oct 14, 1984, p.8

5 Cohen, *op. cit.*

6 *ibid.*

7 Eckstein, *op. cit.*, p. 295. N.b. our chapter 18, fn.44, 45!

the Jewish roots of their faith. He prefers it when Gentiles act like Gentiles! Pointing to anti-Semitic statements by the church father Ignatius, statements which deny and mock the Jewish roots of Christianity, Eckstein lectures at Christians that they need to uphold Ignatius' anti-Jewish statements. The rabbi does not want Christians to reconnect with ancient Messianic Jewish expressions of their faith. He wants to see the middle wall of partition between Jew and Gentile re-erected, for in truth he never really believed that it was broken down in Messiah Yeshua. Unfortunately Eckstein is sowing mistrust of Jewish believers, and is trying to drive a wedge between Messianic Jews and Gentiles. The fellowship that Eckstein is fostering between Jews and Christians can only succeed when Yeshua, His gospel and His Jewish followers are left outside, standing at the door and knocking. Eckstein makes this strategy crystal clear when he says:

> Hebrew Christians are the source of much of the Jewish mistrust of Evangelicals and the discord in their relations... Christians would do far better to expend their funds and energies elsewhere, to dialogue with Jews, and to leave the conversion of Jews to God who may or may not bring it about when the full time of the Gentiles arrives. At least, they ought to abandon and denounce the overly zealous and deceptive means usually employed by various Hebrew Christian groups... Jews have suffered from Christian missionary actions for almost two millennia. They regard the Hebrew Christian movement as but another form of spiritual genocide.[8]

Havdalah - To Distinguish Between the Pure and the Impure

None of this should surprise us. Orthodox rabbis do not usually defend Yeshua, His gospel or His Jewish followers. What does surprise us is the amount of Gentile Christians who are prepared to work with Rabbi Eckstein under these conditions. Evangelical

---

8   *ibid.,* pp. 298-99

Christians need to clearly understand that Eckstein is attempting to woo Christians away from the purity of the gospel while, at the same time, he calls an evangelistic heart for Israel 'impure'. Another Rabbi, Saul or Paul as he was called among the Gentiles, has something he also wants to teach believers about purity of motives:

> I am jealous for you with a godly jealousy. I promised you to one husband, to Messiah, so that I might present you as a pure virgin to Him. But I am afraid that just as Eve was deceived by the serpent's cunning, your minds may somehow be led astray from your sincere and pure devotion to Messiah. For if someone comes to you and preaches a Yeshua other than the Yeshua we preached, or if you receive a different spirit from the one you received, or a different gospel from the one you accepted, you put up with it easily enough.[9]

Bible believing Christians should grieve over anti-Semitic theology and actions, separating themselves from such things and censuring them as well. But is that what some Orthodox Jews really mean when they say that Christians need "to purge themselves and their faith of anti-Semitism and to repent *(ed., of.)* the violence loosed on Jews in the name of Christianity...by expressing humility, real respect, and honest support of Israel?"[10] For many Orthodox Jews this means, among other things, calling a total halt to Jewish evangelism, accepting that Jews do not need to believe in Yeshua, and distancing oneself from Messianic Jews. Can Christians accept these conditions as kosher prerequisites for bringing comfort to Zion?

There is an Orthodox Jewish agenda which attempts to neutralize the gospel and stop it from coming back to Israel, as well as to persuade Christians that Jesus is not for Jews. If Christians do not stop evangelizing Jewish people or supporting Jewish evangelism, then such Orthodox groups proclaim that they will refuse to give

---

9   2 Cor.11:2-4

10   Pnina Peli, Doubting the blessings of Christian Zionism", *JP*, Friday Sept 20 1985, p.15

Evangelical Christians the privilege of blessing them materially and politically. Is this what Isaiah meant by "Comfort, comfort My people!, saith the Lord"?

Comforting the Uncomfortable

The Scriptures shimmer with God's comfort for His people Israel. "'Comfort, O comfort My people' says your God. 'Speak to the heart of Jerusalem and call to her.'"[11] "Shout for joy, O heavens! And rejoice, O earth! Break forth into joyous shouting, O mountains! For the Lord has comforted His people, and will have compassion on His afflicted".[12] Many believers long to comfort the Jewish people as well, to follow after the compassions of their God.[13] Beginning in the 1970's various movements have spontaneously sprung up across the globe, each attempting to express God's compassionate heart for His people Israel. Some of these groups focus on prayer and intercession, others on evangelism and equipping the body of Messiah, and others still on works of comfort and mercy.

But sometimes a disquieting trend surfaces among some comfort ministries to the Jewish people: at times one has to strain to hear any mention of the fact that Jews need to believe the gospel of Yeshua, or that believers should share the gospel with Jewish people, or even that Christians should pray for the salvation of Israel. Have Rabbi Eckstein's preconditions been accepted by Christian Zionism? Why then do some Christian Zionist groups fall silent when it comes to Israel's desperate spiritual condition? What's wrong with this picture? Why is it happening?

"We Are Not Against You!"

Many Christian Zionist ministries were founded in the 1970's and 1980's in the wake of the United Nation's 1974 declaration that 'Zionism is racism'.[14] The pro-Israel sympathies of Western

---

11   Isa. 40:1-2 (my translation)

12   Isa. 49:13 NASB

13   *Cf.*, 1 Cor. 11:1

14   The UN's unprecedented attack on Zionism, the national liberation movement of the Jewish people,

Europe, Africa and Japan had been shaken by the trauma of the Islamic oil embargo. Many nations had responded to Arab pressure by transferring their embassies in Israel from Jerusalem to Tel Aviv. Israelis felt that once again the Islamic Middle East and the Christian West were arrayed against their tiny nation. A Hebrew proverb common in those days was '*Kol ha'olam negdenu!*' ('All the world is against us').

A few brave Gentile believers banded together and formed the International Christian Embassy in Jerusalem (ICEJ). Their desire was to communicate to the Israeli people in no uncertain terms that many Evangelical and Charismatic Christians would not turn their backs on the Jewish state, but would stand by Israel through thick and thin. These believers took a lot of flack over the years over their resolute stand for Israel. Arab Christian Replacement theologians counterattacked, proclaiming that the ICEJ did not represent the Arab Christian world and that the Embassy's pro-Israel stance further marginalized the Christian presence in Muslim society. Liberal Protestants and Catholics roundly condemned the Embassy's evangelical interpretation of the Bible, its recognition of Israel as a partial fulfillment of biblical prophecy, and its unconcealed warmth for the right-wing of Israel's body politic.

In the Orthodox Jewish community, anti-missionaries accused the ICEJ and other such ministries of being undercover missionaries. Some religious parties put pressure on the overwhelmingly secular Israeli government, demanding that they expel Christian Zionist organizations from Israel. Many Christian Zionist leaders felt attacked from all sides. They could personally identify with the words of Psalm 69:9: "(F)or zeal for Your house consumes me, and the insults of those who insult You fall on me."

---

was unjustified on moral and ethical grounds. The support for this resolution was due to the fear unleashed among the industrialized nations of the awesome economic damage that an Islamic oil embargo could cause. This racist UN resolution was rescinded in the days immediately preceding the 1991 Gulf War, as part of an American-proposed package of measures designed to shore up the anti-Sadaam coalition and restrain Israel from defending itself from anticipated Iraqi hostile actions.

When in Rome ...

The State of Israel is not excited about the preaching of the gospel. This is not surprising in light of the long history of Christian anti-Semitism. "The Christian presence in this land has always been a sensitive issue. Missionaries are not welcome, inasmuch as they are seen as having come here with the intention of enticing a Jew to abandon his or her roots."[15] Though Israelis have a large measure of religious freedom, and freedom to evangelize is presently protected by Israeli law, the situation governing visas for foreign religious workers and extended-stay tourists who evangelize is not encouraging. At times Gentile Christians have discovered that their own evangelistic activities have led to governmental refusal to renew visas.

It is important for readers to know that most Christian Zionists outside of the land of Israel are free to evangelize Jewish people. Their right to remain in their countries of residence will not be revoked on religious grounds. Government supported activists will not spy on them or harass them, open their mail or bug their phones. Unfortunately this is no always the case in the State of Israel. Though Israel is one of the few democracies in the Middle East, Orthodox Jewish political parties continue to drum up public sentiment against Messianic Jews and Evangelical Christians by scare tactics and political pressures. They have milked public funds to support their own anti-missionary activists, whose behavior is often illegal and thuggish. Israel's commitment to democracy and to Western religious and civil liberties is being severely tested by these Orthodox Jewish political activists.

The members of those Christian Zionist organizations which operate in Israel live as guests in that country. They know that if they proclaim in public what they believe in private – that Yeshua is Israel's Messiah, and that Jews everywhere need to kiss the Son of God in order to receive true security and salvation – then strategic

15   Johann Lueckhoff, *A Word from Jerusalem: Newsletter of the International Christian Embassy Jerusalem,* Sept./Oct. 1997, p. 2.

Israeli government bodies will deny even more visas, permission to hold street marches will probably be revoked, and the amount of negative press articles will rise dramatically.

As a result of this unfriendly atmosphere, many Christian Zionist groups in Israel have gone through a process of self-censorship. Some have concluded that it is too hard to evangelize Jewish people, and that therefore God will have to save the Jewish people by Himself, in His own good time. One man has said, "Christians have a lot to do before they have even the right to speak to this nation".[16] Other Gentile Christian Zionists focus on garnering political support for the State of Israel, or raising and distributing financial and material support for disadvantaged Jewish people. Some of these believers do share Yeshua's gospel quietly as the opportunity arises.

But this situation has sapped the vitality and witness of many individual believers and of some Christian ministries in the State of Israel today. An example – one Christian ministry sends out monthly prayer guidelines to its network of intercessory groups, studiously avoiding all mention of Jewish believers and other local Israeli Christians. A representative of that ministry told this author that this omission was deliberate, since the mailing also goes to rabbis and Israeli government leaders. Is it kosher Christian Zionism to pray only for the material needs of the Jewish people while simultaneously ignoring the body of Messiah and the work of the gospel in that country, and this in order to avoid problems with Israeli authorities? Who is influencing whom?

Demonic spirits whose job it is to crush and compromise Jewish evangelism whisper that Christians must choose between blessing Israel materially and blessing her spiritually. But this is a false dichotomy. It should not be a case of 'either or' but of 'both and'. The face of Yeshua is truly experienced when Christians do good deeds, plant trees, visit hospitals and dance in the streets of Jerusalem. The compassions of Messiah smell like sweet perfume when Christian

---

16   Marilyn Tripp, "The Christian Embassy Speaks: An Interview with Jan van der Hoeven", *Now - Israel's Weekly Newspaper*, date and p. unknown.

believers serve the Jewish sick, poor or hungry, and when Jewish refugees from the former USSR are transported to and settled in Israel. These are praiseworthy manifestations of Messiah's love to Israel – without preconditions, without hidden agendas, with pure motives.

But who will bring comfort to Israel by sharing the wonderful news that Israel's Comforter, the Messiah Yeshua, has come to His own people? Who will guide the intercessors to the throne of the God of all comfort, petitioning Him to pour out the Spirit of grace and consolations upon Israel? Christian Zionists are commanded by Jesus Himself in the Great Commission to find ways to manifest Yeshua's love to the Jewish people and to the Messianic Jewish remnant by preaching the gospel – without preconditions, without hidden agendas, with pure motives.

The Face of Yeshua

A gradual maturing is happening among many in the Christian Zionist movement. Though initial contacts with Israeli politicians brought a temporarily intoxicating flush of pride to the faces of some Christian Zionist leaders, time has brought a greater measure of sobriety in its wake. Government acceptance has come on many fronts, and today many Messianic ministries are represented at international conferences. But the greatest development within Christian Zionism has occurred in the area of more clearly discerning their own calling – to minister the love and compassion of Messiah in physical ways to Jewish people who would otherwise reject any contact with Christians.

The prophetic Scriptures describe a material ministry that believing Gentiles can have to Jewish people.[17] Though many of these passages focus on the Messianic age to come, the prophets do commend the idea of Gentiles bringing material comfort to Israel as an expression of Messiah's love. As the Christian church

---

17   Isa. 49:22-23: 60:5-12, 16; 61:5-6; Rom.15:26-27 (this Scripture refers to Gentile believers ministering materially to Jewish believers!); *etc.*

moves from arrogance and ignorance concerning the Jews to love and compassion, many believers are looking for ways not only to say "God loves you" but also to demonstrate it. A great desire has been birthed among hundreds of thousands of Christians to 'reach out and bless someone', to put feet to their faith regarding God's affection for the Jewish people. Their longing is to be able to say to Israel, "Behold your God! See how He loves you! He has even put it into our hearts to bless you!"

The Lord is up to something. Hundreds of thousands of Jewish hearts are being changed and softened. Centuries long attitudes of fear, hatred and suspicion toward Christians are being transformed. For the first time in a long time, many Jewish people are seeing real followers of Jesus filled with the love of Jesus for His own Jewish people. Some are even coming to faith in Yeshua as a result. What we are observing here is a process – not the conclusion of that process, but rather a new beginning.

Balancing Love and Truth

This rebirth of Christian affection for the Jewish people is a good thing, and it is a 'God' thing. For the first time in many years a significant movement of Christians exists who are demonstrating God's healing heart for Israel through loving hands and kind eyes. The divine calling of Christian Zionism needs to be recognized and appreciated by the wider body of Messiah, and this includes Jewish missions and Messianic Judaism.

At the same the body of Messiah needs to recognize that, while we need the Christian Zionists, they need us. While all believers should be thankful to God for Yeshua's arms of love extended through Christian Zionists, it is also true that Christian Zionist comfort ministries are not complete without the mouth of Yeshua – other believers passionately interceding for Israel's salvation, clearly communicating Yeshua's offer of atonement to the lost sheep of the House of Israel, and committing their lives and resources to save Jewish lives. Once again it is not a case of 'either or' but of 'both and'!

We all need to exercise care that the clarity and the power of the gospel is not blurred in this process. In the early 1990's an Anglican theologian addressed the International Christian Embassy in Jerusalem seminar at the Feast of Tabernacles and, in passing, advocated 'two-covenant' theology. This unbiblical position holds that Jewish people do not need to believe in Yeshua today since, supposedly, they already have a saving covenant with God. The ICEJ quickly repudiated this aspect of that teaching and pulled that recorded session from conference tape albums. The Embassy is to be commended for clearly refusing to endorse anti-gospel views. However, a few other Christian Zionist groups exist which still allow two-covenant views to be propagated at their conferences.

I appeal to all Christian Zionist leaders: please repeat and clearly affirm in your publications, newsletters and conferences, that the gospel of Yeshua really needs to be preached to the Jewish people, and to the Jew first! The Christians who attend your conferences really need to be reminded that the Jewish people still need the gospel, and that Yeshua still commands us to go to them. Silence may be golden, but speaking clearly is the need of the hour.

Keep Thy Tongue From Evil!

Christian Zionism has done the body of Messiah a service by bringing to the fore issues regarding Israel and evangelism how to speak to the heart of Jerusalem issues that need to be discussed in the broader Christian and Messianic communities. It is my conviction that these discussions should be conducted in the Spirit of Messiah, preferring one another in love, humility and gentleness! In the meantime, no believer who wants Messiah's commendation should carp at the good works clearly being carried out by Christian Zionists, or snipe at their productive ministries.

Those involved in Jewish evangelism need to ask themselves some uncomfortable questions: how much success have our organized efforts met with in evangelizing the broader Jewish community in

Israel and the Diaspora? In light of Yeshua's soon return, does it look like the task of bringing in Israel's salvation will be humanly accomplished by traditional evangelistic methods alone? Can't we allow ourselves to be gracious and kind to other brothers and sisters in Messiah who have differing ministries than ours? Could it be that our potential graciousness is being quenched by fear that there will not be enough financial support in the body of Messiah to go around? But our God is bigger than that fear, and His resources and the affections of His heart are unlimited toward His faithful servants!

The voice of the Holy Spirit cries out in the wilderness to us all, "Clear a way for the Lord! Pave a straight path for the ministries of our God! Build up in Israel a highway of integrity that our Lord can walk upon! Let mountains of opposition to the gospel be brought down, and let the humble ministry of Yeshua be lifted up! Let the rough places where the fear of man hides and where the desire to please people lurks be torn down, and let the rugged terrain of hostility be turned into a broad valley of freedom! Then the glory of the Lord will be revealed through Yeshua's ministry of reconciliation, and all flesh will be comforted and acknowledge Messiah together!"

Arise O Men of God!

A heart for Israel is a gift from God. Those who have received it know that it comes by revelation from the Most High. It is akin to a baptism in the Holy Spirit – an overwhelming experience of God's longing for His people, His fierce love and His broken heart. Most leaders of Christian Zionist ministries have received this revelation and this heart. Years ago the Lord prevailed upon their lives with His passion for the Jewish people. At great personal sacrifice, usually knowing only one step at a time, they have walked the lonely walk of a man of faith, preaching a message of God's love for Israel, His eventual restoration of that people, and His priority for the Jewish nation. These people are true heroes of the faith!

A word of exhortation is in order, though. Yeshua's disciples are called not only to do damage control for unsavory aspects of the Christian Church's past. We are called to be pro-active, to beautify the name of Messiah Yeshua. Lasting peace between Gentile Christians and unbelieving Jews comes only through the cross of the Jewish Messiah, and unshakable comfort is not possible for Israel apart from the nail-scarred hands of the Pierced One. When believing Gentiles rejoice in a fellowship with unbelieving Jews which simultaneously shuns Messianic Jews, we are not talking about a peace of the brave – we are not even talking about a real peace.

Jews and Gentiles can only be reconciled through the atonement of Messiah Yeshua. That is the heart of the apostolic gospel. Thank you, Christian Zionists, for reminding us that the Church of the Living God needs to be Messiah's compassionate heart and healing hands to Israel. Please take it to heart, Christian Zionists, that the Church of the Living God also needs to be Messiah's word of life and salvation to the Jewish people.

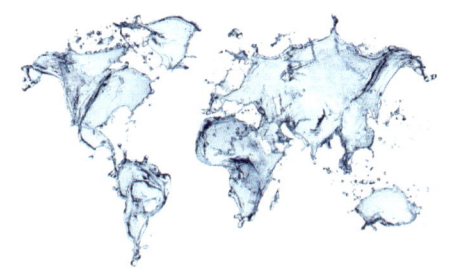

SECTION FIVE:

FOR ZION'S SAKE!

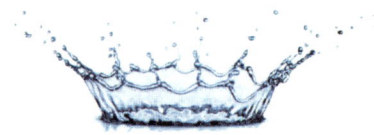

Chapter Thirteen

Zion In The Bible:

"On Earth And As It Is In Heaven"

Tour guides in Israel often have the privilege of introducing Christian pilgrims to the wonders of the Bible heartland. Time and again a surprising exclamation falls from the lips of first time visitors to that country: "I never realized that Jerusalem is an actual three-dimensional city! I never guessed that it would be so earthy, so tangible – so real!" Many Christians' impressions and images of the Holy Land were formed as children in Sunday schools. The brightly colored Bible illustrations found in Sunday School materials do not always dovetail with flesh-and-blood realities.

The sacred sentiments evoked by the sound of the words 'Jerusalem' or 'Zion' also cause many people's spiritual pulses to quicken. For some believers the power of these dreams can nearly eclipse the realities of Jerusalem. In extremely rare instances some tourists visiting Jerusalem actually experience a psychotic reaction to the city, a pathological response nicknamed 'the Jerusalem syndrome.' When suppressed stained-glass fantasies bump into the cool stones of the Old City, watch out for an occasional rise in the weirdness quotient!

A similar though less traumatic paradigm shift can occur when believers theologically confront an earthly and primarily Jewish city, when they had expected a spiritual and international Jerusalem. What connection can there be between earthly Jerusalem and heavenly Zion? The next six chapters examine the historical origins of the hill known as 'Zion', trace the development of its geographical and prophetic calling, and consider those future earth-shaking events which the Scriptures connect with the Mountain of the Lord.

The Canaanite Connection

The original 'inhabitants of Zion were not Jews; in all probability they were Canaanites. In King David's day a Canaanite fortress named Zion (*Tziyon* in Hebrew) was located half-way up the western slope of the Kidron valley. Its walls and ramparts jutted out of an ancient hillside village, a town which was already one thousand years old on the day David was born in Bethlehem. The name of that village is recorded in the Ebla tablets (ca. 2300 B.C.) as *U-ru-sa-li-ma*,[1] and in the Egyptian Execration Texts (ca. 1800 B.C.) as *Rushalimum*.

Jerusalem was also called by another name, 'Jebus' (*Yevus* in Hebrew).[2] Its original Canaanite inhabitants were called Jebusites, a term which means 'dwellers in Jebus.' The Jebusites sometimes shortened this city's name for convenience's sake, turning 'Jerusalem' into the much shorter 'Salem.'[3] Years later, in Asaph's

---

1   H. W. Perkin, 'Tell Mardikh' in *The New International Dictionary of Biblical Archeology*, ed. Edward M. Blaiklock and R.K. Harrison, (Grand Rapids: Zondervan, 1983), pp. 440-42; Pettinato, Giovanni, *Ebla: A New Look at History*, trans. C. Faith Richardson, (Baltimore: Johns Hopkins University Press, 1986), and *The Archives of Ebla: An Empire Inscribed in Clay*, (Garden City: Doubleday & Co., 1981).

2   *Cf.*, Josh. 15:8; 18:28; Judg. 19:10; 1 Chron. 11:4.

3   *Cf.*, Gen. 14:18

day, the writer of Psalm 76:2 remembers these names as synonyms referring to one and the same city – Jerusalem: "(God's) tent is in Salem, His dwelling place in Zion.

Abraham's Commando Raid

In Genesis 14 Abram returns from a successful commando raid in Syria, where he had freed his nephew Lot from desert kidnappers. Arriving in Jerusalem, he brings news of his victory to the kings of Salem and Sodom, meeting them in a valley beside Jerusalem known as 'the King's Valley.'[4]

> After Abram returned from defeating Kedorlaomer and the kings allied with him, the king of Sodom came out to meet him in the Valley of Shaveh (that is, the King's Valley). Then Melchizedek king of Salem brought out bread and wine. He was priest of God Most High, and he blessed Abram, saying, "Blessed be Abram by God Most High, Creator of heaven and earth. And blessed be God Most High, who delivered your enemies into your hand." Then Abram gave him a tenth of everything.[5]

The first reference to Zion/Jerusalem in the Bible describes a Gentile king of Jerusalem who spoke a blessing over Abram. This event took place close to the Jebusite fortress of Zion. Amazingly, God has appointed Melchizedek (Hebrew for 'my king of righteousness'), a righteous priest, as king over Jerusalem in Abraham's day. Melchizedek was a true servant of *El Elyon*, God the Most High. His declaration that God had delivered Abram's enemies into his hand would have prophetic significance for Melchizedek's own Jebusite people in days to come.

Fire in the Fortress

Five hundred years after Abraham's death, Joshua the son of Nun and Eleazar the priest drew up battle plans for the coming invasion of Canaan. Lots were cast according to specific instructions which

---

4   *Cf.*, 2 Sam. 18:18

5   Gen. 14:17-21

the Lord had given to Moses,[6] and the land of Canaan was divided into tribal portions.The tribe of Benjamin was slated to receive the Jebusite town called Jerusalem. Only a few hundred meters south of that town, the projected border between Judah and Benjamin would snake across the southernmost corner of the King's Valley, a stone's throw south of the Canaanite fortress of Zion.[7]

The tribe of Benjamin, however, failed to dislodge the Jebusite residents of Jerusalem or seize the town as part of their inheritance.[8] The warriors of Judah lent a hand to their brother Benjamites, attacking and temporarily conquering Jerusalem. The Book of Judges recounts that they killed many of the city's inhabitants and set Jebus aflame,[9] but within a short period of time the Canaanites returned and rebuilt the town's defenses. The tribe of Benjamin was eventually forced to acknowledge Jebus as "a city of foreigners who are not of the sons of Israel."[10] It was an uneasy peace at best.

Up the Water Spout!

After King Saul died on Mount Gilboa, it did not take long for the men of Judah to crown David as king of their own tribe in Hebron.[11] Seven years later the men of Israel turned their hearts toward David and made a covenant with him, anointing him as king over Israel as well. One of David's first royal decrees to the united Jewish nation was that Jebus be besieged and captured. The plucky Canaanites who sat in the fortress known as Zion controlled the main crossroads of the Judean hills, confident behind their massive stone walls. A prolonged and bloody battle was about to break out.

> The king and his men marched to Jerusalem to attack the Jebusites, who lived there. The Jebusites said to David, "You will not get in here; even the blind and the lame

---

6   Cf., Josh. 14:1-2
7   Cf., Josh. 15:8; 18:11, 16, 21, 28.
8   Cf., Judg. 1:21
9   Cf., Judg. 1:8
10   Judg. 19:12 NASB
11   Cf., 2 Sam.2:7; 5:1-5

can ward you off." They thought, "David cannot get in here." Nevertheless, David captured the fortress of Zion, the City of David. On that day, David said, "Anyone who conquers the Jebusites will have to use the water shaft to reach those 'lame and blind' who are David's enemies." That is why they say, "The 'blind and lame' will not enter the palace." David then took up residence in the fortress and called it the City of David. He built up the area around it, from the supporting terraces inward.[12]

Joab, David's courageous general, probably succeeded in taking the city by climbing up a concealed underground water shaft known today as 'Warren's shaft.' Evidently he was then able to open the bars and gates of Zion from within and, with the help of David's other mighty men, he finally conquered the entire city.[13] From that day onward Zion/Jerusalem would be called by a new name – the City of David.

A Capital Idea

David built his own palace of cedars in Zion[14] and brought the Ark of the Covenant into the City of David as well.[15] Zion became the capital city of Israel, the central seat of government where the king, his family and his officials lived and judged the people of Israel.[16] Psalm 122 was written by King David at the very time when Zion had become the hub of Jewish spiritual, governmental and administrative life. His words evoke the joy of that moment:

Psalm 122
A song of ascents. Of David.
I rejoiced with those who said to me,
"Let us go to the House of the Lord."
Our feet are standing in your gates, O Jerusalem!

---

12   2 Sam. 5:6-9

13   Cf., 1 Chron. 11:6-8

14   Cf., 2 Sam. 5:5,11

15   Cf., 2 Sam. 6:12-17

16   Cf., 2 Sam. 9:7-13; Psa. 122:1-5

Jerusalem is built like a city
that is closely compacted together.
That is where the tribes go up, the tribes of the Lord,
To praise the name of the Lord according
to the statute given to Israel.
There the thrones for judgment stand,
the thrones of the House of David.
Pray for the peace of Jerusalem! May
those who love you be secure.
May there be peace within your walls
and security within your citadels
For the sake of my brothers and friends,
I will say, "Peace be within you!"
For the sake of the house of the Lord our God,
I will seek your prosperity.

The Daughter of Zion

The prophets would eventually use the terms 'Zion' and 'Jerusalem' to refer to the people of Judah or even to the whole people of Israel.[17] Newspapers and TV announcers do the same thing today when they refer to the capital cities of Washington and Moscow, or the government buildings of Whitehall and the Elysée, as metonymies or representatives of those entire countries and specific peoples. An especially endearing term is the pet name 'Daughter of Zion,' a reference to the whole Jewish people, God's tender virgin daughter.[18]

The psalmists got excited describing the beauty and splendor of Mount Zion. This had much to do with the fact that God had chosen this city out of all the great cities in the world to be His own city for time and eternity. Zion would be the home of His chosen people, it would be the throne city of His chosen Davidic dynasty, and it would be the home of His holy Temple where the Shechinah glory would dwell.

17   Eg., Isa. 1:8, 27; 10:24; 51:11; 52:1-10; 59:20-21; 60:14; 61:3; 62:1, 6, 10-12 et al.
18   Cf., 2 Ki. 19:21; Isa. 52:2; Jer. 14:17; Lam. 1:15; 2:13; Zech. 9:9

Psalm 48

Great is the Lord, and most worthy of praise,
In the city of our God, His holy mountain.
It is beautiful in its loftiness, the joy of the whole earth!
Like the utmost heights of Zaphon is Mount Zion,
The city of the Great King.
God is in her citadels;
He has shown Himself to be her fortress...
Like Your name, O God,
Your praise reaches to the ends of the earth;
Your right hand is filled with righteousness.
Mount Zion rejoices,
The villages of Judah are glad because of Your judgments.
Walk about Zion, go around her, count her towers,
Consider well her ramparts, view her citadels,
That you may tell of them to the next generation.
For this God is our God for ever and ever;
He will be our guide even to the end. (vv. 1-3, 10-14)

The Prophetic City

In Deuteronomy God had promised the Jewish people that one day He would reveal the location of a special prophetic city which would become the spiritual center of the Jewish people: "But you shall seek the Lord at the place which the Lord your God shall choose from all your tribes, to establish His name there for His dwelling, and there you shall come."[19] During the reign of King David, God commanded Nathan the prophet to tell David – the time had come to reveal 'that place' and to choose 'that city!'

> And I will provide a place for My people Israel
> ...The Lord declares to you that the Lord Himself
> will establish a house for you: ...I will raise up your
> offspring to succeed you, who will come from your
> own body, and I will establish his kingdom. He is
> the one who will build a house for My Name, and I

---

19   Deut. 12:5 NASB

will establish the throne of his kingdom forever.[20]

When King Solomon dedicated the Temple in Jerusalem and inaugurated its use, he publicly announced what God had privately disclosed to His father David that God had finally chosen Jerusalem to be that chosen city.

> While the whole assembly of Israel was standing there, the king turned around and blessed them. Then he said: "Praise be to the Lord, the God of Israel, who with His own hand has fulfilled what he promised with His own mouth to my father David. For He said, 'Since the day I brought My people Israel out of Egypt, I have not chosen a city in any tribe of Israel to have a temple built for My Name to be there,' ...The Lord has kept the promise He made: I have succeeded David my father and now I sit on the throne of Israel, just as the Lord promised, and I have built the temple for the Name of the Lord, the God of Israel. I have provided a place there for the ark, in which is the covenant of the Lord that He made with our fathers when He brought them out of Egypt."[21]

The choosing of Zion/Jerusalem was not an act of man. The decision to appoint that city as the eternal capital of the Jewish people came from the God of Abraham, Isaac and Jacob. The founder and builder of Jerusalem is God Himself:

> Praise the Lord. How good it is to sing praises to our God, how pleasant and fitting to praise Him! The Lord builds up Jerusalem; He gathers the exiles of Israel. He heals the brokenhearted and binds up their wounds. He determines the number of the stars and calls them each by name. Great is our Lord and mighty in power; His understanding has no limit.[22]

> Thus He brought them to the border of His holy land, to the hill country His right hand had taken. He drove

---

20   2 Sam. 7:10-13

21   1 Ki. 8:14-21

22   Psa. 147:1-5

out nations before them and allotted their lands to them as an inheritance; He settled the tribes of Israel in their homes... (And) He chose the tribe of Judah, Mount Zion, which He loved. He built His sanctuary like the heights, like the earth that He established forever.[23]

For the Lord has chosen Zion, He has desired it for His dwelling: "This is My resting place for ever and ever; here I will sit enthroned, for I have desired it."[24]

His foundation is in the holy mountains. The Lord loves the gates of Zion more than all the other dwelling places of Jacob. Glorious things are spoken of you, O city of God. (Selah)... But of Zion it shall be said, "This one and that one were born in her;" And the Most High Himself will establish her. The Lord will count when He registers the peoples, "This one was born in there." Selah. Then those who sing as well as those who play the flute shall say, "All my springs of joy are in you."[25]

God's choosing of the physical city of Zion/Jerusalem is considered so much a part of His sacred character in the Scriptures that it is even used as a binding pronouncement in face-to-face spiritual confrontation with Satan. The Lord Yeshua declares to Satan as the devil accuses Joshua the high priest on the Day of Atonement: "And the Lord said to Satan, 'The Lord rebuke you Satan! Indeed, the Lord who has chosen Jerusalem rebuke you!'"[26]

God's Country

When God chose Jerusalem, one could say that He was already prejudiced in her favor! The Lord had made up His mind long ago that Israel was the most beautiful land of all the countries in the world. It was there that He would place His jewel, Jerusalem, and

---

23   Psa. 78:54-55, 68-69
24   Psa. 132:13-14
25   Psa. 87:1-7 NASB
26   Zech. 2:2 NASB

His diadem, the Jewish people.[27] Jeremiah the prophet quotes the Lord's very words: "I Myself said, 'How gladly would I treat you like sons and give you a desirable land, the most beautiful inheritance of any nation.'"[28]

A special emotional connection exists between the city of Jerusalem/Zion and the Lord. His overflowing heart of love is aroused for His Jewish people, and every time He thinks about them the very walls of Jerusalem come before His mind's eye.

> But Zion said, "The Lord has forsaken me, the Lord
> has forgotten me." Can a mother forget the baby
> at her breast and have no compassion on the child
> she has borne? Though she may forget, I will not
> forget you! See, I have engraved you on the palms
> of My hands; your walls are ever before Me.[29]

Irrevocably Yours!

The prophets stress the fact that God has irrevocably chosen earthly Zion as His own city for all time. The resurrection of Messiah Yeshua has not obliterated or transformed God's calling on this special city. God Himself vows that He will one day physically return to this earth and make Zion/Jerusalem His world capital once again.

> The sun and moon will be darkened, and the stars no
> longer shine. The Lord will roar from Zion and thunder
> from Jerusalem; the earth and the sky will tremble. But
> the Lord will be a refuge for His people, a stronghold
> for the people of Israel. Then you will know that I, the
> Lord your God, dwell in Zion, My holy hill. Jerusalem
> will be holy; never again will foreigners invade her.[30]

> But Judah will be inhabited forever and Jerusalem for
> all generations. And I will avenge their blood which

---

27 Cf., Isa. 62:1-3

28 Jer. 3:19

29 Isa. 49:14-16

30 Joel 3:15-17

I have not avenged, for the Lord dwells in Zion![31]

One of the Bible's most beautiful blessings concludes: "The Lord bless you from Zion, and may you see the prosperity of Jerusalem all the days of your life. Indeed, may you see your children's children. Peace be upon Israel!"[32] Benjamin Disraeli, the Earl of Beaconsfield and Prime Minister of Great Britain, echoes God's heart both poetically and prophetically when he declared, "The view of Jerusalem is the history of the world; it is more, it is the history of earth and of heaven".[33]

31   Joel 3:20-21 NASB

32   Psa. 128:5-6 NASB

33   Disraeli, Benjamin, *Tancred or The New Crusade*, book 3, chapter 4, originally published 1847 (St. Clair Shores, Michigan: Scholarly Press, 1970)

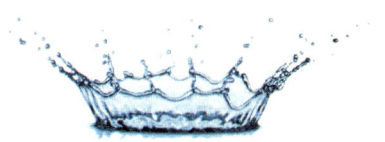

Chapter Fourteen

Messiah Jesus: Zion's Stone Of Stumbling

W hen the subject of Jesus comes up, and why the majority of Jews did not accept Yeshua at His first coming, some Jews and Christians respond in amazingly similar ways. Some Christians ask, "How could the majority of Israel's spiritual leaders not see that Jesus was the Messiah? It's so clear in the Bible – how could they possibly miss it?" On the other hand some Jewish people exclaim, "How could Jesus possibly be the Messiah if our own leaders and rabbis did not accept Him?" These responses are based on two false assumptions: first, if you show people the truth, they will obey it; and second, leaders understand the truth more clearly than common folk do.

The Scriptures point out that Adam and Eve were given clear and accurate instructions by God Himself, yet they chose to disobey. As the Gospel of John wryly notes, "This is the verdict: light has come into the world, but men loved darkness instead of light because their deeds were evil."[1] As to whether leaders have stronger moral fiber than the people they lead, the words of the prophet Micah are clear.

> Hear this, you leaders of the house of Jacob, you rulers
> of the house of Israel, who despise justice and distort
> all that is right; who build Zion with bloodshed, and
> Jerusalem with wickedness. Her leaders judge for a
> bribe, her priests teach for a price, and her prophets tell
> fortunes for money. Yet, they 'lean' upon the Lord and
> say, "Is not the Lord among us? No disaster will come
> upon us." Therefore because of you, Zion will be plowed
> like a field, Jerusalem will become a heap of rubble,
> the Temple hill a mound overgrown with thickets.[2]

Micah's words are not a blanket condemnation of all Jewish leaders throughout all of history. He was speaking specifically about the majority of Israel's leaders in his own generation. His prophecy called out to those leaders to stop using God's name in vain, to repent of their sins against God and man, and to return to the Savior of Israel. Otherwise, the city of Zion and its magnificent Temple would be destroyed.

History Repeats Itself

One hundred years after Micah, Jeremiah found himself on trial for treason before a hung jury. His crime? Prophesying the same things that Micah had said earlier! As the inhabitants of Zion argued back and forth, they came to the realization that, if Micah's prophecy had come from God, Jeremiah could not be condemned for saying the same thing.

> Then Jeremiah said to all the officials and all the people:
> "The Lord sent me to prophesy against this house and
> this city all the things you have heard. Now reform your
> ways and your actions and obey the Lord your God..."
> Then the officials and all the people said to the priests

---

1   Jn. 3:19

2   Mic. 3:9-12

and the prophets, "This man should not be sentenced
to death! He has spoken to us in the name of the Lord
our God. Some of the elders of the land stepped forward
and said to the entire assembly of people, "Micah of
Moresheth prophesied in the days of Hezekiah king
of Judah. He told all the people of Judah, 'This is what
the Lord Almighty says: "Zion will be plowed like
a field, Jerusalem will become a heap of rubble, the
Temple hill a mound overgrown with thickets."' Did
Hezekiah king of Judah or anyone else in Judah put him
to death? Did not Hezekiah fear the Lord and seek His
favor? And did not the Lord relent, so that He did not
bring the disaster He pronounced against them? We
are about to bring a terrible disaster on ourselves!"[3]

The French say *"plus ça change, plus c'est la même!"* – the more things change, the more they remain the same. Though Jeremiah was addressing a different generation than Micah's, the message sadly remained the same – many Jewish leaders of that day had cold hearts and hard eyes when it came to loving God and obeying Him.

Zion - A Charred Remnant

Isaiah, a contemporary of Micah's, spoke of how much suffering the city of Zion and the Jewish nation would undergo before they would embrace the salvation of their God.

Hear, O heavens! Listen, O earth! For the Lord has spoken:
"I reared children and brought them up, but they have
rebelled against Me"...They have forsaken the Lord; they
have spurned the Holy One of Israel and turned their
backs on Him...Why do you persist in rebellion?...Your
country is desolate, your cities burned with fire; your
fields are being stripped by foreigners right before you...
The Daughter of Zion is left like a shelter in a vineyard,
like a hut in a field of melons, like a city under siege...
See how the faithful city has become a harlot!... Zion
will be redeemed with justice, her penitent ones with

---

3   Jer. 26:12-19

righteousness. But rebels and sinners will both be
broken, and those who forsake the Lord will perish.[4]

The God of Israel would take drastic measures to bring His
people's hearts back to Himself. These steps involved lifting His
hand of mercy and protection from the Jewish people[5] and allowing
Satan to bring on the scourges of war, famine, exile and destruction.
Their hearts purified through divine discipline, a remnant of Israel
would finally turn back to Him.

> In that day the remnant of Israel, the survivors of
> the house of Jacob, will no longer rely on him who
> struck them down but will truly rely on the Lord,
> the Holy One of Israel. A remnant will return, a
> remnant of Jacob will return to the Mighty God.
> Though your people, O Israel, be like the sand by
> the sea, only a remnant will return. Destruction has
> been decreed, overwhelming and righteous.[6]

Stumbling Over the Stone

In the Scroll of Isaiah God prophesied that He Himself would
become a spiritual roadblock for the Jewish people. The entire
nation was on a spiritual collision course with the Lord, and He
would not prevent them from crashing into Him. Some would
be brought to repentance through the impact, while many others
would be mortally wounded. The God of Abraham, Isaac and Jacob
would become a stone of stumbling and judgment for His own
chosen people.

> The Lord spoke to me with His strong hand upon me,
> warning me not to follow the way of this people. He
> said: "Do not call conspiracy everything that these
> people call conspiracy; do not fear what they fear, and
> do not dread it. The Lord Almighty is the one you are
> to regard as holy, He is the one you are to fear, He is

---

4   Isa. 1:2-9, 16-28

5   *Cf.*, Zech. 1:12; Ezek. 20:22

6   Isa. 10:20-22

the one you are to dread, and He will be a sanctuary;
but for both houses of Israel He will be a stone that
causes men to stumble and a rock that makes them
fall. And for the people of Jerusalem He will be a trap
and a snare. Many of them will stumble; they will fall
and be broken, they will be snared and captured."[7]

The psalmist also touched on this prophetic theme, noting that one day those who were supposed to be builders and leaders in Israel would reject a stone (an important person) given by God. Ultimately the Lord would lift up that rejected stone and would place it as the capstone, the crowning stone, on the arch of the Lord's divine purposes. God's rejected messenger would become God's honored servant.

I will give You thanks, for You answered me; You have
become my salvation. The stone the builders rejected has
become the capstone; the Lord has done this, and it is
marvelous in our eyes. This is the day the Lord has made;
let us rejoice and be glad in it. O Lord, save us; O Lord,
grant us success. Blessed is he who comes in the name
of the Lord. From the house of the Lord we bless you.[8]

The God of Israel would not only be a stone which causes people to stumble. He would also be a rock of blessing and salvation for everyone seeking refuge under the shadow of His wings. "Therefore hear the word of the Lord, you scoffers who rule this people in Jerusalem...So this is what the Sovereign Lord says: 'See, I lay a stone in Zion, a tested stone, a precious cornerstone for a sure foundation; the one who trusts will never be dismayed.'"[9]

Two Stones and Two Messiahs

The different stones described in Isaiah and in Psalms – a stumbling stone, a rejected stone, and a precious cornerstone – would ultimately find their fulfillment in the man known as

7   Isa. 8:11-15

8   Psa. 118:21-26

9   Isa. 28:14-16

the Messiah of Israel. Godly Jewish people in every generation attempted to penetrate the veil of prophecy and uncover who the Messiah would be and when he would come.[10] Passages like Psalm 2, Isaiah 9, 11, 42, 49 and Amos 9:11-12 were mined for messianic material.[11] A composite picture emerged of a victorious warrior who would destroy all the enemies of Israel, regather the exiled Jewish people and rebuild the ruined Temple on the hill of Zion.[12] This mighty warrior would become known as *Mashiach ben David* (Hebrew for 'the anointed one who is the descendent of David').

At the same time another picture of Messiah emerged from the Scriptures which was very different from the first. This Messiah would suffer tremendously for the sins of his people, and it seemed that he would even taste death on behalf of his nation. Passages such as Zechariah 12:10 and Isaiah 52:13 - 53:12 were examined with a fine-tooth comb, probed for possible leads and sifted for details. Some rabbis concluded this individual was another Messiah, a suffering servant.[13] In Talmudic thought he became known as *Mashiach ben Yoseph* (Hebrew for 'the anointed one who is the descendent of Joseph').

Rabbinic theology allows for two Messiahs – one who suffers to redeem his people, and one who brings military victory to Israel. Among Jews today the suffering Messiah is by and large unknown,

---

10   *Cf.*, 1 Pet.1:10-11. For a rabbinic Targumic messianic interpretation of 'the stone', Targum Jonathan on Isa. 28:16 in *Targum of Isaiah*, trans. and ed. J.F. Stenning (Oxford, 1949); also 1QS 8:5-10 in the Dead Sea Scrolls for a contemporary Qumranic perspective. Also TB (Babylonian Talmud, tractate) Hagigah 5b and Rashi (Rabbi Solomon ben Isaac's Bible commentary) on Isa. 28:16

11   *Cf.*, TB Sanhedrin 96; also the Targum on Isa.4:2; 9:5; 10:27; 11:1, 6; 14:29; 16:1; 28:5; 42:1; 43:10; 52:13; 60:1 etc.

12   Rabbi Moshe ben Maimon (Maimonides) stated in his *Iggeret Teiman* (Epistle to the Yemenite Jews) that the Jewish nation would be able to identify the true *Mashiach ben David* by that one person accomplishing these three deeds (*cf.*, *Moses Maimonides' Epistle to Yemen*, trans. Boaz Cohen, ed. A.S. Halkin (1952).

13   In the Babylonian Talmud (TB Sukkah 52 a-b) the concept of Messiah ben Joseph is proof-texted from Zech. 12:10. Also Rashi, Radak (Rabbi David Kimchi) and Ibn Ezra see Zech. 12 and 13 as referring to Messiah ben Joseph. Rabbinic messianic interpretations of Isa.53 include the Targum, TB Sanhedrin 97b, Midrash Tanchuma, Yalqut Shim'oni, Rabbi Moshe Alshekh and Rabbi Elia de Vidas (these latter rabbis were from Safed). *Cf.*, Driver and Neubauer, *Isaiah 53 According to Jewish Interpreters* (Oxford: Clarendon, 1899 [reprinted Ktav].

while the military figure holds the day. Two helpful analyses of rabbinic source documents from a Messianic perspective are Rachmiel Frydland's *What the Rabbis know about the Messiah*,[14] and Risto Santala's *The Messiah In The Old Testament In The Light Of Rabbinical Writings*.[15]

A Doubletake on One Messiah

The Bible describes two separate messianic tasks, two different messianic missions. Some rabbis had attempted to solve the tension between these two callings by suggesting that two different Messiahs are to come. The first Jewish believers in Jesus proclaimed that Yeshua had fulfilled the first task, the rôle of the suffering Messiah, at His first coming. They announced that Yeshua would be coming back to Planet Earth at the End of Days to fulfill the second leg of the journey – the judgment of the world and the redemption of the remnant of Israel. As well, they announced that the Jewish Messiah would usher in salvation for all Gentiles who believe in Him. Peter and Paul preached not two separate Messiahs but two separate comings of one Messiah Yeshua. In the apostolic gospel two messianic callings blend into one messianic deliverer.

Most Jewish people in Yeshua's day were not looking for a suffering Messiah. The crushing burdens of a cruel Roman occupation caused Israel to cry out for physical deliverance, not for spiritual transformation. One hundred years after Yeshua's resurrection, Rabbi Akiva traveled across the Roman Empire drumming up support for Shim'on Bar-Kochba, who was later proved to be a false messiah. Bar-Kochba's defeat at the hands of the Romans in 135 AD and the subsequent slaughter of Akiva and his followers caused many rabbis to pull back from encouraging messianic hopes and speculations.

But something else had prevented Israel's religious leaders

---

14   Frydland, Rachmiel, *What the Rabbis know about the Messiah*, M.L.O: Columbus 1991, available from Messianic Literature Outreach, P.O. Box 37062, Columbus OH 45222 USA

15   Santala, Risto, *The Messiah In The Old Testament In The Light Of Rabbinical Writings*, Keren Ahvah Meshichit: Jerusalem, 1992, available from Bible and Gospel Service, 15270 Kukkila, Finland.

from accepting Yeshua and His message with an open heart. The chief priests were Sadducees, religious leaders who were also collaborators with Rome. For them Yeshua was a stumbling block because His ministry might irritate the Romans and upset the status quo. Messianic hopes were less important to Annas and Caiaphas than the material survival of their own power base.[16]

On the other hand, the Pharisees understood themselves to be true and righteous shepherds of Israel, and expected any potential Messiah to validate the total package of Pharisaic interpretations of the Torah. Though Yeshua agreed with much of the Pharisaic interpretation of the Mosaic covenant,[17] He insisted that in many cases the Pharisees had missed the heart of God's teachings and were quibbling about minor and external matters.[18] Yeshua prophesied that it was the Pharisees' rejection of Him and not His rejection of them which would contribute to decisive judgment falling upon Zion.[19] Once again, in that generation the majority of Jewish leaders were about to spurn the Holy One of Israel and turn their backs on Him. Isaiah's prophecy of the stones was about to be tragically fulfilled – the Stone of God would now become the Rejected Stone over which Israel would stumble.

The Redemption of the First Born

In Luke's Gospel, Joseph and Mary (*Hebr.* Miriam) brought their baby Yeshua to the hill of Zion in Jerusalem in order to present Him before the Lord.[20] The Book of Exodus commands Jewish parents to dedicate their first-born male children to the Lord in a ceremony known as *pidyon ha-ben*, 'the redemption of the first-born.'[21] Every

---

16 *Cf.,* Jn. 11:45-53

17 *Cf.,* Matt. 23:2-3, 23; also Acts 23:6-9

18 *Cf.,* Matt. 23:24-26; Mk. 7:5-13; Rom. 11:1-2, 15.

19 *Cf.,* Matt. 23:34-39; Matt. 15:12-14: "Then the disciples came to Him and asked, 'Do you know that the Pharisees were offended when they heard this?' He replied, 'Every plant that My heavenly Father has not planted will be pulled up by the roots. Leave them; they are blind guides. If a blind man leads a blind man, both will fall into a pit.'"

20 *Cf.,* Lk. 2:21-38

21 *Cf.,* Exod. 13:1-16; Num. 18:14-16.

new mother would also bring a sin offering for her own purification to the Tent of Meeting or the Temple.[22]

On the Temple Mount of Zion an old Jewish man named Simeon (*Hebr.* Shim'on) lifted baby Yeshua up to dedicate Him. The Holy Spirit of God descended upon righteous Shim'on and filled his mouth with a prophetic word. "Then Shim'on blessed them and said to Miriam, His mother: 'This child is destined to cause the falling and rising of many in Israel, and to be a sign that will be spoken against, so that the thoughts of many hearts will be revealed. And a sword will pierce your own soul too.'"[23] This was the moment all Israel had waited for – the day when Messiah would be revealed to His people Israel. Shim'on proclaimed that Messiah Yeshua had come as Isaiah's prophesied sign, as the Messianic Stone. Those in Israel who would speak against Him would fall, but those Jewish people whose inner heart responded with joyful worship would become the friends of God. The key to Israel's redemption would now be forever linked to the life of Yeshua.

Passing Over the Stone

Yeshua's last week on earth was centered in Jerusalem at the time of the Passover feast. Seated on the back of a donkey, He rode down the Mount of Olives and then up onto Mount Zion. Matthew says that this occurred so "that what was spoken through the prophet might be fulfilled, saying, 'Say to the Daughter of Zion, "Behold your king is coming to you, gentle, and mounted on a donkey, even on a colt, the foal of a beast of burden."'"[24] God's precious Cornerstone had appeared on Mount Zion at Passover. During that week Yeshua challenged the high priests and some of the leading Pharisees concerning their heart attitude to Him. He reminded them of the prophecies describing the Messianic Stone and He called Israel's leaders to repentance.

---

22   *Cf.,* Lev. 12:1-8

23   Lk. 2:34-35

24   Matt. 21:4-5 NASB quoting Zech. 9:9

Yeshua said to them, "Have you never read in the
Scriptures: 'The stone the builders rejected has become
the capstone; the Lord has done this, and it is marvelous
in our eyes?'Therefore I tell you that the kingdom of God
will be taken away from you and given to a people who
will produce its fruit. He who falls on this stone will be
broken to pieces, but he on whom it falls will be crushed."
When the chief priests and the Pharisees heard Yeshua's
parables, they knew He was talking about them.[25]

But within one week the same priests and Pharisees would reject
Yeshua and betray Him to the Romans who in turn would crucify
Him. The Stone of God had begun to fall on the leaders of Israel.

The Rejected Stone of Isaiah 53

The prophet Isaiah had already described this rejection of Messiah
seven hundred years earlier. He prophesied that the Messiah would
come as a servant to His own people, but would be despised, rejected,
ignored, unjustly punished and finally murdered. Nevertheless,
this Servant would make atonement for His own people by offering
up His own sinless life as a guilt offering. After His death He would
live again, and in the fullness of time He would see the success of
His mission – the redemption of many Jews and Gentiles, whose
sins would be paid for by His atoning death.

*See, My servant wi*ll act wisely; He will be raised and
lifted up and highly exalted. Just as there were many
who were appalled at Him – His appearance was so
disfigured beyond that of any man and His form marred
beyond human likeness – so will He sprinkle many
nations, and kings will shut their mouths because of
Him. For what they were not told, they will see, and
what they have not heard, they will understand.

Who has believed our message and to whom has the arm
of the Lord been revealed? He grew up before Him like
a tender shoot, and like a root out of dry ground. He

---

25   Matt. 21:42-45

had no beauty or majesty to attract us to Him, nothing in His appearance that we should desire Him. He was despised and rejected by men, a man of sorrows, and familiar with suffering. Like one from whom men hide their faces He was despised, and we esteemed Him not.

Surely He took up our infirmities and carried our sorrows, yet we considered Him stricken by God, smitten by Him, and afflicted. But He was pierced for our transgressions, He was crushed for our iniquities; the punishment that brought us peace was upon Him, and by His wounds we are healed. We all, like sheep, have gone astray, each of us has turned to his own way; and the Lord has laid on Him the iniquity of us all.

He was oppressed and afflicted, yet He did not open his mouth; He was led like a lamb to the slaughter, and as a sheep before her shearers is silent, so He did not open His mouth. By oppression and judgment He was taken away. And who can speak of His descendants? For He was cut off from the land of the living; for the transgression of my people He was stricken. He was assigned a grave with the wicked, and with the rich in His death, though He had done no violence, nor was any deceit in His mouth.

Yet it was the Lord's will to crush Him and cause Him to suffer, and though the Lord makes His life a guilt offering, He will see His offspring and prolong His days, and the will of the Lord will prosper in His hand. After the suffering of His soul, He will see the light [of life] and be satisfied; by His knowledge My righteous Servant will justify many, and He will bear their iniquities. Therefore I will give Him a portion among the great, and He will divide the spoils with the strong, because He poured out His life unto death, and was numbered with the transgressors. For He bore the sin of many, and made intercession for the transgressors.[26]

---

26   Isa. 52:13 - 53:12

Messiah Yeshua freely offers salvation, yet many prefer to trust in their own religious disciplines and spiritual attainments rather than in His atoning sacrifice. Many Jewish people, like many Gentiles, want to earn their way into heaven. This desire to work one's way into heaven by keeping rules, even God's rules, is a spiritual deception. No one can earn the gift of heaven; it must be received as an undeserved boon. The Apostle Paul noted that Yeshua's offer of undeserved salvation is a major source of stumbling for many Jewish people: "...Israel, who pursued...righteousness, has not attained it. Why not? Because they pursued it not by faith but as if it were by works. They stumbled over the 'stumbling stone.' As it is written: 'See, I lay in Zion a stone that causes men to stumble and a rock that makes them fall, and the one who trusts in Him will never be put to shame.'"[27] Paul knew that the message of a suffering Messiah who grants the gift of undeserved salvation is "a stumbling block to Jews and foolishness to Gentiles."[28]

Preaching the 'Stone' in Jerusalem

The first believers preached the message of Yeshua on Mount Zion, and their initial success[29] brought them to the attention of the Sanhedrin, the religious leaders of the Jewish nation. This parliament was composed of Sadducees and Pharisees, though the high priestly Sadducees chaired and controlled these meetings.

> The priests and the captain of the temple guard and the Sadducees came up to Peter and John while they were speaking to the people. They were greatly disturbed because the apostles were teaching the people and proclaiming in Yeshua the resurrection of the dead. They seized Peter and John, and because it was evening, they put them in jail until the next day. But many who heard the message believed, and the number of men grew to about five thousand. The next day the rulers, elders and

---

27   Rom. 9:31-33

28   1 Cor. 1:23

29   *Cf.*, Acts 2:29, 41, 47

teachers of the law met in Jerusalem. Annas the high priest was there, and so were Caiaphas, John, Alexander and the other men of the High Priest's family. They had Peter and John brought before them and began to question them: "By what power or what name did you do this?"

Then Peter, filled with the Holy Spirit, said to them: "Rulers and elders of the people! If we are being called to account today for an act of kindness shown to a cripple and are asked how he was healed, then know this, you and all the people of Israel: It is by the name of Messiah Yeshua of Nazareth, whom you crucified but whom God raised from the dead, that this man stands before you healed. He is 'the stone you builders rejected, which has become the capstone.' Salvation is found in no one else, for there is no other name under heaven given to men by which we must be saved." When they saw the courage of Peter and John and realized that they were unschooled, ordinary men, they were astonished and they took note that these men had been with Yeshua. But since they could see the man who had been healed standing there with them, there was nothing they could say.[30]

A Living Stone in Zion

Peter was the senior apostle to the Jewish people[31] and ministered among them all his days. Towards the end of his life he wrote a circular letter to Jewish believers scattered across the Roman Empire, encouraging them to stand fast in God's grace, and to draw upon the mighty reserves of the presence of God as they faced persecution. He told his readers that they were like Yeshua, rejected by some men but very precious to God. As he penned the epistle, the ancient prophecies of the Messianic Stone of Zion flowed from his quill:

As you come to Him, the living Stone – rejected by men but chosen by God and precious to Him – you also, like

30   Acts 4:1-14
31   *Cf.*, Gal. 2:7-8

living stones, are being built into a spiritual house to be a holy priesthood, offering spiritual sacrifices acceptable to God through Messiah Yeshua. For in Scripture it says: "See, I lay a stone in Zion, a chosen and precious cornerstone, and the one who trusts in Him will never be put to shame." Now to you who believe, this stone is precious. But to those who do not believe, "The stone the builders rejected has become the capstone, and, "A stone that causes men to stumble and a rock that makes them fall." They stumble because they disobey the message.[32]

Stumbling into Recovery

Paul wanted his Gentile readers to know that even though the majority of the Jewish people's religious leaders have turned their backs on the Messiah, and even though most Jewish people have followed their leaders in this terrible choice, a day is coming when Israel will be freed from that spiritual snare. Though the Jewish people have stumbled, they have not 'wiped out' – they have not fallen irretrievably. Paul reminds the Roman believers that Gentiles have a responsibility and a calling to live so close to the presence of God that the Jewish people will become spiritually jealous.

When that happens, Jewish people will want to drink of the messianic reality that so intoxicates their Gentile neighbors. Then Israel will turn again to Yeshua and, in doing so, open the doors of incredible spiritual blessing for the whole world! "Again I ask: Did (the Jewish people) stumble so as to fall beyond recovery? Not at all! Rather, because of their transgression, salvation has come to the Gentiles to make Israel envious. But if their transgression means riches for the world, and their loss means riches for the Gentiles, how much greater riches will their fullness bring!"[33] Through the manifest presence of God in the lives and the evangelistic witness of Gentile and Jewish believers, the Stumbling Stone will one day become Israel's glorious and precious Cornerstone!

---

32   1 Pet. 2:4-8

33   Rom. 11:8-12

Chapter Fifteen

The Return to Zion

The Land of Promise was not only flowing with milk and honey in Moses' day. A spiritual snare was also waiting for the Jewish people in Canaan – the sexual immorality and witchcraft of the Canaanites. These unclean ways moved God to prophesy destruction against the Canaanites and the Amorites four hundred years earlier, back in Abraham's day.[1] If Israel followed these corrupt practices, they would experience judgment as well.

> Do not defile yourselves in any of these ways, because
> this is how the nations that I am going to drive out
> before you became defiled. Even the land was defiled;
> so I punished it for its sin, and the land vomited out its
> inhabitants... And if you defile the land, it will vomit you
> out as it vomited out the nations that were before you.[2]

In time Israel defiled itself with the ways of the Canaanites. Eight

---

1 *Cf.*, Gen. 15:16
2 Lev. 18:24-28; *cf.*, Deut. 4:24-31

hundred years after Moses, God spoke straight from the heart to Ezekiel as He surveyed the Jewish people's spiritual history.

> Again the word of the Lord came to me: "Son of man, when the people of Israel were living in their own land, they defiled it by their conduct and their actions. Their conduct was like a woman's monthly uncleanness in My sight. So I poured out My wrath on them because they had shed blood in the land and because they had defiled it with their idols. I dispersed them among the nations, and they were scattered through the countries; I judged them according to their conduct and their actions. And wherever they went among the nations they profaned My holy name, for it was said of them, 'These are the Lord's people, and yet they had to leave His land.' I had concern for My holy name, which the house of Israel profaned among the nations where they had gone."[3]

The prophets grieved and wept over Israel's spiritual uncleanness for centuries. Isaiah cried, "Woe is me, for I am ruined! Because I am a man of unclean lips, and I live among a people of unclean lips; For my eyes have seen the King, the Lord of hosts."[4] Jeremiah lamented that "Jerusalem has sinned greatly and so has become unclean...Zion stretches out her hands, but there is no one to comfort her...Jerusalem has become an unclean thing..."[5] Finally God spoke to Ezekiel in Babylon and told him to prophesy that "the people of Israel will eat defiled food among the nations where I will drive them."[6] Disobedient uncleanness in the land led to forced defilement among the Gentiles.

The anguished cry of God's people rose up to Him through Isaiah's prophetic intercession: remember Zion, have compassion on Your people, and honor Your covenant promises of restoration!

All of us have become like one who is unclean, and all

---

3   Ezek. 36:16-21
4   Isa. 6:5 NASB
5   Lam. 1:8, 17
6   Ezek. 4:13

our righteous acts are like filthy rags; we all shrivel up like a leaf, and like the wind our sins sweep us away. No one calls on Your name or strives to lay hold of You; for You have hidden Your face from us and made us waste away because of our sins. Yet, O Lord, You are our Father. We are the clay, You are the potter; we are all the work of Your hand. Do not be angry beyond measure, O Lord; do not remember our sins forever. Oh, look upon us, we pray, for we are all Your people. Your sacred cities have become a desert; even Zion is a desert, Jerusalem a desolation. Our holy and glorious temple, where our fathers praised You, has been burned with fire, and all that we treasured lies in ruins. After all this, O Lord, will You hold Yourself back? Will You keep silent and punish us beyond measure?[7]

It was crucial to prophet and common people to discover where God stood concerning the national calling and choosing of the Jewish people. Had Israel's sins caused God to utterly reject His people, or was there hope that Abraham's dream still applied to the whole Jewish nation? "Restore us to Yourself, O Lord, that we may return; renew our days as of old unless You have utterly rejected us and are angry with us beyond measure."[8]

Six hundred years after Jeremiah, the Lord decisively answered this petition through the mouth of Paul the apostle. "I ask then: Did God reject His people? By no means! ... God did not reject His people whom He foreknew."[9] National restoration for the Jewish people is still on the divine agenda, even in the New Testament age, because God has not stopped loving His chosen people.[10] This same principle of God's love is revealed in the New Covenant as well: "This is love: not that we loved God, but that He loved us...We love because He first loved us."[11]

---

7   Isa. 64:6-12

8   Lam. 5:21-22

9   Rom. 11:1-2

10   *Cf.*, Hos. 2:14-23; Jer. 31:1-4

11   1 Jn. 4:10, 19

He Who Scattered Israel ...

The Hebrew Scriptures speak with one voice: the Jewish people didn't wake up one morning and freely decide to leave the land of Israel in order to spread the light of God across the globe. Instead they were exiled from their own land because of disobedience to the God of their fathers. The Bible calls this a banishment, a great calamity, a ruination, a captivity and a desolation.[12] God Himself exiled and uprooted His people, scattering them among the nations[13] in His furious anger and great wrath.[14] The Jewish people's exile is compared to being stricken with wounds and sickness.[15] It is a time of bereavement, days filled with sorrow, weeping and crying.[16] Violence and devastation, destruction and desolations filled the land of Israel during this time period.[17] History records that the Promised Land was forsaken and hated, with few travelers even passing through.[18]

Ezekiel lists some of the indignities that happened to the Jewish people's national homeland during the Exile. Enemies of Israel claimed the land as their own[19] while they ravaged it and hounded the few Jews still living there. Towns and pasturelands were plundered. The land of Israel suffered the scorn and taunts of these nations for millennia, becoming the object of their ridicule, malicious talk and slander. These enemies' hearts were full of malicious glee toward the Jewish people and their land.

A moving and accurate portrayal of Israel's sufferings during the Exile is found in Isaiah 61:1-7. In this passage Messiah Yeshua reaches out in love to His own banished and captive Jewish nation. His hands are stretched out to all who mourn and grieve in Zion

---

12   *Cf.*, Jer. 16:15; 30:10; 32:42; Isa. 49:8, 19

13   *Cf.*, Jer. 24:5-6; 31:10; Deut. 30:1, 4

14   *Cf.*, Jer. 32:31, 37; Ezek. 20:13, 21

15   *Cf.*, Jer. 30:14-15

16   *Cf.*, Isa. 49:20; 60:20; 61:3; 65:19

17   *Cf.*, Isa. 60:18; 62:4

18   *Cf.*, Isa. 60:15; Mic. 3:12. See also the description of Palestine in Mark Twain's *The Innocents Abroad* in *The Complete Essays of Mark Twain*, (New York: Doubleday, 1963).

19   *Cf.*, Ezek. 36:1-15. All references in the paragraph come from this passage.

– to the poor, the brokenhearted, the captives, and the prisoners in the darkness. He cleans off the ashes, comforts the mourners, and drives away a spirit of despair. He turns His restorative gaze upon the ancient ruins, the places long devastated, and the ruined cities that have been devastated for generations. His compassions are kindled over the fact that Israel has received a double portion of shame and humiliation. In all their afflictions He too is afflicted.

Rachel Weeps for her Children

Jeremiah is known as the weeping prophet. His writings, more than any other, convey the broken heart of God over His people.[20] Jeremiah wept over the destructiveness and suffering that the Exile brought to his people. The ruin of Zion overcame him with grief.

> Oh, that my head were a spring of water and my eyes a fountain of tears! I would weep day and night for the slain of my people... I will weep and wail for the mountains and take up a lament concerning the desert pastures. They are desolate and untraveled, and the lowing of cattle is not heard. The birds of the air have fled and the animals are gone. "I will make Jerusalem a heap of ruins, a haunt of jackals; and I will lay waste the towns of Judah so no one can live there" ... This is what the Lord Almighty says: "Consider now! Call for the wailing women to come; send for the most skillful of them. Let them come quickly and wail over us till our eyes overflow with tears and water streams from our eyelids. The sound of wailing is heard from Zion: 'How ruined we are! How great is our shame! We must leave our land because our houses are in ruins.'" Now, O women, hear the word of the Lord; open your ears to the words of His mouth. Teach your daughters how to wail; teach one another a lament. Death has climbed in through our windows and has entered our fortresses; it has cut off the children from the streets and the young men from the public squares. Say, "This is what the Lord declares: 'The dead bodies of men will lie like refuse on the open field, like cut

---

20   *Cf.*, Jer. 9

grain behind the reaper, with no one to gather them.'"[21]

In another chapter Jeremiah summed up the Jewish people's history, describing a prophetic picture of Rachel the matriarch weeping over the hundreds of thousands of her slaughtered progeny. In the middle of her tears God Himself gently comforts Rachel, promising that her scattered nation would one day return to their homeland.

> "A voice is heard in Ramah, mourning and great weeping,
> Rachel weeping for her children and refusing to be
> comforted, because her children are no more." This is what
> the Lord says: "Restrain your voice from weeping and
> your eyes from tears, for your work will be rewarded,"
> declares the Lord. "They will return from the land of
> the enemy. So there is hope for your future," declares
> the Lord. "Your children will return to their own land. I
> have surely heard Ephraim's moaning... Is not Ephraim
> my dear son, the child in whom I delight? Though I
> often speak against him, I still remember him. Therefore
> my heart yearns for him; I have great compassion for
> him," declares the Lord. "Set up road signs; put up
> guideposts. Take note of the highway, the road that you
> take. Return, O Virgin Israel, return to your towns."[22]

The nation of Israel is told by Jeremiah to leave 'a trail of breadcrumbs' as they are led away to exile in Babylon. They are commanded to pay attention to the route which they take out of the Promised Land. For one day the Jewish people would return by the same way they had departed. The Daughter of Zion will return to Jerusalem and ascend Zion's hill, free at last in her homeland!

The Regathering of Zion

God calls believers everywhere to trumpet a declaration to the world. "Hear the word of the Lord, O nations, and declare in the coastlands afar off, and say, 'He who scattered Israel will gather

---

21   Jer. 9:1, 10-11, 17-22
22   Jer. 31:15-21

him, and keep him as a shepherd keeps his flock.' For the Lord has ransomed Jacob, and redeemed him from the hand of him who was stronger than he. And they shall come and shout for joy on the height of Zion..."[23] Israel's return to her ancestral homeland is as much an act of God as was the original exile. God's faithfulness to restore His Jewish people should also be exciting news to all Gentile followers of Yeshua. Chapter six has already examined many of the Scriptures which describe the Jewish people's homecoming to Zion as a sign and a wonder to the nations.

The Return to Zion is an event prophesied hundreds of times in the Scriptures. The national regathering of the Jewish people on Israel's soil is one of the major prophetic themes of the Bible. "Thus says the Lord God, 'Behold, I will open your graves and cause you to come up out of your graves, My people; and I will bring you into the land of Israel.'"[24]

> I shall bring them back because I have had compassion on them... Their hearts will be glad as if from wine. Indeed, their children will see it and be glad... I will whistle for them to gather them together ... and they will be as numerous as they were before. When I scatter them among the peoples ... in far countries ... they with their children will live and come back. I will bring them back from the land of Egypt and gather them from Assyria. And I will bring them into the land of Gilead and Lebanon until no room can be found for them.[25]

Moses prophesied to the Jewish people that God would bring their exiles back to Israel from the very farthest points of the inhabited earth. New Zealand has the honor of being 'the uttermost parts of the earth'. Jewish people from 'the country of the kiwis' who made aliyah and now reside in Israel are a living fulfillment of Moses' words.

---

23   Jer. 31:10-12 NASB

24   Ezek. 37:12 NASB

25   Zech. 10:6-10 NASB

When all these blessings and curses I have set before
you come upon you and you take them to heart wherever
the Lord your God disperses you among the nations...
the Lord your God will restore your fortunes and have
compassion on you and gather you again from all the
nations where He scattered you. Even if you have been
banished to the most distant land under the heavens, from
there the Lord your God will gather you and bring you
back. He will bring you to the land that belonged to your
fathers, and you will take possession of it. He will make
you more prosperous and numerous than your fathers ...[26]

The first return to the land of Israel occurred in the days of Ezra
and Nehemiah. The prophetic Scriptures call the end-time return to
Israel 'a second return.'

In that day the Lord will reach out His hand a
second time to reclaim the remnant that is left of
His people from Assyria, from Lower Egypt, from
Upper Egypt, from Cush, from Elam, from Babylonia,
from Hamath and from the islands of the sea.He
will raise a banner for the nations and gather the
exiles of Israel; He will assemble the scattered people
of Judah from the four quarters of the earth.[27]

This second return is decidedly different from the first one, in
that the second return is the final return. The Jewish people will
never again experience the totality of a third national exile or a third
national return. "'I will plant Israel in their own land, never again
to be uprooted from the land I have given them,' says the Lord your
God."[28] Isaiah notes that "they will possess the land forever. They
are the shoot I have planted, the work of My hands, for the display
of My splendor."[29]

In the last decade of the twentieth century the number of Jewish

---

26   Deut. 30:1-5
27   Isa. 11:11-12
28   Amos 9:15
29   Isa. 60:21

people returning to Israel has increased by phenomenal proportions. The return to Zion is a process and eventually, at its conclusion, all the earth's Jews will be repatriated to Israel.

> Therefore this is what the Sovereign Lord says: I will now bring Jacob back from captivity and will have compassion on all the people of Israel, and I will be zealous for My holy name... for though I sent them into exile among the nations, I will gather them to their own land, not leaving any behind.[30]

Out of the Frozen North

When the Iron Curtain collapsed in November 1989, few people could envision how this would affect the Jewish people of the former USSR. Within eight years over 750,000 Russian-speaking Jews would pack their suitcases and make their way home to the land of Israel. So far this exodus from the C.I.S. is fifteen times larger than the exodus under Nehemiah and Ezra. Truly, events of biblical proportions are happening in our day!

Two thousand six hundred years ago Jeremiah prophesied about this present exodus from the lands which lie directly north of Israel, including Russia, Ukraine and Belarus.

> Go, proclaim this message toward the north ... "Return, faithless people, declares the Lord, "for I am your husband. I will choose you – one from a town and two from a clan – and bring you to Zion ... In those days the house of Judah will join the house of Israel, and together they will come from a northern land to the land I gave your forefathers as an inheritance."[31]

The exodus from a 'northern land' which has begun in our day will become more powerful and breathtaking than the original exodus under Moses. Its magnitude will actually eclipse the Passover story and replace it as the major act of Jewish restoration

---

30   Ezek. 39:25-28; *cf.,* Isa. 43:5-7

31   Jer. 3:12, 14-18

at the end of days. At its height it will include not only Russian Jews but also their brothers and sisters in North and South America, Europe, Australia, *etc.*

> "... (T)he days are coming," declares the Lord, "when
> men will no longer say, 'As surely as the Lord lives,
> who brought the Israelites out of Egypt,' but they
> will say, 'As surely as the Lord lives, who brought the
> Israelites up out of the land of the north and out of all
> the countries where He had banished them.' For I will
> restore them to the land I gave their forefathers."[32]

Restoration Can Be Measured

An old proverb goes 'Give him an inch – and he'll measure it!' Former President Ronald Reagan once quoted an apocryphal Russian proverb, 'Trust – but verify!' The restoration of the Jewish people to their ancestral homeland is measured and verified in the Bible. The return is a direct act of God, and He takes credit for working out all the details of the entire enterprise. "This is what the Lord says: 'The people who survive the sword will find favor in the desert; I will come to give rest to Israel... I have loved you with an everlasting love; I have drawn you with loving-kindness. *I will build you up again and you will be rebuilt*, O Virgin Israel.'"[33]

Restoration of the Jewish people involves three complementary parts: stopping the destruction, reversing the effects of that destruction, and restoring the situation to its original blessed state.

> "The days are coming," declares the Lord, "when I will
> plant the house of Israel and the house of Judah with the
> offspring of men and of animals. Just as I watched over
> them to uproot and tear down, and to overthrow, destroy
> and bring disaster, so I will watch over them to build and
> to plant," declares the Lord. "I will rejoice in doing them
> good and will assuredly plant them in this land with
> all My heart and soul. This is what the Lord says: As I

32 Jer. 16:13-15; *cf.*, Jer. 23:7-8
33 Jer. 31:2-4 emphases mine

have brought all this great calamity on this people, so I will give them all the prosperity I have promised them... because I will restore their fortunes, declares the Lord."[34]

The final purposes of restoration of the Jewish people extend beyond the borders of Israel proper. God's blessing of Israel, His gifts of peace and prosperity to her – these will cause the whole world to sit up and take notice that God has a loving commitment to the Jewish people.

> Call to Me and I will answer you and tell you great
> and unsearchable things you do not know... I will heal
> My people and will let them enjoy abundant peace and
> security. I will bring Judah and Israel back from captivity
> and will rebuild them as they were before... Then this city
> will bring Me renown, joy, praise and honor before all
> nations on earth that hear of all the good things I do for it;
> and they will be in awe and will tremble at the abundant
> prosperity and peace I provide for it... For I will restore the
> fortunes of the land as they were before,' says the Lord.[35]

God prophesies the restoration of specific geographical areas and cities in Israel which will be rebuilt and repopulated. He describes the ages and gender of the population, their business activities and times of play. The restoration of the Jewish people involves practical physical details, and the Bible gives accurate measurements of the fullness of this restoration.

> Again you will take up your tambourines and go out to
> dance with the joyful. Again you will plant vineyards
> on the hills of Samaria; the farmers will plant them and
> enjoy their fruit. There will be a day when watchmen
> cry out on the hills of Ephraim, "Come, let us go up to
> Zion, to the Lord our God"... See, I will bring them from
> the land of the north and gather them from the ends of
> the earth. Among them will be the blind and the lame,
> expectant mothers and women in labor; a great throng

---

34   Jer. 32:41-44
35   Jer. 33:3, 6-7, 9, 11

will return. They will come with weeping; they will pray
as I bring them back. I will lead them beside streams of
water on a level path where they will not stumble, because
I am Israel's father, and Ephraim is My firstborn son.[36]

Once more fields will be bought in this land of which
you say, "It is a desolate waste, without men or animals,
for it has been handed over to the Babylonians."
Fields will be bought for silver, and deeds will be
signed, sealed and witnessed in the territory of
Benjamin, in the villages around Jerusalem, in the
towns of Judah and in the towns of the hill country,
of the western foothills and of the Negev, because
I will restore their fortunes, declares the Lord.[37]

Some Replacement theologians like to interpret these passages
as applying to the first return under Ezra and Nehemiah. But the
fields and villages described in these Scriptures have not yet tasted
the prosperity and peace promised by God. The nations have not
yet trembled at the material blessing and peace that God will one
day provide for Israel. These passages describe a time yet future,
when the physical blessings from God's hand will be even greater
than the physical destruction seen in Jewish history.

Restoration to God

The land of Israel hasn't yet seen the day of its full restoration.
This is not surprising, for the prophets link the fullness of the land's
restoration to the Jewish people's spiritual restoration. At present
the vast majority of the Jewish population is still in unbelief.[38] Right
now the world watches as God continues to bring His chosen people
back to the promised land. This return to Zion is the dawning of
a new prophetic day. Events which the Bible once described as
occurring in 'years yet future' seem destined for fulfillment in our
own generation. The heartbeat of our planet is beginning to pulse

36   Jer. 31:1-6, 7-9

37   Jer. 32:41-44; *cf.*, Jer. 31:38-40; 33:10-13

38   Chapters 17 and 18 of this book discuss other aspects of the restoration process.

with immediacy.

> In future years...(Israel will be) a land that has recovered
> from war, whose people were gathered from many
> nations to the mountains of Israel, which had long
> been desolate. They had been brought out from the
> nations, and now all of them live in safety...a land of
> unwalled villages;...a peaceful ... people – all of them
> living without walls and without gates and bars.[39]

Yeshua's Passion for Jewish Restoration

The bright flame of God's passion for the restoration of Israel
burns in Isaiah, Jeremiah, Hosea and Zechariah. These prophets
paint the restoration of the Jewish people to Zion in lover's hues.
The yearning of a husband for his beautiful wayward wife, the
alluring and wooing that is part of divine courtship, the tenderness
and comfort between a groom and his bride – this is the passionate
poetry of the Return to Zion!

> For your Maker is your husband ... For a brief moment I
> abandoned you, but with deep compassion I will bring
> you back. In a surge of anger I hid My face from you
> for a moment, but with everlasting kindness I will have
> compassion on you, says the Lord your Redeemer.[40]

> No longer will they call you 'Deserted', or name your
> land 'Desolate'. But you will be called 'Hephzibah', and
> your land 'Beulah'; for the Lord will take delight in you,
> and your land will be married. As a young man marries
> a maiden, so will your sons marry you; as a bridegroom
> rejoices over his bride, so will your God rejoice over you.[41]

> The word of the Lord came to Jeremiah: "Have you not
> noticed that these people are saying, 'The Lord has
> rejected the two kingdoms He chose?' So they despise My

---

39   Ezek. 38:8, 11

40   Isa. 54:5-8

41   Isa. 62:4-5

people and no longer regard them as a nation. This is what the Lord says: "If I have not established My covenant with day and night and the fixed laws of heaven and earth, then I will reject the descendants of Jacob and David My servant and will not choose one of his sons to rule over the descendants of Abraham, Isaac and Jacob. For I will restore their fortunes and have compassion on them."[42]

Therefore I am now going to allure her; I will lead her into the desert and speak tenderly to her. There I will give her back her vineyards, and will make the Valley of Achor a door of hope. There she will sing as in the days of her youth, as in the day she came up out of Egypt. In that day, declares the Lord, you will call Me 'My husband.' You will no longer call Me 'My master'...In that day I will make a covenant for them with the beasts of the field and the birds of the air and the creatures that move along the ground... I will betroth you to Me forever. I will betroth you in righteousness and justice, in love and compassion. I will betroth you in faithfulness, and you will acknowledge the Lord. In that day I will respond, declares the Lord, I will respond to the skies, and they will respond to the earth. And the earth will respond to the grain, the new wine and oil, and they will respond to Jezre'el. I will plant her for Myself in the land. I will show My love to the one I called 'Not my loved one.' I will say to those called 'Not My people,' 'You are My people'; and they will say, 'You are My God.'"[43]

This is what the Lord says: "I will return to Jerusalem with mercy, and there My house will be rebuilt ... Proclaim further: This is what the Lord Almighty says: My towns will again overflow with prosperity, and the Lord will again comfort Zion and choose Jerusalem."[44]

---

42   Jer. 33:23-26
43   Hos. 2:14-23
44   Zech. 1:16-17

The Year of Jubilee

Recently the State of Israel has celebrated the fiftieth anniversary of its independence, a jubilee of fifty years since it has taken its rightful seat as a full member in the community of the nations. Though Israel's 1998 celebration does not occur on the rabbinically computed year of Jubilee, it has nevertheless been a time of accounting and soul searching for the nation. The event was heralded by fifty men blowing ram's horns in a great long blast, and newspapers and television have attempted to ask and answer the great questions 'why Israel?' and 'where are we going now?' Even apart from God, the Jewish people still feel a call on their souls, a higher call that they must answer and somehow become a light to the nations.

> Consecrate the fiftieth year and proclaim liberty
> throughout the land to all its inhabitants. It shall be
> a jubilee for you; each one of you is to return to his
> family property and each to his own clan. The fiftieth
> year shall be a jubilee for you; do not sow and do not
> reap what grows of itself or harvest the untended vines.
> For it is a jubilee and is to be holy for you; eat only
> what is taken directly from the fields ... In this Year of
> Jubilee everyone is to return to his own property.[45]

The Return to Zion and the Mosaic concept of the Year of Jubilee have something in common. In the Year of Jubilee all property reverts to its original owners, all debts are canceled, and liberty is proclaimed throughout the land. When the flood of God's restoration crests over the entire land, these same blessings pour over the entire Jewish people.

The Jubilee year was also known as 'the year of the Lord's favor.'[46] The psalmist knew that a time would come when God would rescue Israel and restore her back to her land. He called this 'the time to show her favor.' "You will arise and have compassion on Zion, for

---

45   Lev. 25:10-13

46   *Cf.*, Isa. 61:2

it is time to show favor to her; the appointed time has come. For her stones are dear to your servants; her very dust moves them to pity."[47] In synagogues across the globe, the prayer of King David the sweet singer of Israel is lifted daily before God, asking Him to pour out His Jubilee favor on Israel by returning them to Zion: "But as for me, my prayer is to You, O Lord, at the time of favor. O God, in the abundance of Your covenant love, answer me with the sureness of Your salvation."[48] When the nation of Israel cries out for the return of Messiah Yeshua, God will answer them with the full power of His restoration and salvation.

Fishers and Hunters

In the late 1930's a Jewish man from Odessa named Vladimir Jabotinsky traveled to Poland with a sobering message. "Jews, get out!" he implored. "Very soon a terrible destruction will happen to European Jewry. Only those who flee to Israel will be spared!" Though he pleaded and argued throughout the Jewish communities of Poland, only a handful believed Jabotinsky's message. Even fewer Jews heeded the message and moved to then British-controlled Palestine. His plan to transfer 1,500,000 Jews from Eastern Europe to Palestine got lost in committee meetings.

Jabotinsky was what the prophet Jeremiah called a 'fisher.' He did not know that his urgent call to the Jewish people was being stirred up by the Lord of Hosts, and that his message was a partial fulfillment of Jeremiah's prophecy.

> But now I will send for many fishermen, declares the Lord, and they will catch them. After that I will send for many hunters, and they will hunt them down on every mountain and hill and from the crevices of the rocks. My eyes are on all their ways; they are not hidden from Me, nor is their sin concealed from My eyes. I will repay them double for their wickedness and their sin, because they have defiled My land with the lifeless forms of their vile images and

47 Psa. 102:13-14
48 Psa. 69:13 my translation

have filled My inheritance with their detestable idols.[49]

Jabotinsky's message for the most part fell on deaf ears. Within five years Hitler's SS were machine-gunning Jewish men and women, grandparents and children, and dumping their nude bodies into yawning pits.

Jeremiah was prophesying about a future time when fishers would first be raised up to woo the Jewish people back to Israel, one by one.[50] We live during this time. As believers in Yeshua encourage their Jewish neighbors and friends to return to Israel, they are fishing among the Jewish people in fulfillment of Jeremiah's prophecy. The Church needs to awaken to the fact that worldwide anti-Semitic persecutions will soon engulf all nations. A day is fast approaching when vast networks of underground railroads will run along secret tracks built by believers. These networks will help channel Jews fleeing these latter-day pogroms to Israel. The time of the hunters will be soon upon us.[51]

Prepare and pray!

---

49   Jer. 16:16-18

50   *Cf.,* Isa. 27:12-13

51   *Cf.,* Jay and Meridel Rawlings, *Fishers and Hunters* (Jerusalem/Chichester: International Vistas Inc./ New Wine Press, 1982-85); Steve Lightle, *Exodus II* (Gwent, UK: Bridge Publishing, 1983-84); Tom Hess, *Let My People Go* (Washington D.C.: Progressive Vision International, 1987).

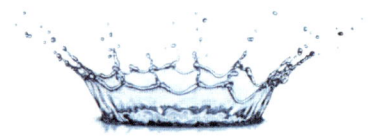

Chapter Sixteen

Zion: The Cup of Trembling

An old Yiddish proverb says *"Men ken nisht tantzn oyf tsvey chas'nes mit eyn tuchis"* – one is not able to dance at two weddings with one behind! It is rare to find a person who can do two things simultaneously and competently. Quality usually suffers in one of the endeavors. In contrast, the Lord of Hosts is able to handle an infinite number of scenarios without losing His cool, and can pull them all off with a perfect balance of wisdom, compassion and justice.

A good example of this balance can be seen in His dealings with the nation of Israel. God is bringing the Jewish people back to their homeland and physically invigorating that country in fulfillment of His promise of restoration. At the same time He is committed to purifying that people and restoring them spiritually – something that can only be done in the furnace of affliction.

The Lord has more than one track operating with the nations as well. On one hand God is causing the world to sit up and pay attention to the amazing return of Israel to their homeland after an exile of 2,600 years. This return to Zion is a sign inviting the nations to repent and to worship. On the other hand the Lord is allowing anti-Semitism to flourish (which will bring judgment on the Gentiles and destruction to many Jews) and is preparing to use Zion and Jerusalem as His divine 'tar-baby'– fatally ensnaring the peoples who attempt to wipe out the Jewish nation and the State of Israel.

The International Gentile Conspiracy

Neo-Nazi groups and communist radicals often speak darkly of an international Jewish conspiracy which strives for world domination. Most of them are unaware that the Scriptures do expose a hidden conspiracy which even today is moving to achieve its goal of world domination. What may surprise some readers is that there are no Jews in this secret conspiracy – it is totally Gentile! King David describes this secret Gentile cabal in Psalm 2: "Why do the nations conspire and the peoples plot in vain?The kings of the earth take their stand and the rulers gather together against the Lord and against His Anointed One. 'Let us break their chains,' they say, 'and throw off their fetters.'"[1]

This conspiracy links different world leaders who have at least two points in common – a hatred for the God of the Bible, and a loathing for His chosen Jewish people. These men and women despise Judeo-Christian ethics. They oppose reintroducing biblical morality into the marketplace of ideas and politics. They scorn belief in a God who holds nations responsible to obey Scriptural standards. Ultimately their desire for world peace and a prosperous – new world order will move them first to shun the State of Israel and then to wage a military campaign against it.

One of the guiding principles of this conspiratorial world view is that anything can be obtained for the right price: even the hot flames of Arab-Israeli hostilities can be cooled by combining political

1   Psa. 2:1-2

pressures (the 'stick') and offers of prosperity and political influence (the 'carrot'). With enough manipulation terrorist and terrorized can be forced to sit down and sign memoranda of understanding, 'making peace' when there is no peace.

However, the child who points out that the emperor has no clothes, the prophet who says that real peace must involve reciprocity, reconciliation and restitution – not just signed 'documents of paper – is immediately marginalized as 'an impediment to the peace process.' International television news networks aid this flowering world conspiracy by shaping world opinion, identifying who is the 'promoter of peace' and who is the 'provoker of war' in this process. Current politically correct wisdom holds that an Israeli government which holds on to all of Jerusalem, refuses to give up more of the West Bank, and rejects a Palestinian state is definitely an obstacle to world peace. As man in rebellion against God tries to establish a secular peace, he will eventually conclude that both the borders God ordained for Israel as well as the tenacious Jewish people are his primary obstacles to world peace.

The Wars of Israel and Ishmael

Prophetic words given to Ishmael and Esau four thousand years ago still shape the present destiny of the Middle East. Any nation which wants to further a lasting peace process should consider these prophecies carefully. They chart out the path to ultimate resolution and reconciliation between Arab and Jew. Unhappily that path leads directly through the cauldron of decisive military conflagration.

This saga began when the Angel of the Lord appeared to pregnant Hagar and told her that she would bear a son who would possess a powerful destiny.

> I will so increase your descendants that
> they will be too numerous to count
>
> ... You are now with child and you will have a son. You

shall name him Ishmael, for the Lord has heard of your
misery. He will be a wild donkey of a man; his hand will
be against everyone and everyone's hand against him,
and he will live in hostility toward all his brothers.[2]

A short time later God gave Abraham other
details about Ishmael's prophetic future.

And as for Ishmael, I have heard you: I will surely
bless him; I will make him fruitful and will greatly
increase his numbers. He will be the father of twelve
rulers, and I will make him into a great nation.
But My covenant I will establish with Isaac, whom
Sarah will bear to you by this time next year.[3]

The Arab descendants of Ishmael would become a group of
mighty nations. The prophetic word adds that these peoples would
be stubborn and fiercely independent – the traits of an untamed
and wild donkey. God Himself prophesies that the Arab peoples
would be suspicious and antagonistic with each other, with the
Jewish people, and with all nations. At the root of this tension
between Isaac and Ishmael is God's covenant – though both nations
would be blessed, only Isaac's would be chosen. This has remained
the sore point between Arab and Jew from the beginning of biblical
history to the present day.

The same type of spiritual rivalry characterized the relationship
between Isaac's two sons Esau and Jacob. Now it was Jacob's destiny
to be the chosen one, and this was confirmed by a prophetic word
to Rebekah when the twins were still in her womb.

The babies jostled each other within her, and she
said, "Why is this happening to me?" So she went to
inquire of the Lord. The Lord said to her, "Two nations
are in your womb, and two peoples from within you
will be separated; one people will be stronger than

---

2 Gen. 16:10-12
3 Gen. 17:20-21; *cf.*, Gen. 21:12-13, 17-18

the other, and the older will serve the younger."[4]

Later on Esau despised his own birthright and sold it to his brother Jacob on a binding oath.[5] The Book to the Hebrews notes that a root of bitterness sprang up in Esau's heart after God affirmed that Jacob would indeed possess the promise.

> See to it that no one comes short of the grace of God; that
> no root of bitterness springing up causes trouble, and by
> it many be defiled; that there be no immoral or godless
> person like Esau, who sold his birthright for a single meal.
> For you know that even afterwards, when he desired
> to inherit the blessing, he was rejected, for he found no
> place for repentance, though he sought for it with tears.[6]

This bitter root has spiritually defiled the majority of the Arab peoples. Satan has complicated matters by using Islam to fan the flames of hatred toward the Jewish people – first among the Arabs, and then through them to the rest of the Islamized world. Islam has perpetuated this spiritual striving, elevating it to the level of a religious commandment. Today Esau's physical and spiritual descendants still seek to recover what has irrevocably been given to Jacob's descendants.

But Isaac's prophetic words to Jacob are clear: "May nations serve you and peoples bow down to you. Be lord over your brothers, and may the sons of your mother bow down to you. May those who curse you be cursed and those who bless you be blessed."[7] The Abrahamic covenant's blessings and curses have protected and will protect the Jewish people throughout history – and not the Arab people.

Isaac also prophesies to Esau that the future relationship between Jews and Arabs would be a rocky one.

"I have made [Jacob] lord over you and have made all his

---

4   Gen. 25:22-23

5   *Cf.*, Gen. 25:31-34

6   Hebr. 12:15-17

7   Gen. 27:28-29

relatives his servants, and I have sustained him with grain
and new wine... Your dwelling will be away from the
earth's richness, away from the dew of heaven above. You
will live by the sword and you will serve your brother.
But when you grow restless, you will throw his yoke
from off your neck." Esau held a grudge against Jacob
because of the blessing his father had given him. He said
to himself, "The days of mourning for my father are near;
then I will kill my brother Jacob." When Rebekah was
told what her older son Esau had said, she sent for her
younger son Jacob and said to him, "Your brother Esau
is consoling himself with the thought of killing you."[8]

According to the prophecy of Esau's own father, the Arab
descendants of Esau would become desert dwellers and would be
known for pillage and murder. Today, deep within the historical
memory of many of Esau's children, a murderous hatred and a
destructive jealousy toward the children of Jacob still burns. Peace
treaties will not heal this hatred. United Nations resolutions will
not slake the fire of these flames. Only national Arab repentance
before the God of Jacob in the person of Yeshua, and an acceptance
of God's choosing of the Jewish people will bring complete healing
to the descendants of Ishmael and Esau.

Isaiah speaks of a day yet future when many Arab peoples will
turn to the God of Jacob and find His healing. This will not be a
day of defeat for the Arab nations, but rather an entrance into true
victory and blessing as the rift in Abraham's family will finally
be healed. Ishmael and Esau will at last find joy and covenantal
blessing as they embrace their Jewish cousins.

In that day there will be an altar to the Lord in the heart
of Egypt, and a monument to the Lord at its border. So
the Lord will make himself known to the Egyptians,
and in that day they will acknowledge the Lord... In that
day there will be a highway from Egypt to Assyria. The
Assyrians will go to Egypt and the Egyptians to Assyria.

---

8   Gen. 27:37, 39-42

> The Egyptians and Assyrians will worship together. In that day Israel will be the third, along with Egypt and Assyria, a blessing on the earth. The Lord Almighty will bless them, saying, "Blessed be Egypt My people, Assyria My handiwork, and Israel My inheritance."[9]

One of the keys to peace between the sons of Ishmael and the sons of Israel lies in the hands of the Jewish people. When God grants Israel grace, humility and revelation, the Jewish people will be able to honor and respect Ishmael and Esau as Abraham and Isaac's firstborn sons – though God's promise remains Isaac's and Jacob's inheritance. Even though Abraham's earthly family remains very dysfunctional, believers should remember that the Arab nation is the Jewish people's elder brother. Pray that the fractured physical family of Abraham will be healed in fullness, and that the Jewish people grow deep enough in grace to bless and honor their Arab brothers. Pray that God will so transform Arab and Jewish hearts that Jews will request wise and godly counsel from their Arab brothers (unlike the secular Oslo peace process), and that Arabs will gladly share their "older brotherly" wisdom and protection with younger brother Jacob, the Jewish people whom God calls 'the firstborn son among all the nations.'[10]

Counterfeit Monotheism and the Arab Nation

As the world moves closer to 'the end of the age', God is unwrapping various strategies which He has hidden since before the creation of the world. We humans are aware of only the dullest glimmer of a few of these strategies (*e.g.*: the fullness of unity and love which Yeshua prayed for in John 17:21-23; the fullness of Messiah revealed in the maturation of the body of believers, prophesied in Eph.4:11-16; the fullness of Israel's salvation which will lead to life from the dead for the whole earth - Rom.11:12, 15; *etc.*).

At the same time, the prophetic Scriptures note that Satan also

---

9   Isa. 19:19, 21, 23-25

10   *cf.*, Exod.4:22-23

has his own infernal game plan, one important aspect of which focuses on the persecution and destruction of both Jews and true Christians. Insight into one aspect of these strategies is found on the Temple Mount in Jerusalem. Inside the Dome of the Rock, Arabic words written in beautiful gold leaf calligraphy shed light on this. The founding inscription of the Golden Dome proclaims: "O People of the Book, do not overstep proper limitations... and speak only the truth about God. The Messiah Yeshua, son of Mary, is only a messenger of God... Believe therefore in God and His messengers, and do not say 'Three'...God is only one God. Far be it from His glory that He should have a son." This golden inscription quoting from the Koran clearly denies the deity of Messiah Yeshua, His incarnation, and the deity of the Holy Spirit. In this sacred shrine of Islam, the central place afforded to this anti-Christian declaration is no accident.

Most people in the world would say that there is a great brotherhood of three monotheistic religions – Judaism, Christianity and Islam. As a result, many Christians and Jews have concluded that Moslems actually worship the God of the Bible, albeit in a distorted or inferior way. Some Christian evangelistic ministries to Muslims even state that Allah is simply another name for Jehovah, and teach that these two names really are interchangeable.

Is this truly the case? Yeshua once said that "you will know them by their fruits" (Matthew 7:13-23). He was talking about false prophets who come in sheep's clothing but who are actually ravenous wolves. Yeshua encourages us to look at the fruit of the tree: a bad tree bears bad fruit. In that light, consider the following about Islam.

The deity known as 'Allah' was once the name of a tribal deity/ demon of the Saudi Arabian peninsula. This spirit was worshipped by many Arabs as a local deity. When a spirit came to Muhammad posing as Jibril or the angel Gabriel, he told Muhammad that Allah is actually the God of the Bible. This spirit gave Muhammad many revelations, including the following – God has rejected the Jews;

Jesus is not God's Son (cf. 1 John 2:18-23); there is no Trinity; the Bible, both Old and New Testaments, has been deliberately distorted by Jews and Christians to the point where it is no longer the word of God; Yeshua never died on the cross; it is a 'divine' commandment to persecute Jews and Christians, to defeat them in battle and then to consign them either to eternal slavery or to death.

These teachings are definitely bad spiritual fruit! The spirit who communicated these teachings to Muhammad is not the God of the Bible. He is a demon. It follows that Allah is not Jehovah, and Islam is not a monotheistic religion. Islam worships a demon and calls that demon 'the one true God.' This is not true monotheism. It is a false monotheism. It is actually a demonic counterfeit of true monotheism.

The Centrality of Jerusalem

Something else to consider: today Islam says that it has three holy cities – first Mecca, then Medina (both in Saudi Arabia), and finally Jerusalem. Be aware that this order is another strategic deception. Jerusalem may officially come third on the Islam's list, but Jerusalem sets modern Islamic passions aflame in a way that leave Mecca and Medina far behind. The world may think that Jerusalem is of lesser importance for Islam, but Muslims see a Jewish-controlled Jerusalem as an unjust insult against Islam which needs to be corrected. Behind this seething hatred lies Satan, who has not forgotten Zion's unchanging divine priority and its true spiritual importance. Since God has chosen to love Israel, Satan has chosen to hate her!

In the meantime the prince of darkness pursues his own plans for Jerusalem and the Jewish people. His present first goal is to rip Jerusalem away from the regathered Jewish people by making eastern Jerusalem the capital of a Palestinian state. His second goal is to turn the Gentile world against the Jewish people and the State of Israel with an aim to destroying both. Here his strategies include catalyzing world anger against the Jewish people for their resolve to hold on to the Promised Land; stampeding world economic panic as a result of future Arab oil embargoes; and escalating worldwide anti-Semitism as a response to petroleum pressures. Finally, Satan will fight to protect both the present demonic worship-centers he has established on the Temple Mount (the Dome of the Rock and the Al-Aqsa mosque) as well as the one he will yet establish. The Temple Mount is the mountain that God Himself calls 'The Mountain of the Lord' (cf., 2 Thessalonians 2:3-5 and Isaiah 2), and it is the piece of real estate from which Yeshua will one day reign over all the earth.

Keeping these three points in mind, the Islamic agenda to win world support for the establishment of an Islamic and Arab 'Palestine' on the West Bank with East Jerusalem as its capital is not a spiritually neutral event. Bluntly stated, a false and demonic monotheism is attempting to re-establish demonic control over the land of the Jewish people. This counterfeit monotheism is determined not to lose its grasp on the Mountain of the Lord. And it is trying to convince the world (including many Christians) to support it politically in this endeavor! In this sense Islam can accurately be defined as espousing a 'double Replacement theology' – it not only claims to be the divinely approved inheritor of Israel's blessings (which it says now belong to Muslims alone); it also claims that Muslims alone are the heirs of Israel's land (which it now calls Palestine).

Arab believers and Jewish Restoration

Jewish and Arab Messianic believers in Israel may share the same land, eat in the same restaurants, pay taxes to the same government, but they do not often share the same theology. Jewish believers ardently long to see the restoration of the Jewish people spiritually and physically, while Arab believers' focus is on the spread of the gospel among Arabs, and some of them hope for the establishment of a Palestinian state. Israeli Arab believers are confronted with a most painful dilemma: should they rejoice and side with developing Palestinian nationalistic aspirations, or should they see themselves as loyal citizens of a primarily Jewish state, one in which they are less than fully honored citizens?

This ambivalence of identity and schizophrenic mode of existence has led some Arab believers to embrace a theology which will allow them to downplay, ignore or deny God's present restoration of Israel and His future plans for a reborn Jewish state. Instead of recognizing that the Lord is restoring Jacob (something that requires great spiritual courage, honesty and humility), these believers redefine the issue, pointing out that there are different schools of eschatological interpretation in Christian theology. As a result, they feel that they do not need to subscribe to a view which assigns priority to the Jewish people in their own land. According to this viewpoint, whether the restoration of Israel is of God or of colonialistic Zionism is only a matter of opinion.

Yeshua has once again taken His Jewish thermometer and this time He has stuck it into the mouth of Palestinian believers. What will their spiritual temperature be? Pray that Arab hearts will be transformed, and that His judgment will not have to declare, "You know how to interpret the appearance of the earth and the sky. How is it that you don't know how to interpret this present time?"[11]

Life From the Dead for the Arab Nation

One of the surprising side effects of future Jewish restoration, physical and spiritual, is that when life from the dead happens for Israel, the blessings of the gospel will also flow to the Arab world through reborn Jewish evangelists. The power of such a scenario needs to be understood in the right context in order to be fully appreciated!

Islam has certain basic beliefs. Some of these are that the Jewish people rejected Yeshua; that Christians are heretical because of their belief in the Trinity; that Islam is a more powerful religion and is a superior form of faith; and that any doctrine found in the Christian or Jewish Scriptures which disagrees with Islamic teachings is a

---

11 Lk. 12:56

deliberate and wicked distortion of the real truth.

Imagine what will happen to these not so sacred cows when Spirit-filled Messianic Jews arrive on Arab soil overshadowed by the power of God! Imagine the popular response when these Hebrew evangelists heal the sick, raise the dead, cast out demons and declare that Yeshua is indeed the Messiah and the Son of the Living God. Consider what the Arab spiritual response would be to a bold Jewish declaration of the gospel in the power of the Spirit – in Saudi Arabia and Syria, in Qatar and Kuwait, in Baghdad and Bahrain! What a blessed day that will be, when the atoning blood of Messiah Yeshua re-unites Jew and Arab, healing the Semitic schism of the centuries! Life from the dead is coming not just to Israel, but also through Israel to the whole Muslim world!

The Mother of all Arab-Israeli Wars

The August air of Tel Aviv was muggy and oppressive. But the brass-like voice pouring out of the taxi's radio speaker cut through the heat with pointed sharpness. Sadaam Hussein was announcing his intention to rain down Scud missiles filled with binary chemical weapons on the streets of Tel Aviv. As his tanks rolled through the streets of Kuwait City in August 1991, he declared that the mother of all wars had begun – a war which would not end until the Arab nation had liberated Al Kuds, the Holy City of Jerusalem.

Sadaam Hussein was not the first Arab ruler in history who threatened to destroy Israel. Centuries ago the author of Psalm 83 was probably describing an ancient Middle Eastern war of his own day, a battle where the enemies of the Jewish people gathered and consolidated forces against the Jewish state. As the attack drew near, the psalmist interceded with God, reminding Him that an attack on the Jewish people is an attack on the God Himself.

> O God, do not keep silent; be not quiet, O God, be not still. See how Your enemies are astir, how Your foes rear their heads. With cunning they conspire against Your people; they plot against those You cherish. "Come,"

they say, "let us destroy them as a nation, that the name
of Israel be remembered no more." With one mind they
plot together; they form an alliance against You…[12]

The Arab-Israeli wars of 1948, '56, '67, '73, '78 and '82 as well as
the present day manifestations of *jihad* (Islamic wars of destruction)
like *Intifada* and suicide bombers, all reflect the same attitude to the
Jewish people as do the 'enemies' found in Psalm 83. These same
enemies of Israel still exist in the same countries, and since these
countries still are making military preparations for the destruction
of Israel, the scenario described in Psalm 83 most likely will find a
future fulfillment as well. Psalm 83 is a prophetic picture of a future
Arab attack on the country of Israel.

Psalm 83:6-8 lists the aggressor countries: Edom and the
Ishmaelites (southern Jordan and Saudi Arabia), Moab (central
Jordan) and the Hagrites (Syrian and Arabian deserts) Gebal
(southern Jordan), Ammon (central Jordan in the area of Amman)
and Amalek (the Sinai desert), Philistia (the area of the present
Gaza Strip), the people of Tyre (southern Lebanon) and Assyria
(eastern Syria and Iraq). Though some of these countries may have
signed peace treaties with Israel, the Scriptures prophesy that these
countries will one day make a covenantal agreement between
themselves directed against the God of Jacob and toward the
destruction of the Jewish people.[13]

The psalmist asks God to defeat and destroy these armies who
say, "Let us possess for ourselves the pastures of God," – a term
which means 'the land of Israel.' He pleads,

> Make them like tumbleweed, O my God, like chaff before
> the wind. As fire consumes the forest or a flame sets the
> mountains ablaze, so pursue them with Your tempest
> and terrify them with Your storm. Cover their faces with
> shame so that men will seek Your name, O Lord. May
> they ever be ashamed and dismayed; may they perish

---

12   Psa. 83:1-5
13   Psa. 83:4-5

in disgrace. Let them know that You, whose name is the
Lord – that You alone are the Most High over all the earth.

This is not simply a future scenario. At the writing of this book
Syria has 1,100 North Korean-made Scud missiles armed with VX
nerve gas warheads aimed at the houses of Tel Aviv and Tiberias.
Iran has purchased two nuclear bombs from former Soviet arsenals,
and it is testing a version of the Soviet SS-4 (the '*Shihab*') which will
allow it to deliver chemical or nuclear-tipped missiles to Israel's
doorstep by mid-1999. Iraq continues to stockpile biological and
chemical weapons (anthrax, aflatoxin and sarin) for use in a future
war with the Jewish state.

In chapter eight of this book Revelation 12:13 was considered.
"When the dragon saw that he had been hurled to the earth, he
pursued the woman who had given birth to the male child." Satan's
most strategic target has always been the Jewish people and, as the
events of Psalm 83 move closer to fulfillment, one should expect an
intensification of warfare (both spiritual and physical) against the
Jewish people.

Gog - The Invader of Israel

The prophet Ezekiel describes a future Middle Eastern war in
chapters 38 and 39 of his book. Rabbis have called this battle *the
Wars of Gog and Magog*. The participants in this battle are listed,
a confederation of Arab, Islamic and Turkic nations: Persia (Iran),
Cush (Sudan/Ethiopia), Put (Libya), Magog (formerly the ancient
Scythian homeland north and northeast of the Black Sea, presently
in southern Russia between Crimea and Muslim Azerbaijan),
Meshech and Tubal (both in modern Turkey), Gomer and Beth-
Togarmah (both are ancient names for Turkic areas on the Black
Sea, possibly extending up to Ukraine). As well, Sheba (Yemen)
and Dedan (Saudi Arabia) take a lively commercial interest in the
proceedings.

> The word of the Lord came to me: "Son of man, set your
> face against Gog, of the land of Magog, the chief prince

of Meshech and Tubal; prophesy against him and say:
'This is what the Sovereign Lord says: I am against you,
O Gog, chief prince of Meshech and Tubal. I will turn
you around, put hooks in your jaws and bring you out
with your whole army – your horses, your horsemen fully
armed, and a great horde with large and small shields,
all of them brandishing their swords. Persia, Cush and
Put will be with them, all with shields and helmets, also
Gomer with all its troops, and Beth Togarmah from the
far north with all its troops – the many nations with you.
Get ready; be prepared, you and all the hordes gathered
about you, and take command of them. After many days
you will be called to arms. In future years you will invade
a land that has recovered from war, whose people were
gathered from many nations to the mountains of Israel,
which had long been desolate. They had been brought out
from the nations, and now all of them live in safety. You
and all your troops and the many nations with you will
go up, advancing like a storm; you will be like a cloud
covering the land.' This is what the Sovereign Lord says:
'On that day thoughts will come into your mind and you
will devise an evil scheme. You will say, 'I will invade
a land of unwalled villages; I will attack a peaceful and
unsuspecting people –all of them living without walls
and without gates and bars. I will plunder and loot and
turn my hand against the resettled ruins and the people
gathered from the nations, rich in livestock and goods,
living at the center of the world.'[14] Sheba and Dedan and
the merchants of Tarshish and all her villages will say
to you, 'Have you come to plunder? Have you gathered
your hordes to loot, to carry off silver and gold, to take
away livestock and goods and to seize much plunder?'"[15]

The Spirit of God led Ezekiel to prophesy some important
strategic information. God Himself will put a hook in the jaws
of these nations and will reel them in toward a military invasion

---

14   I have substituted the NIV's 'land' and replaced it with the NASB's 'world'. The Hebrew word is
eretz which can be translated as either word.

15   Ezek. 38:1-13

of Israel. Stronger than all the anti-Semitism and the greed here stand the purposes of God, who is bringing these nations to a day of reckoning. The Jewish people are described in this passage as having been regathered and brought out from many nations to the mountains of Israel. There they have resettled the ruined cities and rebuilt their industry and infrastructure with a measure of prosperity and blessing. Their safety and security is described as being in their own hands. That is an accurate depiction of the present day State of Israel. This war also takes place 'after many days' and 'in future years' – a signpost of the end-time period of human history.

> Therefore, son of man, prophesy and say to Gog: "This is what the Sovereign Lord says: In that day, when My people Israel are living in safety, will you not take notice of it? You will come from your place in the far north, you and many nations with you, all of them riding on horses, a great horde, a mighty army. You will advance against My people Israel like a cloud that covers the land. In days to come, O Gog, I will bring you against My land, so that the nations may know Me when I show Myself holy through you before their eyes. This is what the Sovereign Lord says: Are you not the one I spoke of in former days by My servants the prophets of Israel? At that time they prophesied for years that I would bring you against them."[16]

The great invasion comes out of the far north, drawn by a God it does not believe in. This confederacy is brought against Israel to fulfill a purpose about which it is totally in the dark – to become as cannon fodder before the Lord of the armies of Israel. The other nations of the world will see God defending Israel from Gog on that day. They will observe God showing Himself holy as He defeats and destroys Israel's enemies.

> And I shall set My glory among the nations; and
> all the nations will see My judgment which I have

---

16   Ezek. 38:14-17

executed, and My hand which I have laid on them.
And the house of Israel will know that I am the Lord
their God from that day onward... When I bring
them back from the peoples and gather them from
the lands of their enemies, then I shall be sanctified
through them in the sight of many nations.[17]

The Holy Spirit reminds Ezekiel's readers that many of the Hebrew prophets repeatedly prophesied to the Jewish people concerning this invasion ("Are you not the one I spoke of in former days by My servants the prophets of Israel? At that time they prophesied for years that I would bring you against them").[18] Some of these earlier prophecies may have been included in the biblical record,[19] but Ezekiel's word is by far the clearest of them all.

A description of how God will personally defeat the Gog invasion forces follows:

This is what will happen in that day: when Gog attacks
the land of Israel, My hot anger will be aroused, declares
the Sovereign Lord. In My zeal and fiery wrath I declare
that at that time there shall be a great earthquake in the
land of Israel. The fish of the sea, the birds of the air,
the beasts of the field, every creature that moves along
the ground, and all the people on the face of the earth
will tremble at My presence. The mountains will be
overturned, the cliffs will crumble and every wall will
fall to the ground. I will summon a sword against Gog
on all My mountains, declares the Sovereign Lord. Every
man's sword will be against his brother. I will execute
judgment upon him with plague and bloodshed; I will
pour down torrents of rain, hailstones and burning sulfur
on him and on his troops and on the many nations with
him. And so I will show My greatness and My holiness,
and I will make Myself known in the sight of many
nations. Then they will know that I am the Lord.[20]

---

17   Ezek. 39:21, 22, 27 NASB

18   Ezek. 38:16-17

19   *Cf.,* Isa. 34:1-8

20   Ezek. 38:18-23

It is clear that an invasion of Israel led by Turkish and Islamic forces could only occur were Turkey's present pro-Western alignment severely altered. Such a shift would in turn create radical changes in the NATO alliance. However, this would not surprise students of modern Turkey. The Turkish fundamentalist Islamic Party's rise to dominance in the 1996 elections has indelibly altered the political landscape of that country. It has shaken the worldview of those who believed that Turkey would always remain pro-Western. Were a future American government to withdraw its support from Israel, Ezekiel's military scenario would look even more credible to modern eyes.

Desert Storm Revisited

The Bible prophesies more than one war against the tiny country of Israel which is still future. Whereas the Gog invasion of Ezekiel will involve mostly Near Eastern countries, the other future firefight will involve all the nations of the world. This campaign will have similarities to the Desert Shield/Desert Storm campaign of 1990-91, with two important exceptions. First, international participation in the forces allied against Israel will be overwhelming. Second, the target city will not be Baghdad but Jerusalem.

> In those days and at that time, when I restore the fortunes
> of Judah and Jerusalem, I will gather all nations and
> bring them down to the Valley of Jehoshaphat. There I
> will enter into judgment against them concerning My
> inheritance, My people Israel, for they scattered My
> people among the nations and divided up My land...[21]

The military goal of this war will be to establish internationally recognized and enforced borders for two states: the present state of Israel and the future state of Palestine. In order to achieve this goal, the international military confederation will have to neutralize the Israel Defense Forces. Great destruction will result, and all Jewish people who live over the Green Line in East Jerusalem (approximately

---

21   Joel 3:1-2

80% of Jerusalem's Jewish population) will be forcibly evicted to the western side of the city. The eastern side of Jerusalem will be declared off-limits to Jewish people and will become exclusively Arab. Though Jews will be allowed to live on the western side of Jerusalem, the trauma and destruction involved in this battle will shake the city to its spiritual foundations.

> In the whole land (*or earth, ed.*), declares the Lord,
> two-thirds will be struck down and perish; yet one-
> third will be left in it. This third I will bring into
> the fire; I will refine them like silver and test them
> like gold... A day of the Lord is coming when your
> plunder will be divided among you. I will gather all
> the nations to Jerusalem to fight against it; the city will
> be captured, the houses ransacked, and the women
> raped. Half of the city will go into exile, but the rest
> of the people will not be taken from the city.[22]

This war will certainly be a high water mark for worldwide anti-Semitism. Two-thirds of all Jewish people in the land of Israel (or quite possibly in the whole world – the Hebrew word *eretz* allows either interpretation) will be murdered. In other words, this future holocaust will be twice as horrific as the Nazi slaughter.[23] Israel's confidence in its own ability to defend itself will be shattered and the Jewish people will begin to wrestle with God, asking the same anguished questions as did the writer of Psalm 79.

Psalm 79
A psalm of Asaph.

O God, the nations have invaded Your inheritance;
They have defiled Your holy Temple,
  they have reduced Jerusalem to rubble.

---

22 Zech. 13:8-9; 14:1-2. The Hebrew word *eretz* can mean either land or earth, depending on the context.

23 In the Nazi holocaust six million Jewish people were murdered out of a world Jewish population of 18 million. This was a destruction of one-third of the Jewish people. The future holocaust will comprise two-thirds of the Jewish people. The official world Jewish population today stands at nearly 15 million.

They have given the dead bodies of Your servants
as food to the birds of the air,
The flesh of Your saints to the beasts of the earth.
They have poured out blood
like water all around Jerusalem,
And there is no one to bury the dead.
We are objects of reproach to our neighbors,
of scorn and derision to those around us.
How long, O Lord? Will You be angry forever?
How long will Your jealousy burn like fire?
Pour out Your wrath on the nations
that do not acknowledge You,
On the kingdoms that do not call on Your name;
For they have devoured Jacob
and destroyed his homeland.
Do not hold against us the sins of the fathers;
May Your mercy come quickly to meet us,
For we are in desperate need.
Help us, O God our Savior, for the glory of Your name;
Deliver us and forgive our sins for Your name's sake.
Why should the nations say, "Where is their God?"
Before our eyes, make known among the nations
That You avenge the outpoured blood of Your servants.
May the groans of the prisoners come before You;
By the strength of Your arm
preserve those condemned to die.
Pay back into the laps of our neighbors seven times
The reproach they have hurled at You, O Lord.
Then we Your people, the sheep of Your pasture,
will praise You forever;
From generation to generation we will recount Your praise.

The prophet Daniel was confronted with the fact of Jerusalem's future invasion and partial destruction. An angel revealed to him that even this terrible tragedy will be greatly used in God's hand to accomplish redemption for His chosen people. "The man clothed in linen, who was above the waters of the river, lifted his right hand and his left hand toward heaven, and I heard him swear by Him who lives forever, saying, 'It will be for a time, times and half a time. When the power of the holy people has been finally broken, all these things will be completed.'"[24] It seems that what Daniel heard about is the same as the invasion of Zechariah 14, and that this will be the proverbial straw that breaks the camel's back. As Isaiah says,

> In that day the remnant of Israel, the survivors of
> the house of Jacob, will no longer rely on him who
> struck them down but will truly rely on the Lord,
> the Holy One of Israel. A remnant will return, a
> remnant of Jacob will return to the Mighty God.
> Though your people, O Israel, be like the sand by
> the sea, only a remnant will return. Destruction has
> been decreed, overwhelming and righteous.[25]

The Cup of Poison

As the nations surge down to Israel and sweep over it like a massive flooding river, God suddenly exposes a secret weapon hidden in the palm of His hand for millennia, gleaming gold in the sunlight of His power. Zechariah calls it 'God's cup of poison,' a cup that sends nations reeling backwards in horror and pain.

> This is the word of the Lord concerning Israel. The Lord,
> who stretches out the heavens, who lays the foundation
> of the earth, and who forms the spirit of man within
> him, declares: "I am going to make Jerusalem a cup that
> sends all the surrounding peoples reeling. Judah will
> be besieged as well as Jerusalem. On that day, when all
> the nations of the earth are gathered against her, I will
> make Jerusalem an immovable rock for all the nations.
> All who try to move it will injure themselves."[26]

The secret weapon is actually the golden city of Jerusalem. The armies of the world have assembled, so they think, in order to deal decisively with that troublesome city and that obstinate people.

---

24   Dan. 12:7
25   Isa. 10:20-22
26   Zech. 12:1-9

Their solution to the heart of the frustrating Mid-East conflict is to take Israeli sovereignty away from half of Jerusalem and despoil the Jewish people in the process. But as they try to lift and dislodge this city, to establish a peace whose builder and maker is man, the weight of Jerusalem begins to get heavier. God exponentially increases the burden and the spiritual pressure on these armies and their leaders until spiritual hernias begin to bulge and then explode all along the beltline of these nations. God's Abrahamic promise of curse for curse reaches a zenith of judgment for the nations who lift up their hand against Israel. Though the world's desire is to deliver a death-blow to Israel's sovereignty, security and survival, the Lord has other plans.

The prophets describe God's judgment against the nations as being like a cup of poisonous wine. "In the hand of the Lord is a cup full of foaming wine mixed with spices; He pours it out, and all the wicked of the earth drink it down to its very dregs."[27]

In a vision Jeremiah was once commanded by God to engage in a prophetic gesture – to force the nations to imbibe poisonous wine from a divine chalice. The wine of God's fury is the punishment He will pour out on all the nations, those which have conspired and plotted together against the Lord, against His Anointed One, against His Jewish people and against His capital city of Jerusalem.

> Take from My hand this cup filled with the wine of My
> wrath and make all the nations to whom I send you
> drink it. When they drink it, they will stagger and go
> mad because of the sword I will send among them...
> Drink, get drunk and vomit, and fall to rise no more
> because of the sword I will send among you... The Lord
> will roar from on high; He will thunder from His holy
> dwelling... He will shout like those who tread the grapes,
> shout against all who live on the earth. The tumult will
> resound to the ends of the earth, for the Lord will bring
> charges against the nations; He will bring judgment
> on all mankind and put the wicked to the sword...

---

27 Psa. 75:8

Look! Disaster is spreading from nation to nation; a mighty storm is rising from the ends of the earth.[28]

A Time of Trouble for Jacob

Trouble is not only coming for the world; it is also on its way for the Jewish people, said the prophets of Israel. A period of time is marked off in the Scriptures as 'the time of Jacob's trouble.' It is slated to occur at the end of days, when the nation of Israel is being regathered to its ancestral homeland. The full fury of Satan will be turned against the Jewish people in that day with agonizing results.

> The days are coming, declares the Lord, when I will bring My people Israel and Judah back from captivity and restore them to the land I gave their forefathers to possess... These are the words the Lord spoke concerning Israel and Judah:... Cries of fear are heard – terror, not peace. Ask and see: can a man bear children? Then why do I see every strong man with his hands on his stomach like a woman in labor, every face turned deathly pale? How awful that day will be! None will be like it. It will be a time of trouble for Jacob, but he will be saved out of it.[29]

Further on in the same passage in Jeremiah, it says that Israel will once again bear the yoke of the nations upon their necks. For a brief time they will be enslaved and plundered, despoiled and oppressed.[30] An angel speaking to Daniel the seer gave him other details about that time.

"At that time Michael, the great prince who protects your people, will arise. There will be a time of distress such as has not happened from the beginning of nations until then. But at that time your people, everyone whose name is found written in the book, will be delivered."[31]

Michael is the archangel who is in charge of Israel's defense and

28   Jer. 25: 15-16, 27, 30-32; *cf.*, Ezek. 23:28-34; Hab. 2:15-16; Rev. 14:10; 16:19; 17:4: 18:6.

29   Jer. 30:3-7

30   *Cf.*, Jer. 30:8-24; Joel 3:2-7

31   Dan. 12:1

preservation. His rising up is due to the need to protect the Jewish people from total destruction. His mandate will be to save the remnant of the Jewish people, that one-third who turn to Messiah Yeshua in repentance. Sitting on the Mount of Olives, Yeshua described those days: "How dreadful it will be in those days for pregnant women and nursing mothers! There will be great distress in the land and wrath against this people"[32]

> So when you see standing in the holy place 'the abomination that causes desolation,' spoken of through the prophet Daniel (let the reader understand) then let those who are in Judea flee to the mountains. Let no one on the roof of his house go down to take anything out of the house. Let no one in the field go back to get his cloak. How dreadful it will be in those days for pregnant women and nursing mothers! Pray that your flight will not take place in winter or on the Sabbath. For then there will be great distress, unequaled from the beginning of the world until now – and never to be equaled again. If those days had not been cut short, no one would survive, but for the sake of the elect those days will be shortened. At that time if anyone says to you, "Look, here is the Messiah!" or, "There he is!" do not believe it. For false messiahs and false prophets will appear and perform great signs and miracles to deceive even the elect – if that were possible. See, I have told you ahead of time. So if anyone tells you, "There he is, out in the desert," do not go out, or, "Here he is, in the inner rooms," do not believe it. For as lightning that comes from the east is visible even in the west, so will be the coming of the Son of Man.[33]

Though Israel will undergo tremendous anguish and suffering, she will be purified and rescued as a result. Paul the Apostle recognized this divine pattern regarding Israel's purging and salvation when he prophesied, "There will be tribulation and distress for every human being who does evil, first to the Jew, then

---

32 Luke 21:23

33 Matt. 24:15-28

to the Gentile"[34] Ezekiel description of this face-to-face encounter between the Jewish people and their righteous God rings down the corridors of time.

> You say, "We want to be like the Gentiles, like the peoples of the world, who serve wood and stone." But what you have in mind will never happen. As surely as I live, declares the Lord God, I shall be king over you with a mighty hand and with an outstretched arm and with wrath poured out. And I shall bring you out from the peoples and gather you from out of the countries where you are scattered, with a mighty hand and with an outstretched arm and with wrath poured out. And I will bring you into the wilderness of the peoples and there I shall enter into judgment with you, face to face. As I entered into judgment with your fathers in the wilderness of the land of Egypt, so I will judge you, declares the Lord God. And I shall make you pass under the rod, and I shall bring you into the bond of the covenant; and I shall purge from you the rebels and those who revolt against Me. I shall bring them out of the land where they are presently living, but they will not enter the land of Israel. Thus you will know that I am the Lord.[35]

Though some may find these prophecies unnerving, and though our natural tendency is to brush away words of judgment, the Book of Amos declares how important it is to open one's heart to these oracles of the living God. "For behold, I am commanding, and I will shake the house of Israel among all the nations as grain is shaken in a sieve, but not a kernel will fall to the ground. All the sinners of My people will die by the sword, those who say, 'The calamity will not overtake or confront us.'"[36]

---

34 Rom. 2:9 my translation

35 Ezek. 20:32-38 synthesis of NIV and NASB and my translation

36 Amos 9:9-10 NASB

Chapter Seventeen

A Redeemer Will Come To Zion

The return of Messiah to Jerusalem is one of the greatest themes of the ages. Many believers in Yeshua are unaware that most of the biblical descriptions of Yeshua's second coming center around the Jewish people and the city of Zion/Jerusalem. These Jewish aspects of Messiah's return will now be considered.

The Day of Vengeance of Our God

Yeshua's first sermon in His hometown synagogue of Nazareth was based on Isaiah 61. That passage paints a picture of events which began that day in a Galilean synagogue, but the ultimate fulfillment awaits the day of Messiah's return. Unrolling the scroll of the prophet, Yeshua proclaimed:

> The Spirit of the Sovereign Lord is on Me, because
> the Lord has anointed Me to preach good news to the
> poor. He has sent Me to bind up the brokenhearted,
> to proclaim freedom for the captives and release
> from darkness for the prisoners, to proclaim the

> year of the Lord's favor and the day of vengeance of
> our God, to comfort all who mourn ... in Zion.[1]

At His first coming Yeshua proclaimed 'the year of the Lord's favor', another term for the year of jubilee. When the jubilee year arrives, all debts are forgiven. Yeshua declared that, at His first advent, grace and forgiveness would be freely offered and sins and spiritual debts would be forgiven to all who believe. The second phrase, the 'day of vengeance of our God', is quite another matter. This term describes events which occur about the time of Messiah's return. On that day God will blaze forth in anger to save His beleaguered Jewish people. He will be amazed that so very few people will be standing with the Jewish nation and interceding for them.

> The Lord saw, and it was displeasing in His sight
> that there was no justice. And He saw that there was
> no one, and was appalled that there was no one to
> intercede. Then His own arm worked salvation for Him
> and His righteousness sustained Him. And He put on
> righteousness like a breastplate, and a helmet of salvation
> on His head; and He put on garments of vengeance for
> clothing, and wrapped Himself with zeal as a mantle.
> According to what they have done, so will He repay –
> wrath to His adversaries, retribution to His enemies.
> He will repay the coastlands their due...For He will
> come like a pent-up flood that the breath of the Lord
> drives along. The Redeemer will come to Zion, to those
> in Jacob who repent of their sins, declares the Lord.[2]

The Scriptures emphasize that the wrath of the Lord, His vengeance and divine retribution[3] will be directed against the world forces who will stick their finger into the apple of God's eye. His flaming anger will be roused like that of a she-bear defending her endangered cubs. "Ho Zion!... After glory He has sent Me against

---

1   Isa. 61:1-3

2   Isa. 59:15b-20 synthesis of NIV and NASB

3   *Cf.*, Isa. 35:4

the nations which plunder you (for he who touches you touches the apple of His eye),...Be silent, all flesh, before the Lord, for He is aroused from His holy habitation."[4]

God's day of vengeance will come with great destruction what the Bible calls 'divine desolations.' "Come and see the works of the Lord, the desolations He has brought on the earth."[5] When God locks horns with Satan, devastation will occur on an unprecedented scale. The very maelstrom of these events, King David prophesied, will be the hill of Zion, the city of Jerusalem.

> The One enthroned in heaven laughs; the Lord scoffs
> at them. Then He rebukes them in His anger and
> terrifies them in His wrath, saying, "I have installed
> My King on Zion, My holy hill... Ask of Me, and I will
> make the nations Your inheritance, the ends of the
> earth Your possession. You will rule them with an iron
> scepter; You will dash them to pieces like pottery."[6]

The Second Coming of Yeshua is one of the foundations and fundamentals of the New Covenant faith. Since we are still living in the 'times of the Gentiles,' however, and since most theologizing has been done by Gentiles unsympathetic to a prophetic future for Israel, the Jewish element central to His return has often been given short shrift. One aspect of the Second Coming that is often overlooked describes the Lord's return as a tornado of gale force bearing down on the haters of Israel. In accordance with the Abrahamic Covenant's curse-for-curse, God will now curse those who have cursed the Jewish people.

> In that day, declares the Lord Almighty, I will break
> the yoke off their necks and will tear off their bonds;
> no longer will foreigners enslave them ... But all who
> devour you will be devoured; all your enemies will go
> into exile. Those who plunder you will be plundered;
> all who make spoil of you I will despoil...I will punish

---

4   Zech. 2:7a, 8, 13 NASB; cf., Psa. 46:4-11

5   Psa. 46:8

6   Psa. 2: 4-6, 8-9

all who oppress them...See, the storm of the Lord will burst out in wrath, a driving wind swirling down on the heads of the wicked. The fierce anger of the Lord will not turn back until He fully accomplishes the purposes of His heart. In days to come you will understand this.[7]

(T)he hand of the Lord will be made known to His servants, but His fury will be shown to His foes. See, the Lord is coming with fire, and His chariots are like a whirlwind; He will bring down His anger with fury, and His rebuke with flames of fire. For with fire and with His sword the Lord will execute judgment upon all men, and many will be those slain by the Lord.[8]

Trampling Out the Vintage

One of the Father's burning desires is to see His kingdom come and His will be done on earth as it is in Heaven. In Heaven sickness, disease and death do not exist, and neither does anti-Semitism. When Messiah Yeshua returns to trample on the grapes of wrath, He will crush anti-Semitism once and for all. He will execute vengeance on all the nations who have shaken a rebel's fist in the face of God, and He will establish justice for the Jewish people.

Who is this coming from Edom, from Bozrah, with His garments stained crimson? Who is this, robed in splendor, striding forward in the greatness of His strength? "It is I, speaking in righteousness, mighty to save." Why are Your garments red, like those of one treading the winepress? "I have trodden the winepress alone; from the nations no one was with Me. I trampled them in My anger and trod them down in My wrath; their blood spattered My garments, and I stained all My clothing. For the day of vengeance was in My heart, and the year of My redemption has come. I looked, but there was no one to help, I was appalled that no one gave support; so My own arm worked salvation for Me, and My own wrath sustained Me. I

---

7   Jer. 30:8, 16, 20, 23-24; *cf.,* Joel 3:7

8   Isa. 66:14-16

trampled the nations in My anger; in My wrath I made them drunk and poured their blood on the ground."[9]

The Lion of Judah will roar from Zion and make the whole earth tremble. The day of reckoning will arrive for all those who reject Israel and attempt to destroy her.

In those days and at that time, when I restore the fortunes of Judah and Jerusalem, I will gather all nations and…I will enter into judgment against them concerning My inheritance, My people Israel…Multitudes, multitudes in the valley of decision! For the day of the Lord is near in the valley of decision. The sun and moon will be darkened, and the stars no longer shine. The Lord will roar from Zion and thunder from Jerusalem; the earth and the sky will tremble. But the Lord will be a refuge for His people, a stronghold for the people of Israel. Then you will know that I, the Lord your God, dwell in Zion, My holy hill. Jerusalem will be holy; never again will foreigners invade her.[10]

Jewish Power Encounters

One of the names of God is 'The Fear of Isaac.'[11] Though this term probably refers to Isaac's reverential awe as he stood before the God of his father Abraham, the Scriptures tell us that on the day of God's vengeance there will be a fear of Isaac, a dread of the Jewish people, falling on the armies of the world.[12]

The earth will become desolate because of its inhabitants, as the result of their deeds … As in the days when you came out of Egypt, I will show them My wonders. Nations will see and be ashamed, deprived of all their power. They will lay their hands on their mouths and their ears will become deaf. They will lick dust like a snake, like creatures that crawl on the ground. They

---

9   Isa. 63:1-6

10   Joel 3:1-2, 14-17

11   Gen. 31:42

12   *Cf.*, Exod. 1:11-13; 15:15-17; Psa. 53:3-6; 105:36-38; Isa. 2:19-21

will come trembling out of their dens; they will turn in
fear to the Lord our God and will be afraid of you.[13]

Miracles as mighty as in the days of Moses will occur, and
perhaps even greater wonders as well.[14] The power of God will
saturate those Messianic Jews who hold to the testimony of Yeshua.
Like the two witnesses of Revelation 11, they will minister power
through healing, miracles and judgment to Israel and the nations.
Terror will fall on many as a result of their ministry.[15]

A radical reversal of roles will occur at this time: Gentile
attacking Israel will suddenly fall defeated before their intended
Jewish victims. Those who come to thrash Zion will abruptly find
themselves being threshed!

> O Daughter of Zion,...now many nations are gathered
> against you. They say, "Let her be defiled, let our eyes
> gloat over Zion!" But they do not know the thoughts of the
> Lord; they do not understand His plan, He who gathers
> them like sheaves to the threshing floor. Rise and thresh,
> O Daughter of Zion, for I will give you horns of iron; I
> will give you hoofs of bronze and you will break to pieces
> many nations. You will devote their ill-gotten gains to
> the Lord, their wealth to the Lord of all the earth.[16]

The Bible indicates that military victories will be given to a
reborn Israeli army at this time. Most probably this is the same
fighting force as the exceedingly great army of Ezekiel 37. The
Scriptures conceal more than reveal on this point. One day God
will break forth with greater light and understanding concerning
these matters.

> On that day I will make the leaders of Judah like a firepot
> in a woodpile, like a flaming torch among sheaves. They
> will consume right and left all the surrounding peoples,
> but Jerusalem will remain intact in her place ... On that

13   Micah 7:13, 15-17
14   *Cf.*, Jn. 14:12
15   *Cf.*, Rev. 11:3-14
16   Mic. 4:10-13

day the Lord will shield those who live in Jerusalem, so that the feeblest among them will be like David, and the house of David will be like God, like the Angel of the Lord going before them. On that day I will set out to destroy all the nations that attack Jerusalem.[17]

Touchdown on the Mount of Olives

Messiah Yeshua will return to the city of Zion and His feet will walk again on the hills of Jerusalem. Zechariah tells us that the catalyst for His return will be the Gentile conquest and oppression of Jerusalem's Jewish residents, spearheaded by the anti-Messiah's international military confederation. Immediately after Yeshua's final destruction of those armies, Messiah will take up His royal Davidic throne in Zion and begin to reign over the entire earth.

Then the Lord will go out and fight against those nations, as He fights in the day of battle. On that day His feet will stand on the Mount of Olives, east of Jerusalem, and the Mount of Olives will be split in two from east to west, forming a great valley, with half of the mountain moving north and half moving south ... The Lord will be king over the whole earth. On that day there will be one Lord, and His name the only name.[18]

This entire process is laid out as a panorama in Psalm 110. The Messiah readies Himself for the day of vengeance, and His youthful armies jump to attention in military formation.[19] Yeshua then leaps into the fray, crushing the forces of His foes. After the victory has been won, the Lion of Judah refreshes Himself like a lion stopping at a brook to drink water. No one dares to steal his prey from Him. Yeshua rules majestic over His enemies from the City of David.

The Lord says to My Lord: "Sit at My right hand until I make Your enemies a footstool for Your feet." The Lord

---

17 Zech. 12:4-9

18 Zech. 14:3-4, 9

19 The term translated 'be willing' is *hityatzev,* a Hebrew word meaning 'to show up in military formation or rank'.

will extend Your mighty scepter from Zion; You will
rule in the midst of Your enemies. Your troops will be
willing on Your day of battle. Arrayed in holy majesty,
from the womb of the dawn You will receive the dew
of your youth ... The Lord is at Your right hand; He
will crush kings on the day of His wrath. He will judge
the nations, heaping up the dead and crushing the
rulers of the whole earth. He will drink from a brook
beside the way; therefore He will lift up His head.[20]

Judgment in Jehoshaphat's Valley

The judgment of the nations will take place in the Kidron Valley
east of the Temple Mount, soon after Yeshua's triumphant Second
Coming. This valley is also known as the King's Valley and the
Valley of 'Jehovah Judges' (*Yehóshaphát* in Hebrew). All the nations of
the world will be brought there and their leaders will be questioned
personally, one at a time, by Messiah Yeshua. These leaders will be
judged for dividing Jerusalem up into two sectors, for downsizing
the borders of the Jewish state,1 and for removing half of the Jewish
population from East Jerusalem.[21]

On that day each person's saving faith in Yeshua (or lack of it) will
be obvious to all, and clearly demonstrated by his or her answer
to only one question, "How did you treat the Jewish people?" On
the day of Jehoshaphat true faith in Yeshua will be recognized by
precious fruit – works of compassionate love which save Jewish
lives.[22] The 'day of decision' will make one point crystal clear: 'to do
the works of Jesus' has special reference to saving Jewish lives.

> In those days and at that time, when I restore the fortunes
> of Judah and Jerusalem, I will gather all nations and
> bring them down to the Valley of Jehoshaphat. There I
> will enter into judgment against them concerning My
> inheritance, My people Israel, for they scattered My

---

20   Psa. 110:1-3, 5-7; *cf.,* 1 Chron. 16:8, 12, 30-31, 33, 35

21   *Cf.,* Zech. 14:1-2

22   *Cf.,* Ja. 2:14-26

people among the nations and divided up My land.[23]

In the Gospels Yeshua calls this future judgment 'the separation of the sheep from the goats.' In the Middle East to this day shepherds allow goats and sheep to mingle together, separating them only at the shearing season. Yeshua will separate mankind into two groups – those destined for His kingdom, and those destined for eternal fire. The basis for judgment will be how each person treated 'the least of the brothers of Yeshua.' The Book to the Hebrews says that the brothers of Yeshua are His flesh-and-blood relatives, the Jewish people. "For surely it is not is not angels He helps, but Abraham's descendants. For this reason He had to be made like His brothers in every way, in order that He might become a merciful and faithful high priest in service to God, and that He might make atonement for the sins of the people."[24]

> When the Son of Man comes in His glory, and all the
> angels with Him, He will sit on His throne in heavenly
> glory. All the nations will be gathered before Him,
> and He will separate the people one from another as a
> shepherd separates the sheep from the goats. He will
> put the sheep on His right and the goats on His left.
> Then the King will say to those on His right, "Come, you
> who are blessed by My Father; take your inheritance,
> the kingdom prepared for you since the creation of the
> world. For I was hungry and you gave Me something to
> eat, I was thirsty and you gave Me something to drink,
> I was a stranger and you invited Me in, I needed clothes
> and you clothed Me, I was sick and you looked after
> Me, I was in prison and you came to visit Me." Then the
> righteous will answer Him, "Lord, when did we see You
> hungry and feed You, or thirsty and give You something
> to drink? When did we see You a stranger and invite
> You in, or needing clothes and clothe You? When did
> we see You sick or in prison and go to visit You?" The
> King will reply, "I tell you the truth, whatever you did

---

23 Joel 3:1-2
24 Heb. 2:16-17; *cf.*, John 1:11; Gal. 4:4-5

for one of the least of these brothers of Mine, you did for Me." Then He will say to those on His left, "Depart from Me, you who are cursed, into the eternal fire prepared for the devil and his angels. For I was hungry and you gave Me nothing to eat, I was thirsty and you gave Me nothing to drink, I was a stranger and you did not invite Me in, I needed clothes and you did not clothe Me, I was sick and in prison and you did not look after Me." They also will answer, "Lord, when did we see You hungry or thirsty or a stranger or needing clothes or sick or in prison, and did not help You?" He will reply, "I tell you the truth, whatever you did not do for one of the least of these, you did not do for Me." Then they will go away to eternal punishment, but the righteous to eternal life.[25]

Jerusalem of Gold

God operates on more than one track at a time. He is able to keep many different plates spinning smoothly and simultaneously. As we turn from the Gentile track to consider God's dealings with the Jewish nation, let's consider: what is happening to Israel during this same time period? How does the nation survive its face to face encounter with God in the wilderness of the peoples?[26]

One of God's many names is 'the Hope of Israel, its Savior in times of distress'.[27] The Bible says that God does not willingly bring affliction or grief to mankind,[28] and that the Lord does not want any human being to choose an eternal fate separate from God. But sometimes it is during times of distress that men and women listen best to God. C.S. Lewis once said, "Pain insists on being attended to. God whispers to us in our pleasures, speaks in our conscience, but shouts in our pains; it is His megaphone to rouse a deaf world."[29] Isaiah agrees: "Lord, they came to You in their distress; when You

---

25   Matt. 25:31-46

26   *Cf.,* Ezek. 20:35 *ff.*

27   Jer. 14:8

28   *Cf.,* 2 Pet.3:9; Lam. 3:33

29   C.S. Lewis, *The Problem of Pain,* Fountain Books, Glasgow, 1977, VI.81

disciplined them, they could barely whisper a prayer."[30]

The Jewish people have gone through centuries, indeed millennia of distress, and they would have been totally destroyed had it not been for the fact that the Guardian of Israel never slumbers or sleeps.[31] His hand of mercy and preservation is what has kept the Hebrew nation alive. But there really is a divine goal behind Israel's national distresses –to bring the nation to repent for the wrong decision (and their leaders' wrong decision) to reject Messiah Yeshua. Hosea sums up this whole process, even prophesying what Israel's future prayer of repentance to the Lord will be:

> Then I will go away and return to My place until they
> acknowledge their guilt and seek My face. In their
> affliction they will earnestly seek Me…"Come, let us
> return to the Lord. He has torn us to pieces but He
> will heal us; He has injured us but He will bind up
> our wounds. After two days He will revive us; on the
> third day He will restore us, that we may live in His
> presence. Let us acknowledge the Lord; let us press
> on to acknowledge Him. As surely as the sun rises,
> He will appear; He will come to us like the winter
> rains, like the spring rains that water the earth."[32]

The fires of Jewish history will ultimately be used by God to turn the heart of His stubborn chosen people back to Himself. Though He is not the author of anti-Semitism, God is not below using the wrath of men to refine and purify His people. "See, I have refined you … I have tested you in the furnace of affliction."[33] As a result of this final time of distress, the agony of Jewish suffering will be transformed into the ecstasy of a reborn Israeli nation. "This third I will bring into the fire; I will refine them like silver and test them like gold. They will call on My name and I will answer them; I will

---

30   Isa. 26:16; *cf.*, Jer. 15:11; Judg. 2:10-23

31   *Cf.*, Psa. 121:4

32   Hosea 5:14- 6:3

33   Isa. 48:10; *cf.*, Psa. 76:10; Isa. 10:5, 25; 13:3-5; Jer. 10:25

say, 'They are My people,' and they will say, 'The Lord is our God.'"[34]

The Holy Spirit will begin to blow on the hearts of Zion and Jerusalem, quickening repentance and confession of sin. All Israel which survives the worldwide anti-Semitic persecution will receive a spiritual revelation of the Messiahship of Yeshua, His deity and the power of His atoning blood. "And I will pour out on the house of David and the inhabitants of Jerusalem a Spirit of grace and supplication. They will look on Me, the One they have pierced, and they will mourn for Him as one mourns for an only child, and grieve bitterly for Him as one grieves for a firstborn son."[35] The stage is now set for the full expression of the New Covenant.

The Jewish New Covenant

Two thousand six hundred years ago God promised Jeremiah that He would make a new covenant with the Jewish people. The New Covenant will be unlike the Mosaic Torah in some ways. It will be a different treaty with differing emphases and obligations. At its heart will be Yeshua's everlasting atonement, not a yearly Yom Kippur sacrifice. Every Jewish man, woman, boy and girl will have a personal and intimate relationship with the God of Israel and will have the teachings of God written on his or her heart. Though many of these aspects are the present experience of Jews and Gentiles who follow Yeshua today, the New Covenant has not yet been realized in national fullness for the Jewish people. But when the Spirit of grace and supplications is poured out, Jeremiah's prophecy over the Hebrew people will become a living national reality.

> "Behold days are coming," declares the Lord, "when I
> will cut a new covenant with the house of Israel and
> with the house of Judah. It will not be like the covenant

---

34   Zech. 13:9

35   Zech. 12:10. There seems to be some cloudiness in the Scriptures as to the exact order of events surrounding Zech.12:10. Rev.1:7 applies a similar scenario to the nations as well. Does Zech. 12:10 occur first, and catalyze Rev.1:7? If Zech.12:10 describes the national regeneration of Israel, does it occur before Zech,14:1-2? The answers to these questions remain unclear. Pray that the Lord will grant greater prophetic clarity to the body of Messiah on these matters.

I cut with their fathers in the day when I took them by
the hand to lead them out of Egypt, for they broke My
covenant, though I was a husband to them, " declares
the Lord. "For this is the covenant which I will cut with
the house of Israel after those days," declares the Lord.
"I will put My teaching inside them and on their hearts
will I write it. I will be their God, and they will be My
people. No more will they teach every man his neighbor
and every man his brother, saying, 'Know the Lord,' for
they will all know Me, from the smallest of them up to
the biggest," declares the Lord. "For I will forgive their
perversity and their sins I will remember no more."[36]

A magnificent page of Jewish history now begins, the greatest
aspect of it being that, for the first time in history, the entire people
of Israel will make their boast totally in the Lord.[37] The nation will
be so deliriously in love with the God of Jacob, that individuals
will scribble Yeshua's name on their hands, change their names to
belonging to the God of Israel', etc.

For I will pour water on the thirsty land, and streams
on the dry ground; I will pour out My Spirit on your
offspring, and My blessing on your descendants. They
will spring up like grass in a meadow, like poplar trees
by flowing streams. One will say, 'I belong to the Lord';
another will call himself by the name of Jacob; still
another will write on his hand, 'The Lord's,' and will take
the name 'Israel.' This is what the Lord says – Israel's
King and Redeemer, the Lord Almighty: I am the first
and I am the last; apart from Me there is no God.[38]

The ancient promise made to Abraham, that his physical children
would be a spiritual blessing to the whole world, now becomes
reality. Moses' prophecy of a Jewish nation with circumcised hearts

---

36   Jer. 31:31-34 my translation. The Hebrew word *Torah* in v. 32, often translated as 'Law' following
     the Septuagint, comes from the root *yrh* (yarah) and means teaching or instruction, as in the modern
     Hebrew word for teacher *morah*.

37   *Cf.*, Isa. 45:23-25

38   Isa. 44:3-6

is now actualized. The Spirit of God fills the hearts and mouths of Zion's children with prophetic fire, never to depart again.

> "The Redeemer will come to Zion, to those in Jacob who repent of their sins," declares the Lord. "As for Me, this is My covenant with them, says the Lord. My Spirit, who is on you, and My words that I have put in your mouth will not depart from your mouth, or from the mouths of your children, or from the mouths of their descendants from this time on and forever," says the Lord.[39]

The Apostle Paul knew this last passage well. One of his closing thoughts in the eleventh chapter of Romans quotes these above verses, stressing that Isaiah's Israel and Isaiah's Zion are the Jewish people, who now will fully enter into the blessings of the New Covenant through Yeshua, Israel's Redeemer.

> I do not want you to be ignorant of this mystery, brothers, so that you may not be conceited: Israel has experienced a hardening in part until the full number of the Gentiles has come in. And so all Israel will be saved, as it is written: 'The Deliverer will come from Zion; He will turn godlessness away from Jacob. And this is My covenant with them when I take away their sins.' As far as the gospel is concerned, they are enemies on your account; but as far as election is concerned, they are loved on account of the patriarchs, for God's gifts and His call are irrevocable.[40]

All in the Family?

Believers have pored over the Scriptures referred to in this chapter, attempting to discover what percentage of the Jewish people will be saved. Some have wrestled with the words 'all Israel,' tentatively concluding that that term is only a generalization for a large majority of Jewish people. This position would hold that

39 Isa. 59:20-21
40 Rom. 11:25-29

many Jews will be regenerated in that day, but not all. But when God says 'all' does He really mean 'all?' Jeremiah cuts the Gordian knot with his own decisive contribution.

Describing Israel's prophetic return to her homeland (which in this passage includes territories now belonging to southern Syria and northern Jordan), the Lord declares that 'all' really does mean 'all.'

> But I will bring Israel back to his own pasture and he will graze on Carmel and Bashan; his appetite will be satisfied on the hills of Ephraim and Gilead. In those days, at that time, declares the Lord, search will be made for Israel's guilt, but there will be none, and for the sins of Judah, but none will be found, for I will forgive the remnant I spare.[41]

When Will These Things Be?

Lovers of Zion have attempted to discover exactly when Israel will undergo national salvation. The traditional Dispensational position is that this will occur during the last few days of the Tribulation. Most other theologies have not invested much time or interest on this question. What do the Scriptures say? Is there any ironclad biblical word which will clear up the matter?

It seems that the Bible is not as dogmatic in presenting its own time-line as many of us might wish. Even in Yeshua's day many brilliant scribes, Pharisees and apostles did not immediately comprehend that a gap existed between Messiah's first and second coming, and did not understand the 'suffering servant' aspect of Messiah's ministry. So also in our day some gaps in our understanding of eschatological chronology probably still exist! Our goal should not be to invest the lion's share of our efforts in trying to unlock the date of Israel's salvation. The nation of Israel may come to the Lord three minutes before Yeshua returns, or it may even be three days, three months or three years before that moment. The priority is to give God and ourselves no peace, calling out to Him in intercession and

---

41   Jer. 50:19-20

reaching out to the Jewish people in evangelism, until He makes a Jerusalem a praise in all the earth.

Proclaim Liberty Throughout The Land!

The Jubilee Year is a year of rejoicing. All debts are wiped out, all slaves are freed, and all ancestral land is returned to its original owners. When Messiah returns to Zion, the hope that has burned in Jewish breasts throughout the long years of exile will finally be realized in fullness: the centuries of Jewish subjugation, mourning and humiliation will be over. Micah expresses this Messianic longing eloquently.

> Do not rejoice over me, O my enemy. Though I fall I will rise; though I dwell in darkness the Lord is a light for me. I will bear the indignation of the Lord because I have sinned against Him, until He pleads my case and executes justice for me. He will bring me out to the light, and I will see His righteousness. Then my enemy will see, and shame will cover her who said to me, "Where is the Lord your God?" My eyes will look on her; at that time she will be trampled down like the mire of the streets.[42]

At last the Jewish people will be free from fear of attack and terrorism. Zephaniah prophesies about that day: "The Lord has taken away your punishment. He has turned back your enemy. The Lord, the King of Israel, is with you; never again will you fear any harm."[43] Isaiah adds, "No longer will violence be heard in your land, nor ruin or destruction within your borders, but you will call your walls Salvation and your gates Praise...and your days of sorrow will end. Then will all your people be righteous and they will possess the land forever."[44] God's first-born son among the nations, the Jewish people, will come into the double portion of his inheritance.

Instead of their shame My people will receive a double

---

42   Micah 7:8-10
43   Zeph. 3:15
44   Isa. 60:18, 20-21

portion, and instead of disgrace they will rejoice in
their inheritance; and so they will inherit a double
portion in their land, and everlasting joy will be theirs
... In My faithfulness I will reward them and make an
everlasting covenant with them. Their descendants
will be known among the nations and their offspring
among the peoples. All who see them will acknowledge
that they are a people the Lord has blessed.[45]

The ministry of mighty angels will attend the return of any
believing Jews still scattered to the four points of the compass as
a result of the anti-Semitic persecutions. "And He will send His
angels with a loud trumpet call, and they will gather His elect
from the four winds, from one end of the earth to the ends of the
heavens."[46] The shofar blast of God will resound across the face of
the earth, calling back the Jewish people to their motherland.

In that day the Lord will thresh from the flowing
Euphrates to the Wadi of Egypt, and you, O Israelites,
will be gathered up one by one. And in that day a great
trumpet will sound. Those who were perishing in Assyria
and those who were exiled in Egypt will come and
worship the Lord on the holy mountain in Jerusalem.[47]

The Russians have a proverb, "A boil is no problem under the
other fellow's armpit." When a tragedy affects you personally, it
takes on a totally different dimension. The same is true of the other
side of the coin, when it comes to blessing. Today, perhaps only
those Gentiles who are open-hearted and attuned to the sufferings
of the Jewish people can grasp how important the promises of
Jewish restoration are to Jewish people, and how powerfully their
fulfillment will affect the Jewish nation. With this in mind, one can
understand better why God calls upon all believers everywhere to
lift up their voices and intercede with the Father for Zion's sake

45   Isa. 61:7-9; cf., Isa. 51:9-11

46   synthesis of Matt. 24:31 and Mark 13:27. Note also how Matt. 24:30 uses Zech. 12:10 in a broader
      context, referring to universal repentance.

47   Isa. 27:12-13

– for the sake of the final restoration of the Jewish nation.

> For Zion's sake I will not keep silent, for Jerusalem's sake I will not remain quiet, till her righteousness shines out like the dawn, her salvation like a blazing torch. The nations will see your righteousness, and all kings your glory; you will be called by a new name that the mouth of the Lord will bestow. You will be a crown of splendor in the Lord's hand, a royal diadem in the hand of your God. No longer will they call you 'Deserted,' or name your land 'Desolate.' But you will be called 'Hephzibah,' and your land 'Beulah;' for the Lord will take delight in you, and your land will be married. As a young man marries a maiden, so will your sons marry you; as a bridegroom rejoices over his bride, so will your God rejoice over you. I have posted watchmen on your walls, O Jerusalem; they will never be silent day or night. You who call on the Lord, give yourselves no rest, and give Him no rest till He establishes Jerusalem and makes her the praise of the earth. The Lord has sworn by His right hand and by His mighty arm: "Never again will I give your grain as food for your enemies, and never again will foreigners drink the new wine for which you have toiled; but those who harvest it will eat it and praise the Lord, and those who gather the grapes will drink it in the courts of My sanctuary." Pass through, pass through the gates! Prepare the way for the people. Build up, build up the highway! Remove the stones. Raise a banner for the nations. The Lord has made proclamation to the ends of the earth: "Say to the Daughter of Zion, 'See, your Savior comes! See, His reward is with Him, and His recompense accompanies Him.'" They will be called the Holy People, the Redeemed of the Lord; and you will be called Sought After, the City No Longer Deserted.[48]

We Shall Not Be Moved!

When the Redeemer comes back to Zion, He will pour out His blessings of prosperity and provision over the people and the land.

---

48   Isa. 62:1-12; *cf.*, Isa. 65:19-24

God's cornucopia of abundance will not be stolen again from the Jewish people or ravaged by war. The land of milk and honey will blossom as the rose.

> The days are coming, declares the Lord, when the reaper will be overtaken by the plowman and the planter by the one treading grapes. New wine will drip from the mountains and flow from all the hills. I will bring back My exiled people Israel; they will rebuild the ruined cities and live in them. They will plant vineyards and drink their wine; they will make gardens and eat their fruit. I will plant Israel in their own land, never again to be uprooted from the land I have given them, says the Lord your God.[49]

It is not unusual to hear the word 'Jew' used negatively today, as in 'to Jew someone down.' All these anti-Semitic slurs will cease when the Lord returns, and the Deuteronomic curses[50] will dissolve to give way to Abrahamic blessings.

> This is what the Lord Almighty says: "I will save My people from the countries of the east and the west. I will bring them back to live in Jerusalem; they will be My people, and I will be faithful and righteous to them as their God...As you have been an object of cursing among the nations, O Judah and Israel, so will I save you, and you will be a blessing. Do not be afraid, but let your hands be strong."[51]

> Then the Lord will be jealous for His land and take pity on His people. The Lord will reply to them: "I am sending you grain, new wine and oil, enough to satisfy you fully; never again will I make you an object of scorn to the nations"...Be not afraid, O land; be glad and rejoice. Surely the Lord has done great things. Be not afraid, O wild animals, for the open pastures

---

49   Amos 9:8-15; *cf.*, Isa. 35:1-10; Ezek. 36: 7-15

50   *Cf.*, Deut. 28:15-20, 37

51   Zech. 8:1-15

are becoming green. The trees are bearing their fruit;
the fig tree and the vine yield their riches. Be glad, O
people of Zion, rejoice in the Lord your God, for He
has given you the autumn rains in righteousness. He
sends you abundant showers, both autumn and spring
rains, as before. The threshing floors will be filled with
grain; the vats will overflow with new wine and oil.[52]

The picture that the Scriptures paint of the Jewish people in their land once again is like a flock of contented sheep, peacefully chewing their cud on the mountainous Carmel Ridge beside Haifa, up on the windswept Golan Heights, in the green valleys of the West Bank and on the plateaus of northern Jordan. "But I will bring Israel back to his own graze on Carmel and Bashan; his appetite will be satisfied on the hills of Ephraim and Gilead."[53]

God has prophesied about Israel's restoration in very specific geographical terms. He has given specific promises concerning specific pieces of real estate, about hills and valleys with specific names. These places and place names are not symbols of something else. These place names still represent actual plots of land real Jewish places prepared for real Jewish people. Three-dimensional physical blessings will shower down on the Jewish people in space-time reality!

The days are coming, declares the Lord, when this
city will be rebuilt for Me from the Tower of Hananel
to the Corner Gate. The measuring line will stretch
from there straight to the hill of Gareb and then
turn to Goah. The whole valley where dead bodies
and ashes are thrown, and all the terraces out to
the Kidron Valley on the east as far as the corner of
the Horse Gate, will be holy to the Lord. The city
will never again be uprooted or demolished.[54]

One of the most touching and heart-warming prophecies about

---

52   Joel 2:18-19, 21-24; *cf.,* Hos. 2:14-23

53   Jer. 50:19

54   Jer. 31:38-40; *cf.,* 30:18-22; 31:23-25

the restoration of the Jewish people describes the returning and restored nation as precious jewels, as tiaras, as bridal garments covering the land of Israel. Isaiah prophesied that the land of Israel will be speechless for shock, and then the earth itself will utter words as if in a Narnia novel, saying: "I thought my people had been destroyed in the Holocaust, slaughtered by the anti-Messiah, assimilated and diluted beyond remedy. How can it be that they have returned to me in greater number and with more life than ever before?"

> Your sons hasten back, and those who laid you waste
> depart from you. Lift up your eyes and look around;
> all your sons gather and come to you. As surely as
> I live, declares the Lord, you will wear them all as
> ornaments; you will put them on like a bride. Though
> you were ruined and made desolate and your land
> laid waste, now you will be too small for your people,
> and those who devoured you will be far away. The
> children born during your bereavement will yet say in
> your hearing, "This place is too small for us; give us
> more space to live in." Then you will say in your heart,
> "Who bore me these? I was bereaved and barren; I was
> exiled and rejected. Who brought these up? I was left
> all alone, but these – where have they come from?"[55]

Which Comes First – The Chicken Or The Teshuvah?

One of the questions that students of prophecy often ask concerning the restoration of Israel is this: Do the Jewish people repent and turn to Yeshua before they return to the land of Israel, or do they return to the land first and only then look on the One they have pierced? Two different schools of thought exist on this question. Those who hold to a 'land first' position are usually ardent advocates of *aliyah*, Jewish immigration to Israel. Sometimes those who are hesitant about evangelizing the Jewish people also prefer this position, concluding that the salvation of Israel is

---

55   Isa. 49:17-21

totally someone else's problem – perhaps God's! Those who hold to a 'repentance first' position often live in the Diaspora and are usually more openly involved in evangelism. The Hebrew word for repentance is *teshuvah*. So which comes first – the *aliyah* or the *teshuvah*?

Those who hold to *teshuvah* first present Scripture verses like Nehemiah 1:8-9.

> Remember the instruction You gave Your servant Moses, saying, "If you are unfaithful, I will scatter you among the nations, but if you return to Me and obey My commands, then even if your exiled people are at the farthest horizon, I will gather them from there and bring them to the place I have chosen as a dwelling for My Name."

Another passage with much merit is Deuteronomy 30:1-5.

> When all these blessings and curses I have set before you come upon you and you take them to heart wherever the Lord your God disperses you among the nations, and when you and your children return to the Lord your God and obey Him with all your heart and with all your soul according to everything I command you today, then the Lord your God will restore your fortunes and have compassion on you and gather you again from all the nations where He scattered you. Even if you have been banished to the most distant land under the heavens, from there the Lord your God will gather you and bring you back. He will bring you to the land that belonged to your fathers, and you will take possession of it. He will make you more prosperous and numerous than your fathers.

A last Bible verse with this perspective is Zechariah 10:9. "Though I scatter them among the peoples, yet in distant lands they will remember Me. They and their children will survive, and they will return."

In the last two Scripture passages quoted above (Zechariah and Deuteronomy), it should be noted that in both cases the immediate context stresses God's sovereign work in the hearts of Israel, quickening their desire to return. The Deuteronomy passage continues with, "The Lord your God will circumcise your hearts and the hearts of your descendants, so that you may love Him with all your heart and with all your soul, and live."[56] In Zechariah's case, six different verbs are used emphasizing divine activity in bringing a spirit of repentance and salvation to the remnant of the Jewish people.

> I will strengthen the house of Judah and save the house of Joseph. I will restore them because I have compassion on them...Their children will see it and be joyful; their hearts will rejoice in the Lord...Surely I will redeem them; they will be as numerous as before. Though I scatter them among the peoples, yet in distant lands they will remember Me. They and their children will survive, and they will return...I will strengthen them in the Lord and in His name they will walk, declares the Lord.[57]

These above passages reveal that God is able to do more than one thing at a time and more than one thing in the same place. He is obviously bringing Jewish people back to the land today in biblical proportions. But He is also bringing salvation in Messiah Yeshua to many Jewish hearts in every place where the gospel is preached. The large number of Russian-speaking Jews turning to the Lord in the former USSR is ample proof that many Jewish people are repenting prior to their return to Zion.

There's No Place Like Home

On the other hand, the majority of Scripture passages dealing with repentance and return overwhelmingly reflect the same scenario – a return to the land is followed by a national repentance. Four clear examples of this are presented here.

> My eyes will watch over them for their good, and I will bring them back to this land. I will build them up and

56   Deut. 30:6
57   Zech. 10:6-12

not tear them down; I will plant them and not uproot them. I will give them a heart to know me, that I am the Lord. They will be My people, and I will be their God, for they will return to Me with all their heart.[58]

I will surely gather them from all the lands where I banish them in My furious anger and great wrath; I will bring them back to this place and let them live in safety. They will be My people, and I will be their God. I will give them singleness of heart and action, so that they will always fear Me for their own good and the good of their children after them. I will make an everlasting covenant with them: I will never stop doing good to them, and I will inspire them to fear Me, so that they will never turn away from Me. I will rejoice in doing them good and will assuredly plant them in this land with all My heart and soul.[59]

For I will take you out of the nations; I will gather you from all the countries and bring you back into your own land. I will sprinkle clean water on you, and you will be clean; I will cleanse you from all your impurities and from all your idols. I will give you a new heart and put a new spirit in you; I will remove from you your heart of stone and give you a heart of flesh. And I will put My Spirit in you and move you to follow My decrees and be careful to keep My laws.[60]

This is what the Sovereign Lord says to these bones: I will make breath enter you, and you will come to life. I will attach tendons to you and make flesh come upon you and cover you with skin; I will put breath in you, and you will come to life. Then you will know that I am the Lord... O My people, I am going to open your graves and bring you up from them; I will bring you back to the land of Israel.

---

58   Jer. 24:6-7
59   Jer. 32:37-41
60   Ezek. 36:24-27; *cf.*, vv.22, 38; 39:27-28

Then you, My people, will know that I am the Lord, when
I open your graves and bring you up from them. I will
put My Spirit in you and you will live, and I will settle
you in your own land. Then you will know that I the Lord
have spoken, and I have done it, declares the Lord.[61]

The above Scripture passages allow us to conclude that, along
with evangelistic fruit in the countries of the Diaspora, God does
have a major game plan involving the restoration of a large number
of Jewish people to the land in unbelief. This seems to be followed
by a divinely instigated national Jewish revival which sweeps at
least one third[62] of all Israel into a personal relationship with the
God of Jacob.

Purge in the Desert

Another ingredient must be added into the prophetic mixing
bowl. In Ezekiel 20 God prophesies that a major judgment will fall
on many Jewish people as they are being divinely brought back
toward the land of Israel. These are the rebels and the ones who
reject Yeshua. It seems that their fate will be to experience a purge
similar to that of Korah and his comrades in Numbers 16. For this
group of Jewish people, repentance does not occur at all – whether
in the Diaspora or on the soil of Israel.

I will bring you from the nations and gather you from
the countries where you have been scattered – with
a mighty hand and an outstretched arm and with
outpoured wrath. I will bring you into the desert of the
nations and there, face to face, I will execute judgment
upon you. As I judged your fathers in the desert of
the land of Egypt, so I will judge you, declares the
Sovereign Lord. I will take note of you as you pass
under My rod, and I will bring you into the bond of the
covenant. I will purge you of those who revolt and rebel
against Me. Although I will bring them out of the land

---

61   Ezek. 37:5-6, 12-13. But note the order in 37:14: Spirit, settlement, knowledge. In contrast Ezek.
      36:24-27 puts the infilling of the Spirit after the return of the nation to their land.

62   For more biblical background see chapter 16's heading 'Desert Storm Revisited.'

where they are living, yet they will not enter the land of Israel. Then you will know that I am the Lord.[63]

Dancing at Two Weddings

This brief study shows that God, who does all things well, is able to do at least two things at a time. Only He can successfully dance at two weddings! The Lord of all the earth is simultaneously engaged in a two-pronged work of restoration with the Jewish people, as He promised in Isaiah 49. There the prophet declares that God is restoring them physically to the land ('gathering them back') in order to heal their backslidings ('bringing Jacob back').[64] He is raising up the banner of a physically restored Jewish people, and at the same time He is restoring[65] the spirit of the remnant of Israel to Himself.

> And now says the Lord, who formed Me from the womb to be His servant to bring Jacob back to Him in order that Israel might be gathered to Him ... "It is too small a thing that you should be My servant to raise up the tribes of Jacob and to restore the preserved ones of Israel. I will also make You a light of the Gentiles, so that My salvation may reach to the ends of the earth" ... Thus says the Lord, "In a favorable time I have answered You, and in a day of salvation I have helped You; and I will keep You and give You for a covenant of the people, to restore the land, to make them inherit the desolate heritages."[66]

The rhythm of God's word guides us back to the basics and focuses our attention on the essentials. Our main calling isn't to figure out how God's restoration of Israel breaks down into percentages

---

63   Ezek. 20:34-38; *cf.*, 36:33; 39:29 NASB

64   The Hebrew word for 'bring back' is *sbb* (shobab), having the meaning of restoring a backslider; *e.g.*, Jer. 3:22 - *Shuvu banim shovavim* (Return, o sons who go back/backsliding sons).

65   Isaiah uses the verb *l'hashiv* from the root *sub* (shuv), from which root the word *teshuvah* (repentance) also is derived.

66   Isa. 49:5-6, 8 NASB. God is actually doing more than two redemptive acts here. At the same time as He is restoring Israel, He also bringing light to the Gentiles and reaping a massive salvation-harvest from among all the nations!

of physical and spiritual activity, nor is it to chart and defend an inerrant time-line regarding the exact sequence of eschatological events. Whether Israel comes to faith primarily in the land or among the nations, the divine call to intercession and evangelism remains the same: "For thus says the Lord, 'Sing aloud with gladness for Jacob, and shout among the chiefs of the nations; Proclaim, give praise, and say, 'O Lord, save Thy people, the remnant of Israel.'"[67]

---

67   Jer. 31:7 NASB

Chapter Eighteen

Zion: The House of Prayer for All Nations

It was Yeshua's last day on earth. Within a few minutes He would be taken away from the apostles and ascend to the right hand of the Father. Like Elisha on the day Elijah was snatched away, the disciples had one burning question in their hearts, one final request. When will the kingdom of David be physically restored to the Jewish people?

> So when they met together, they asked Him, "Lord, are you at this time going to restore the kingdom to Israel?" He said to them: "It is not for you to know the times or dates the Father has set by His own authority. But you will receive power when the Holy Spirit comes on you; and you will be My witnesses in Jerusalem, and in all Judea and Samaria, and to the ends of the earth."[1]

Yeshua did not rebuke them, say that their understanding was faulty, or roll His eyes and declare "How long must I bear with an

---

1 Acts 1:6-8

evil and unbelieving generation!" The Messiah, just as ardently as His apostles, looked forward to the physical restoration of the Messianic kingdom to Israel. It is true, He told them, that the Father has set specific times and dates when that event will take place. But access to this revelatory information is off-limits to mankind.

The Reality of Restoration

The reality of the full restoration of the kingdom has always been a Jewish messianic hope. The Orthodox Prayer Book quotes from Lamentations 5:21, "*Chadesh yamenu k'kedem*" (Renew our days as in ancient times)! Recently the subject of restoration has also begun to move to the forefront of Christian eschatology. The Charismatic movement and the Church of Christ have each in their own way struggled with the Scriptures, trying to discern God's patterns as He restores the pure truths of the gospel, the Scriptures, the body of Messiah, lay ministry, the spiritual gifts, prayer, intercession and revival. The restoration of Israel is occurring at the same time as restoration is touching these other streams, though some believers are unaware of God's dealings and heart on this matter.

Many believers have shied away from considering the restoration of Israel, having been taught that God will no longer fulfill His physical promises to the Jewish people. For these people, passages such as Micah 4:1-8 raise questions which are hard to answer and which, it seems, few believers have considered. The theme of this chapter, God's 'House of Prayer for All Nations,' will be considered in light of the restoration of Israel.

One thousand years before the apostles asked Yeshua when the restoration of Zion/Jerusalem would occur, the psalmist declared that God has already appointed a specific time and date for that prophetic event. God's restoration of Jerusalem will one day affect even the physical stones and dust of that city. Zion's restoration is close to the heart of God and should be very close to the hearts of all God's children as well. Normally even the mention of that city should stir up compassion in believers' hearts.

But You, O Lord, sit enthroned forever; Your renown endures through all generations. You will arise and have compassion on Zion, for it is time to show favor to her; the appointed time has come. For her stones are dear to Your servants; her very dust moves them to pity. The nations will fear the name of the Lord, all the kings of the earth will revere Your glory.[2]

At Home In The Temple

After Yeshua ascended to the Father, the first Messianic Jews returned to Jerusalem and waited there for the Father's promise. After the Holy Spirit filled them with courage and power on the Jewish Feast of Pentecost, they became bold witnesses for Messiah Yeshua in all of Jerusalem. Much of their time was spent on the biblical ridge of Zion praying, teaching and evangelizing on the Temple Mount. "Every day they continued to meet together in the Temple courts."[3] Peter and John would go up to the Temple for afternoon prayer at the time of the *mincha* service.[4] "All the believers used to meet together in Solomon's Colonnade,"[5] a covered corridor on the Temple Mount. Once "an angel commanded the apostles, 'Go, stand in the Temple courts,' he said, 'and tell the people the full message of this new life'... Day after day, in the Temple courts and from house to house, they never stopped teaching and proclaiming the good news that Yeshua is the Messiah."[6]

When Paul visited Jerusalem he too went up to the Temple Mount to pray, first ceremonially cleansing himself in a Jewish ritual bath, a *mikveh*, before entering the Temple courts.[7] Once, while praying in the Temple precincts, Paul fell into a trance and received a divine visitation.[8] The earliest believers accepted that Temple worship was

---

2 Psa. 102:12-15

3 Acts 2:46

4 *Cf.*, Acts 3:1

5 Acts 5:12

6 Acts 5:20, 42; *cf.*, Acts 21:20-24

7 Acts 24:18

8 Acts 22:17

part of the Jewish people's divine inheritance, as Paul said, "For I could wish that I myself were cursed and cut off from Messiah for the sake of my brothers, those of my own race, the people of Israel. Theirs is the adoption as sons; theirs the divine Glory, the covenants, the receiving of the law, the Temple worship and the promises."[9]

This snapshot of early apostolic life in Jerusalem may raise some unsettling questions. Now that these Jewish believers were under grace, why did they continue to fellowship in the Temple? Were the preachers of the apostolic gospel perhaps unaware of their new freedom in Messiah? How could the apostles worship in a Temple that would be soon be destroyed, as Yeshua had prophesied?[10] How could Paul and the other Messianic Jewish believers participate in bringing sacrifices to the Temple, since they all knew that these physical offerings could add nothing to the atonement of Yeshua?[11] Doesn't belief in Yeshua mean that there is no more place for a physical Temple? If this is indeed true, why then did the apostles believe that God would one day physically restore the kingdom to Israel and that a future Temple would stand again in Jerusalem?[12] How did they integrate these different perspectives while preserving the purity of their faith? Do the Scriptures give us any keys to answer these questions?

The New World Order

The Scriptures tell us that Jerusalem will one day be the capital of the world, home to a world Supreme Court and a reborn and sanctified 'United Nations.' Zion will also be the spiritual center of the earth, since Yeshua Himself will reign from Jerusalem and will honor it with His presence.

In the last days the mountain of the Lord's Temple will

---

9   Rom. 9:3-4

10   Matt. 23:37-39; 24:1-3; Mk. 13:1-4; Lk. 21:5-7

11   Heb. 10:1-12. Paul saw no contradiction between this truth and the apostolic counsel of Acts 21:23-24.

12   *Eg.*, 2 Thess. 2:3-5; Rev. 11:1-2, 17, 19

be established as chief among the mountains; it will be raised above the hills, and peoples will stream to it. Many nations will come and say, "Come, let us go up to the mountain of the Lord, to the House of the God of Jacob. He will teach us His ways, so that we may walk in His paths. The teaching will go out from Zion, the word of the Lord from Jerusalem. He will judge between many peoples and will settle disputes for strong nations far and wide."[13]

The centrality and preeminence of Jerusalem at the End of Days is a prophetic theme throughout the Bible. Jeremiah says, "At that time they will call Jerusalem 'The Throne of the Lord', and all nations will gather in Jerusalem to honor the name of the Lord."[14] The psalmist agrees, "So the name of the Lord will be declared in Zion and His praise in Jerusalem when the peoples and the kingdoms assemble to worship the Lord."[15] Isaiah adds, "The moon will be abashed, the sun ashamed; for the Lord Almighty will reign on Mount Zion and in Jerusalem, and before its elders, gloriously."[16]

Zion's physical restoration ties in with a prophecy in the Book of Amos. "In that day I will restore David's fallen tent. I will repair its broken places, restore its ruins, and build it as it used to be, so that they may possess the remnant of Edom and all the nations that bear My name, declares the Lord, who will do these things."[17]

What did Amos mean by the term 'David's fallen tent,' and how did 'it used to be?' 'David's tent' refers to the mighty dynasty of the House of David, the kingly line and rule established by God's irrevocable covenant in Second Samuel chapter seven.[18] This wonderful dynasty was severely weakened when five-sixths of the kingdom split off and broke away during the days of Rehoboam.[19] Instead of one smooth national edifice, the Jewish people were

---

13 Mic. 4:1-3; *cf.*, Isa. 2:1-3

14 Jer. 3:19

15 Psa. 102:21-22

16 Isa. 24:23

17 Amos 9:11-12

18 2 Sam. 7:27; 1 Chron. 17:10, 25; Psa. 89:1-4, 27-37

19 1 Ki. 12:1-19

broken in two – Israel in the north and Judah in the south. Within two hundred years Isaiah was bemoaning the damage done to the lineage of David, comparing the once glorious dynasty to a burned and smoldering tree stump.[20] But there was hope for David's fallen tent: it was revealed to Isaiah that a green sprig would shoot up from the ravaged tree-stump of Jesse, and from the roots of David's House a messianic Branch would arise and bear fruit.[21] Isaiah prophesied that one day the Messiah son of David would come and re-establish his forefather's rule over all the Jewish people.

The Good Old Days

The high point of the Davidic dynasty in history past, 'how it used to be,' occurred during the latter part of David's reign and the first part of Solomon's rule.[22] Father and son ruled the surrounding countries east and north of Israel, and Israel's enemies were all on the defensive. The Jewish people's resulting peace and prosperity became the envy of the Middle East.[23]

But the prophetic Scriptures declare that the zenith of the Davidic dynasty is still future. Its scope will be international. David's descendant the Messiah will reign over the whole earth, exercising leadership and dominance from Jerusalem. "Of the increase of His government and peace there will be no end. He will reign on David's throne and over his kingdom, establishing and upholding it with justice and righteousness from that time on and forever. The zeal of the Lord Almighty will accomplish this."[24] "In that day the Root of Jesse will stand as a banner for the peoples; the nations will rally to Him, and His place of rest will be glorious."[25] The psalmists add other important details:

---

20   Isa. 6:13; 7:13-14; 11:1. Jesse was David's father, and the Davidic king was also known among the Jewish people as 'the root of Jesse,' he who sprang from David's loins.

21   Isa. 11:1

22   2 Sam.6-8; 1 Ki. 4:21-34

23   1 Ki. 10:1-10

24   Isa. 9:7

25   Isa. 11:10

He will rule from sea to sea and from the River to the ends of the earth. The desert tribes will bow before him and his enemies will lick the dust. The kings of Tarshish and of distant shores will bring tribute to him; the kings of Sheba and Seba will present him gifts. All kings will bow down to him and all nations will serve him.[26]

I will crush his foes before him and strike down his adversaries. My faithful love will be with him, and through My name his horn will be exalted. I will set his hand over the sea, his right hand over the rivers. He will call out to Me, 'You are my Father, my God, the Rock my Savior.' I will also appoint him My firstborn, the most exalted of the kings of the earth. I will maintain My love to him forever, and My covenant with him will never fail. I will establish his line forever, his throne as long as the heavens endure.[27]

The apostles believed wholeheartedly that Yeshua was the Messiah, the glorious Son of David. They once asked Him what governmental authority they would receive when the Davidic kingdom would be established on earth. Yeshua promised Peter and the apostles that they would share in His Davidic authority when He returned to sit on David's throne.[28]

Peter answered Him, "We have left everything to follow You! What then will there be for us?" Yeshua said to them, "I tell you the truth, at the renewal of all things, when the Son of Man sits on His glorious throne, you who have followed Me will also sit on twelve thrones, judging the twelve tribes of Israel."[29]

26   Psa. 72:8-11

27   Psa. 89:23-29

28   Lk. 1:31-33: "You will be with child and give birth to a son, and you are to give Him the name Yeshua. He will be great and will be called the Son of the Most High. The Lord God will give Him the throne of His father David, and He will reign over the house of Jacob forever; His kingdom will never end.

29   Matt. 19:27-28

Dinner is Served!

When Messiah takes up His throne, great spiritual riches will stream out of Jerusalem. On the Mount of Zion a once-in-a-lifetime Messianic Banquet will be served to all the nations, a magnificent supper which is still the subject of traditional Jewish songs. On that day the power of death and disease over the whole earth will be drastically curtailed,[30] and the Jewish people will never again suffer disgrace and humiliation at the hands of the Gentile world.

> On this mountain the Lord Almighty will prepare a feast of rich food for all peoples, a banquet of aged wine "the best of meats and the finest of wines. On this mountain He will destroy the shroud that enfolds all peoples, the sheet that covers all nations; He will swallow up death forever. The Sovereign Lord will wipe away the tears from all faces; He will remove the disgrace of His people from all the earth... The hand of the Lord will rest on this mountain.[31]

In the day of Messiah's glory the nations of the world will discover that "the way to happiness and freedom ... comes from submitting to Israel's God and the people chosen to be a blessing to the world."[32] On a weekly and monthly basis they will send emissaries to Mount Zion to worship the Lord. "From one New Moon to another and from one Sabbath to another, all mankind will come and bow down before Me, says the Lord."[33] The Hebrew calendar will become the internationally accepted calendar and the Jewish feast days (Sabbath, New Moon, Passover and Tabernacles) will be celebrated throughout the world.[34]

Gentile delight in the God of Israel, in the priority of the Jewish

---

30 Isa. 33:24; 65:20 where death still exists though it will be severely curtailed and will only be the result of personal sin.

31 Isa. 25:6-10

32 Saucy, Robert L., *The Case* for Progressive Dispensationalism (Grand Rapids: Zondervan, 1993) p. 303.

33 Isa. 66:23

34 *Cf.,* Lev. 23:1-4. God describes the Hebrew calendar and the feast cycle as His own personal calendar though, at the present time, He accommodates Himself to the differing calendars of mankind.

people and in the centrality of Jerusalem will go hand in hand in that day. "When the Lord will have compassion on Jacob and again choose Israel, and settle them in their own land, then strangers will join them and attach themselves to the house of Jacob."[35] "In those days ten men from all languages and nations will take firm hold of one Jew by the hem of his robe and say, 'Let us go with you, because we have heard that God is with you.'"[36]

Daniel and the Temple of Doom

Since the Scriptures speak warmly of a restoration of the Jewish people, some Christians have concluded that the present plans of a few ultra-Orthodox Israeli groups to rebuild a Temple on Mount Zion are also worthy of support. Some confusion exists in Christian circles as to whether a Third Temple[37] would fulfill prophecy negatively or positively.

The Bible actually refers to the existence of two future Temples. The Third Temple will be decidedly negative, while the Fourth Temple will be decidedly positive. In his letter to the believers of Thessalonica, Paul reminds them that he had repeatedly taught them that the Anti-Christ, the man of lawlessness, would come to Mount Zion, enter the Temple and demand worship for himself which should properly be given only to God.

> Don't let anyone deceive you in any way, for that
> day will not come until the rebellion occurs and the
> man of lawlessness is revealed, the man doomed to
> destruction. He will oppose and will exalt himself
> over everything that is called God or is worshipped, so
> that he sets himself up in God's Temple, proclaiming
> himself to be God. Don't you remember that when
> I was with you I used to tell you these things?[38]

---

35 Isa. 14:1 NASB

36 Zech. 8:23

37 The First Temple was built by Solomon. The Second Temple was begun by Zerubbabel, expanded by the Maccabees and completed by Herod the Great. The Third and Fourth Temples are still future.

38 2 Thess. 2:3-5. For a differing position see *Israel, the Church and the Last Days*, by Dan Juster and Keith Intrater, Destiny Image, Shippensburg, 1990.

The Third Temple will be the stage upon which the Anti-Messiah will be exposed. The present Orthodox Jewish move to rebuild the Temple is unwittingly playing into the sinister hands of Satan. Satan's goal is to create a counterfeit Temple on Mount Zion and there to reveal a counterfeit 'messiah.' His scheme is to counterfeit God's holy revelation of the real Messiah on Mount Zion. The current preparations to rebuild the Jerusalem Temple are not worthy of believers' support.

This Third Temple is described in two other places, and in both cases the context is very dark. An angel tells John the Revelator that both Jerusalem and the courts of a future Temple will be desecrated by Gentiles for 42 months.

> I was given a reed like a measuring rod and was told, "Go and measure the Temple of God and the altar, and count the worshipers there. But exclude the outer court; do not measure it, because it has been given to the Gentiles. They will trample on the holy city for 42 months."[39]

Daniel the prophet was told by the angel Gabriel that the Messiah would come to Israel but be rejected and murdered. Some time after that the city of Jerusalem and the Second Temple would be destroyed. Then, at the end of the age, a man would arise whose ethnic origin would be tied to the Romans, the nation which destroyed the Second Temple in 70 AD. This man would set up some kind of idol called an 'abomination which causes destruction' in a rebuilt Third Temple.

> He will confirm a covenant with many for one 'seven.' In the middle of the 'seven' he will put an end to sacrifice and offering. And on a wing [of the Temple] he will set up an abomination that causes desolation, until the end that is decreed is poured out on him.[40]

The Third Temple will be the place where the 'abomination of desolation' (perhaps this is the same as the statue or image of the

39   Rev. 11:1-2
40   Dan. 9:27

'beast' described in Revelation 13) will be set up and worshipped. This Temple will not be a Temple of Delight but a Temple of Doom.

Full Speed Reverse?

Some believers find it distressing to consider the prospect of any rebuilt Jewish Temple, whether positive or negative. Some believe that Messiah has done away with Temples, and that we are now His temple.[41] Others feel that the flow of revelation has progressed from earthly and carnal to heavenly and spiritual. It is their opinion that a return to a physical Temple on Mount Zion would be a reactionary move – 'full speed reverse!' When these believers run into texts like Ezekiel 40-48 and Isaiah 56, they often 'transform' the meaning of these Scriptures through the use of allegory into poetic descriptions of the Christian Church.

But is it going backwards to believe that God's kingdom will one day be established on earth as it is in Heaven? Is it carnal to interpret the Scriptures as their Hebrew hearers would have done? Perhaps a question more to the point would be: Why do some Christians today react in trepidation when the subject of a rebuilt Temple on Mount Zion comes up? Why are some of us uneasy about such a House, when the apostles all felt at home in the Temple?

It's All Greek To Me!

The Christian Church has its foundations and origins in the Jewish world, but it has also been strongly influenced by Greek philosophies and the ancient Hellenistic world. One Christian philosopher has commented that the "element of the Greek spirit had great influence on ... the Christian movement in the first three centuries. At the same time it was the factor which was operative at the bottom of some of the heresies which arose."[42] Part of this Greek

---

41   Believers' physical bodies are certainly called the temple of the Holy Spirit in 1 Cor. 3:16-17, 19 and
      2 Cor. 6:16 , and believers' physical bodies are corporately and symbolically described as a temple in
      Eph. 2:21. Yeshua referred to His own physical body as a temple in Jn. 2:19-21. These figurative uses
      do not claim to invalidate the biblical prophetic words which affirm the rebuilding of a physical
      Temple in Jerusalem. It is not a case of 'either or' but of 'both and.'

42   Stobe, Ralph, *Christianity and Classical Civilization* (Grand Rapids: Eerdmans, 1950), p. 49.

influence was a basic belief in Platonic dualism.

> Platonism holds that there are two worlds: the visible, material world and the invisible, spiritual world. The visible or phenomenal world is in tension with the invisible or conceptual world. Because it is imperfect and a source of evil, the material world is inferior to that of the spiritual. In this view, the human soul originates in the heavenly realm, from which it fell into the realm of matter. Though human beings find themselves related to both these worlds, they long for release from their physical bodies so that their true selves (their souls) might take flight back to the permanent world of the celestial and divine.[43]

Hebrew thought which has been influenced by the Bible has come to conclusions radically different from Platonism. God created matter and the world, and prior to the Fall it was originally good in every way and untainted by sin. God is bringing salvation into this world, and eventually will fully redeem and sanctify His physical creation. Most important for this discussion, Hebrew expectation knows that God's restoration will occur in the physical world. For example, the expectation that the body will be physically resurrected is a happy Hebrew thought, whereas the Greeks thought of physical resurrection as primitive and obscene, longing to be free of flesh and blood. The Jewish hope for restoration is linked to space and time. That hope is based on God's concrete promises to a real Semitic people who inhabit a tangible Middle Eastern piece of real estate. The biblical worldview is that restoration happens in the real three-dimensional world and to physical bodies.

Karl Barth has noted: "The Bible...is a Jewish book. It cannot be read and understood and expounded unless we are prepared to become Jews with the Jews."[44] The Hebrew prophets expected

---

43 Wilson, Marvin R., *Our Father Abraham: Jewish Roots of the Christian Faith* (Grand Rapids: Eerdmans, 1989), p. 168

44 Barth, Karl, *Church Dogmatics*, trans. Geoffrey W. Bromiley, et al. (Edinburgh: T. & T. Clark, 1956), 1/2:511

physical restoration for Israel and all the nations. Both a Temple and a House of Prayer for Israel and all the nations are an integral part of that vision.

The Heavenly Temple

As the nation of Israel waited fearfully at the foot of Mount Sinai, God was giving Moses an amazing revelation of Heaven. Moses' spiritual eyes were opened and he began to see the outline of a radiant building – a Temple in Heaven! The Lord told Moses to pay close attention to this Sanctuary and to memorize exactly how everything in the Heavenly Temple was constructed. Soon Moses would carry out God's command to build an exact replica of this Temple on earth, reflecting the glorious original which is in Heaven.

> Then have them make a sanctuary for Me, and I will dwell among them. Make this tabernacle and all its furnishings exactly like the pattern I will show you[45]...A talent of pure gold is to be used for the lampstand and all these accessories. See that you make them according to the pattern shown you on the mountain.[46]

> The Lord said to Moses, "Speak to Aaron and say to him, 'When you set up the seven lamps, they are to light the area in front of the lampstand.' Aaron did so; he set up the lamps so that they faced forward on the lampstand, just as the Lord commanded Moses. This is how the lampstand was made: it was made of hammered gold from its base to its blossoms. The lampstand was made exactly like the pattern the Lord had shown Moses.[47]

Divine Architecture

Centuries later Stephen, filled with the Holy Spirit, reminded his listeners of the Temple's Heavenly architectural origin. "Our

---

45   Exod. 25:8-9
46   Exod. 25:39-40
47   Num. 8:1-4

forefathers had the Tabernacle of the Testimony with them in the desert. It had been made as God directed Moses, according to the pattern he had seen."[48] The anonymous writer of the Book to the Hebrews expounds on the subject of the Heavenly Temple, affirming Moses' and Stephen's revelation as accurate.

> The point of what we are saying is this: we do have such a high priest, who sat down at the right hand of the throne of the Majesty in heaven, and who serves in the sanctuary, the true Tabernacle set up by the Lord, not by man. If He were on earth, He would not be a priest, for there are already men who offer the gifts prescribed by the law. They serve at a sanctuary that is a copy and shadow of what is in heaven. This is why Moses was warned when he was about to build the tabernacle: "See to it that you make everything according to the pattern shown you on the mountain."[49]

The architectural plans for both the Tabernacle in Heaven and the Temple on earth were drawn up by God Himself. The activity of the Levitical priests on earth was designed by God to mirror and foreshadow Yeshua's activity as our great High Priest in Heaven. Just as the earthly High Priest would enter the Holy of Holies once a year on Yom Kippur to offer the blood of atonement, so Yeshua entered the Heavenly inner sanctuary, passed through a Heavenly curtain and came into the presence of the Father.

> In fact, the law requires that nearly everything be cleansed with blood, and without the shedding of blood there is no forgiveness. It was necessary, then, for the copies of the heavenly things to be purified with these sacrifices, but the heavenly things themselves with better sacrifices than these. For Messiah did not enter a man-made sanctuary that was only a copy of the true one; He entered Heaven itself, now to appear for us in God's presence. Nor did He enter Heaven to offer Himself again and again, the

---

48   Acts 7:44
49   Heb. 8:1-5

way the high priest enters the Most Holy Place every year
with blood that is not his own. Then Messiah would have
had to suffer many times since the creation of the world.
But now He has appeared once for all at the end of the
ages to do away with sin by the sacrifice of Himself.[50]

The writer of the Book of Hebrews says that these details about
the Temple in Heaven are given to believers everywhere for
encouragement, so that we might be wooed into the very presence
of God without fear or guilt.

Therefore, brothers, since we have confidence to
enter the Most Holy Place by the blood of Yeshua,
... and since we have a great priest over the House
of God, let us draw near to God with a sincere
heart in full assurance of faith, having our hearts
sprinkled to cleanse us from a guilty conscience
and having our bodies washed with pure water.[51]

Another astounding description of the Heavenly Temple is
found in Isaiah 6 where the prophet is commissioned anew to go
to his people. Isaiah is brought into the Heavenly Temple to the
very Throne of God. Mighty angels surround the Lord, and the
room is full of glory and smoke. Isaiah beholds the thresholds
and doorposts of the Heavenly Sanctuary, as well as an altar of
atonement complete with coals and tongs.

In the year that King Uzziah died, I saw the Lord seated
on a throne, high and exalted, and the train of His robe
filled the Temple. Above Him were seraphs, each with six
wings: with two wings they covered their faces, with two
they covered their feet, and with two they were flying.
And they were calling to one another: "Holy, holy, holy is
the Lord Almighty; the whole earth is full of His glory."
At the sound of their voices the doorposts and thresholds
shook and the Temple was filled with smoke. Then one
of the seraphs flew to me with a live coal in his hand,

---

50   Heb. 9:22-26; *cf.*, Heb. 6:19-20; 7:22, 24-25; 10:11-14
51   Heb. 10:19, 21-22

which he had taken with tongs from the altar. With it he touched my mouth and said, "See, this has touched your lips; your guilt is taken away and your sin atoned for."[52]

Many other prophets had a similar revelation of the Heavenly Temple, as the following brief quotes demonstrate: "Hear, O peoples, all of you, listen, O earth and all who are in it, that the Sovereign Lord may witness against you, the Lord from His holy Temple. Look! The Lord is coming from His dwelling place; He comes down and treads the high places of the earth"[53] "But the Lord is in His holy Temple; let all the earth be silent before Him."[54]

The Eternal Heavenly Temple

The resurrection of Messiah Yeshua has not done away with this Heavenly Temple. The Heavenly Temple remains the abode of God, the seat of His glorious rule. Yeshua promises the overcoming Jewish and Gentile believers of Philadelphia in Asia Minor that in eternity they will dwell securely in God's Heavenly Temple. "To Him who overcomes I will make a pillar in the Temple of My God. Never again will he leave it."[55] The martyrs of the Great Tribulation will stand "before the Throne of God and serve Him day and night in His Temple; and He who sits on the Throne will spread His tent over them."[56]

At one point in his stupendous vision, John saw that "God's Temple in Heaven was opened, and within His Temple was seen the Ark of His Covenant. And there came flashes of lightning, rumblings, peals of thunder, an earthquake and a great hailstorm."[57] Further on in the vision, John says, "After this I looked and in Heaven the Temple, that is, the Tabernacle of the Testimony, was opened ... And the Temple was filled with smoke from the glory of God and

---

52   Isa. 6:1-4, 6-7
53   Mic. 1:2-3
54   Hab. 2:20
55   Rev. 3:12
56   Rev. 7:15
57   Rev. 11:19; *cf.* 14:15, 17; 15:6; 16:1, 17

from His power, and no one could enter the Temple until the seven plagues of the seven angels were completed."[58]

Six hundred earthly years before John the Revelator, Daniel the seer was given a fiery vision of that same Temple in Heaven.

> As I looked, thrones were set in place, and the Ancient of Days took His seat. His clothing was as white as snow; the hair of His head was white like wool. His throne was flaming with fire, and its wheels were all ablaze. A river of fire was flowing, coming out from before Him. Thousands upon thousands attended Him; ten thousand times ten thousand stood before Him. The court was seated, and the books were opened ... In my vision at night I looked, and there before me was One like a son of man, coming with the clouds of heaven. He approached the Ancient of Days and was led into His presence.[59]

Throughout eternity the Temple of God has stood, stands and will continue to stand in Heaven. This biblical fact should not surprise us. God is both King and Redeemer, and His palace is also His Temple. Since God is pleased to let mankind know about the existence of His Heavenly Temple, we should not be stumbled or offended when He commands us to build a true-to-scale copy of His Heavenly Temple here on earth.

On Earth as it is in Heaven

The Fourth Temple in Jerusalem will be a spiritual magnet for the whole world because it will be the abode of Messiah Yeshua.

> Many peoples and the inhabitants of many cities will yet come, and the inhabitants of one city will go to another and say, "Let us go at once to entreat the Lord and seek the Lord Almighty. I myself am going." And many peoples and powerful nations will come to Jerusalem to seek the Lord Almighty and to entreat Him.[60]

---

58   Rev. 15:5, 8
59   Dan. 7:9-10, 13
60   Zech. 8:20-23

In that day no believer will be denied access to the Temple courts. Deep spiritual fellowship and joy will flow between Jews and Gentiles, and the central place of meeting, worship and celebration will be the Temple Mount.

> Let no foreigner who has bound himself to the Lord
> say, "The Lord will surely exclude me from His people."
> And let not any eunuch complain, "I am only a dry
> tree." For this is what the Lord says: "To the eunuchs
> who keep My Sabbaths, who choose what pleases Me
> and hold fast to My covenant – to them I will give
> within My temple and its walls a memorial and a name
> better than sons and daughters; I will give them an
> everlasting name that will not be cut off. And foreigners
> who bind themselves to the Lord to serve Him, to love
> the name of the Lord, and to worship Him, all who
> keep the Sabbath without desecrating it and who hold
> fast to My covenant – these I will bring to My holy
> mountain and give them joy in My House of prayer.
> Their burnt offerings and sacrifices will be accepted on
> My altar; for My house will be called 'a House of Prayer
> for All Nations.'" The Sovereign Lord declares – He
> who gathers the exiles of Israel – "I will gather still
> others to them besides those already gathered."[61]

God Himself will choose some Gentiles to conduct Temple worship and participate in priestly ministry from among the nations who helped bring the Jewish people back to Jerusalem and to the Temple Mount.

> And they will bring all your brothers, from all the nations,
> to My holy mountain in Jerusalem as an offering to the
> Lord – on horses, in chariots and wagons, and on mules
> and camels, says the Lord. They will bring them, as the
> Israelites bring their grain offerings, to the Temple of the
> Lord in ceremonially clean vessels. And I will select some

---

61   Isa. 56:3-8. Yeshua interpreted the term 'A House of Prayer for All Nations' in Isaiah 56 as referring
to a physical Temple; *cf.*, Mk. 11:14-18.

of them also to be priests and Levites, says the Lord.[62]

A yearly international pilgrimage to Jerusalem will center around the Feast of Tabernacles. Attendance at this feast will be compulsory, and most nations will respond with joy and celebration. The nation of Egypt is prophetically singled out as a potential troublemaker, a country whose heart may be somewhat cool toward Israel and less than fully dependent on God for its physical survival.

> Then the survivors from all the nations that have attacked Jerusalem will go up year after year to worship the King, the Lord Almighty, and to celebrate the Feast of Tabernacles. If any of the peoples of the earth do not go up to Jerusalem to worship the King, the Lord Almighty, they will have no rain. If the Egyptian people do not go up and take part, they will have no rain. The Lord will bring on them the plague He inflicts on the nations that do not go up to celebrate the Feast of Tabernacles. This will be the punishment of Egypt and the punishment of all the nations that do not go up to celebrate the Feast of Tabernacles.[63]

Footrest of the Lord

God even has a special name for this future Temple. He calls it 'the place of My feet' – a place for Him to rest His feet while on the earth, a divine footrest! "The glory of Lebanon will come to you, the pine, the fir and the cypress together, to adorn the place of My sanctuary; and I will glorify the place of My feet ... but you will call your walls Salvation and your gates Praise."[64] "While the man was standing beside me, I heard Someone speaking to me from inside the Temple. He said: 'Son of man, this is the place of My throne and the place for the soles of My feet. This is where I will live among the Israelites forever.'"[65]

---

62   Isa. 66:20-23

63   Zech. 14:16-19. For a more positive aspect of Egypt's future relationship to Israel see Isa.19:18-25

64   Isa. 60:13, 18

65   Ezek. 43:6-7

The Scriptures describe the joys of daily Jewish life when Messiah Yeshua reigns from Mount Zion. Israelis will be able to finish work at the end of the day and travel to Jerusalem to meet their God. The sanctuary priests (who will be predominantly Jewish) will be delighted with their working conditions, and all the nations of the world will be appreciative towards the Jewish people. For the first time in history the entire nation of Israel will be filled with a servant's heart, and all the nations of the world will be drawn closer to the face of God by looking at the lives of the Jewish people.

> I will build you up again and you will be rebuilt, O Virgin Israel... There will be a day when watchmen cry out on the hills of Ephraim, 'Come, let us go up to Zion, to the Lord our God.' ... They will come and shout for joy on the heights of Zion ... I will satisfy the priests with abundance, and My people will be filled with My bounty, declares the Lord.[66]

> Yet in the towns of Judah and the streets of Jerusalem ... there will be heard once more the sounds of joy and gladness, the voices of bride and bridegroom, and the voices of those who bring thank offerings to the House of the Lord, saying, "Give thanks to the Lord Almighty, for the Lord is good; His love endures forever." For I will restore the fortunes of the land as they were before, says the Lord.[67]

> And you will be called priests of the Lord, you will be named ministers of our God. You will feed on the wealth of nations, and in their riches you will boast ... Their descendants will be known among the nations and their offspring among the peoples. All who see them will acknowledge that they are a people the Lord has blessed.[68]

---

66   Jer. 31:4, 6, 12, 14
67   Jer. 33:10-11
68   Isa. 61:1-11

Holiness Unto the Lord

The Temple will be a place of holiness. The very presence of God will be manifested there as Messiah Yeshua reigns from Mount Zion. As a matter of fact, all of Jerusalem will be bathed in a special holiness, irradiated by the Holy Spirit of God.

> In that day the Branch of the Lord will be beautiful and glorious, and the fruit of the land will be the pride and glory of the survivors in Israel. Those who are left in Zion, who remain in Jerusalem, will be called holy, all who are recorded among the living in Jerusalem. The Lord will wash away the filth of the women of Zion; He will cleanse the bloodstains from Jerusalem by a spirit of judgment and a spirit of fire. Then the Lord will create over all of Mount Zion and over those who assemble there a cloud of smoke by day and a glow of flaming fire by night; over all the glory will be a canopy. It will be a shelter and shade from the heat of the day, and a refuge and hiding place from the storm and rain.[69]

Zechariah tells us that even the stoves and cookware of Jerusalem's inhabitants will be sanctified by the physical nearness of God. As a result, a visit to Jerusalem will be a spiritual experience of the most exhilarating kind.

> On that day 'Holy To The Lord' will be inscribed on the bells of the horses, and the cooking pots in the Lord's House will be like the sacred bowls in front of the altar. Every pot in Jerusalem and Judah will be holy to the Lord Almighty, and all who come to sacrifice will take some of the pots and cook in them. And on that day there will no longer be a Canaanite in the House of the Lord Almighty.[70]

In the Book of Ezekiel a prophetic word is spoken over the descendants of the tribe of Levi. In Ezekiel's day some of them had given in to idolatry and had led the people of Israel astray. God promises to remember the deeds of these particular ones

69   Isa. 4:2-6
70   Zech. 14:20-21

throughout the generations and, when the Temple is finally rebuilt, He will not allow the descendants of these specific Levitical families to minister in the Holy Place and the Most Holy Place. They will be allowed to have the consolation of a public ministry, but the greatest privilege, ministering in secret before the very presence of God, will be withheld from them.

> The Levites who went far from Me when Israel went astray and who wandered from Me after their idols must bear the consequences of their sin. They may serve in My sanctuary, having charge of the gates of the Temple and serving in it ... and stand before the people and serve them. But because they served them in the presence of their idols and made the house of Israel fall into sin, therefore I have sworn with uplifted hand that they must bear the consequences of their sin, declares the Sovereign Lord. They are not to come near to serve Me as priests or come near any of My holy things or My most holy offerings; they must bear the shame of their detestable practices. Yet I will put them in charge of the duties of the Temple and all the work that is to be done in it. But the priests, who are Levites and descendants of Zadok and who faithfully carried out the duties of My sanctuary when the Israelites went astray from Me, are to come near to minister before Me; ... They alone are to enter My sanctuary; they alone are to come near My table to minister before Me and perform My service.[71]

The roads leading into Jerusalem will be known as *Derech HaKadosh*, the Holy Highway. The Negev and Aravah deserts will be transformed into a lush paradise, and lakes and rivers will appear out of arid soil. Isaiah prophesies that a holy Jewish people will skip along a holy Hebrew highway, laughing and singing joyous Israeli

---

71   Ezek. 44:10-16. For a penetrating application of this principle to ministry today, see David Fitzpatrick's *Issues of the Heart/Let My People Go* (Antioch: Issachar, 1992) available from Issachar Ministries, 2612 Mountain Laurel Drive, Antioch, TN 37013. The sacrifices and offerings in this future Temple described in Ezekiel 40-46 can be understood as commemorative and instructional: they commemorate the atoning death of Yeshua, they remind the worshiper of the great cost Messiah has paid in His own blood, and they serve as a sobering testimony to the wages of sin.

songs.

> Like the crocus, [the desert] will burst into bloom; it will
> rejoice greatly and shout for joy. The glory of Lebanon
> will be given to it, the splendor of Carmel and Sharon;
> they will see the glory of the Lord, the splendor of our
> God ... Then will the eyes of the blind be opened and
> the ears of the deaf unstopped. Then will the lame leap
> like a deer, and the mute tongue shout for joy. Water will
> gush forth in the wilderness and streams in the desert.
> The burning sand will become a pool, the thirsty ground
> bubbling springs. In the haunts where jackals once lay,
> grass and reeds and papyrus will grow. And a highway
> will be there; it will be called the Way of Holiness. The
> unclean will not journey on it; it will be for those who
> walk in that Way; wicked fools will not go about on it. No
> lion will be there, nor will any ferocious beast get up on
> it; they will not be found there. But only the redeemed
> will walk there, and the ransomed of the Lord will
> return. They will enter Zion with singing; everlasting joy
> will crown their heads. Gladness and joy will overtake
> them, and sorrow and sighing will flee away.[72]

There'll Be Some Changes Made!

The prophets describe geographical changes which will take place in the Days of the Messiah. The final borders of Israel will be established never to be redrawn.[73] The land promised to Abraham, Isaac and Jacob will at last be their possession and the possession of the entire Jewish people. The Book of Hebrews says that Abraham was called by God to the country of Canaan and was promised that he would one day receive that territory as a physical inheritance. But Abraham never inherited this promise while he was alive. Abraham died looking forward to the day when God Himself would establish Abraham's physical inheritance. The God who had

---

72 Isa. 35:1-10

73 Ezek. 47:13-20

given Abraham the prophetic promise of the land of Israel, Jehovah Jireh, would one day see to it that Jerusalem would be established as the chief city among the mountains.'

> By faith Abraham, when called to go to a place he would later receive as his inheritance, obeyed and went, even though he did not know where he was going. By faith he made his home in the promised land like a stranger in a foreign country; he lived in tents, as did Isaac and Jacob, who were heirs with him of the same promise. For he was looking forward to the city with foundations, whose architect and builder is God.[74]

The city of Jerusalem and its Hill of Zion will be internationally known as the City of Festivals and Feasts, as a city characterized by peace and tranquillity. A river will come out from under the threshold of the Temple and pour east, transforming the Dead Sea into a living body of water with its own fishing industry.[75] As the river flows westward, it will turn Jerusalem into 'the Venice of the Middle East.'

> Look upon Zion, the city of our festivals; your eyes will see Jerusalem, a peaceful abode, a tent that will not be moved; its stakes will never be pulled up, nor any of its ropes broken. There the Lord will be our Mighty One. It will be like a place of broad rivers and streams. No galley with oars will ride them, no mighty ship will sail them. For the Lord is our judge, the Lord is our lawgiver, the Lord is our king; it is He who will save us...No one living in Zion will say, "I am ill"; and the sins of those who dwell there will be forgiven.[76]

Isaiah describes the fullness of the day of restoration. "The Lord will surely comfort Zion and will look with compassion on all her ruins; He will make her deserts like Eden, her wastelands like the garden of the Lord. Joy and gladness will be found in her,

---

74   Heb. 11:8-10; *cf.,* Psa. 78:69; 87:1; Isa.14:32 where God is the Builder and Establisher of Jerusalem.

75   Ezek. 47:1-12; Zech. 14:8

76   Isa. 33:20-22, 24

thanksgiving and the sound of singing."[77] Micah stresses that the Davidic king and the Davidic kingdom will be fully restored to the Jewish people, as in days of old. "As for you, O watchtower of the flock, O stronghold of the Daughter of Zion, the former dominion will be restored to you; kingship will come to the Daughter of Jerusalem."[78]

> But be glad and rejoice forever in what I will create, for
> I will create Jerusalem to be a delight and its people
> a joy. I will rejoice over Jerusalem and take delight in
> My people; the sound of weeping and of crying will be
> heard in it no more. Never again will there be in it an
> infant who lives but a few days, or an old man who does
> not live out his years; he who dies at a hundred will be
> thought a mere youth; he who fails to reach a hundred
> will be considered accursed. They will build houses
> and dwell in them; they will plant vineyards and eat
> their fruit. No longer will they build houses and others
> live in them, or plant and others eat. For as the days
> of a tree, so will be the days of My people; My chosen
> ones will long enjoy the works of their hands. They will
> not toil in vain or bear children doomed to misfortune;
> for they will be a people blessed by the Lord, they and
> their descendants with them. Before they call I will
> answer; while they are still speaking I will hear.[79]

Gentiles in the Promised Land

Along with the full restoration of the Jewish people to their own homeland, God will bring restoration to all nations, each in their own appointed homeland. At the same time there will be some Gentiles who will have bound themselves and their destiny to the Jewish people, as Ruth did to Naomi. These non-Jews will live among their newfound Jewish family with full rights and full

---

77 Isa. 51:1-3; *cf.*, 52:7-9

78 Mic. 4:1-8

79 Isa. 65:18-24

acceptance.

> You are to allot it as an inheritance for yourselves
> and for the aliens who have settled among you and
> who have children. You are to consider them as
> native-born Israelites; along with you they are to be
> allotted an inheritance among the tribes of Israel. In
> whatever tribe the alien settles, there you are to give
> him his inheritance, declares the Sovereign Lord.[80]

The Ultimate Temple

The 'House of Prayer for All Nations' is described in Ezekiel 40 - 47 as the Temple in Zion. This magnificent structure will be the site of prayer gatherings for all the nations of the world. It is probable that the Temple's courtyard[81] will be used for public prayer and worship of God, as well as for intercession, thanksgiving and praise. The Lord Himself will be present on the Temple Mount for many of these activities, as it is written: "And the name of the city from that time on will be: The Lord Is There."[82] The Glory of God, the *Shechinah*, will fill this Temple, like the Holy Spirit filled Solomon's Temple on its day of dedication.[83]

> Then the man brought me by way of the north gate to
> the front of the Temple. I looked and saw the glory of
> the Lord filling the Temple of the Lord, and I fell face
> down[84]... Son of man, describe the Temple to the people
> of Israel, that they may be ashamed of their sins. Let
> them consider the plan, and if they are ashamed of all
> they have done, make known to them the design of
> the Temple – its arrangement, its exits and entrances
> – its whole design and all its regulations and laws.
> Write these down before them so that they may be

---

80   Ezek. 47:22-23

81   Ezek. 40:17

82   Ezek. 48:35

83   1 Ki.8:10-11 "When the priests withdrew from the Holy Place, the cloud filled the Temple of the Lord. And the priests could not perform their service because of the cloud, for the glory of the Lord filled His Temple"; *cf.*, Isa. 6:4

84   Ezek. 44:4

faithful to its design and follow all its regulations.[85]

Ezekiel's Temple is described in great detail. The architectural measurements of gateways and porticos, alcoves, courtyards and walls are accurately specified. Bas-reliefs of lions, palm trees and double-faced cherubs are laid out. Never in history has a Temple been constructed with Ezekiel's dimensions and design. His prophetic blueprint remains to be built on Mount Zion in days yet future.

Are There Mountains In Heaven?

The earthly city of Jerusalem is called the Holy City seven times in the Bible.[86] It is also called Zion 161 times in the Scriptures. This is the city where Yeshua will reign as Messiah for one thousand years, where the Fourth Temple will be built, and where space-time history as we have known it will eventually come to an end. As the millennial reign of Messiah Yeshua son of David draws to a close,[87] this present universe (called 'the first heaven and the first earth') will be consumed in a 'big bang.' The Apostle Peter describes this future event.

> The heavens will disappear with a roar; the elements will
> be destroyed by fire, and the earth and everything in it
> will be laid bare ... (E)verything will be destroyed in this
> way ... That day will bring about the destruction of the
> heavens by fire, and the elements will melt in the heat. But
> in keeping with His promise we are looking forward to a
> new heaven and a new earth, the home of righteousness.[88]

In the Book of Revelation, John sees the same future event in a prophetic vision, but one further revelation is imparted to him.

> Then I saw a great white throne and Him who was
> seated on it. Earth and sky fled from His presence,

---

85   Ezek. 43:10-11

86   Neh. 11:1, 18; Isa. 48:2; 52:1; Dan. 9:24; Matt. 4:5; 27:53; Rev. 11:2.

87   Rev. 20:4-7

88   2 Pet. 3:10-13

and there was no place for them. Then I saw a new heaven and a new earth, for the first heaven and the first earth had passed away, and there was no longer any sea. I saw the Holy City, the New Jerusalem, coming down out of heaven from God, prepared as a bride beautifully dressed for her husband.[89]

Heaven Came Down

John has a vision of a holy city in Heaven called the New Jerusalem, which descends from Heaven and seems to touch down on the soil of the New Earth. In a handful of Bible verses a place located somewhere in Heaven is described as the Holy City,[90] the New Jerusalem,[91] the Heavenly Jerusalem,[92] and the City of the living God.[93] This city is described as "coming down out of Heaven from God, prepared as a bride beautifully dressed for her husband."[94] John is careful to say, not that the city is the bride, but that it looks like a bride. This city is the eternal abode of all the saints. That is where the Bride of Messiah will dwell forever. Only those whose names are written in the Lamb's book of life will enter the city. All the redeemed, whether kings of the earth or commoners of the nations, will be brought into this city where their lives will be illuminated by its light.[95]

This city will be the place where God's original promise to the Jewish people ("Then have them make a sanctuary for Me, and I will dwell among them") finds a fulfillment which also encompasses the whole of mankind. There all the redeemed of all the ages will gaze undisturbed on the face of God. The Heavenly Jerusalem warmly receives both the Messianic Jewish believers of earthly Jerusalem and all believers from all the nations.

---

89   Rev. 20:11; 21:1-2

90   Rev. 21:2, 10; 22:19

91   Rev. 3:12; 21:2; *cf.*, 21:10 where it is simply called Jerusalem.

92   Heb. 12:22

93   *ibid.*; *cf.*, Rev. 3:12 'the city of My God'

94   Rev. 21:2

95   Rev. 22:5, 14

> Now the dwelling of God is with men, and He will
> live with them. They will be His people, and God
> Himself will be with them and be their God ... The
> throne of God and of the Lamb will be in the city, and
> His servants will serve Him. They will see His face,
> and His name will be on their foreheads. There will
> be no more night. They will not need the light of a
> lamp or the light of the sun, for the Lord God will give
> them light. And they will reign for ever and ever.[96]

Only once in the Scriptures is the glorious title 'Mount Zion' used to describe a place in Heaven. As there is an earthly Temple and an earthly Jerusalem, and a corresponding Heavenly Temple and a Heavenly Jerusalem, so there is also a Heavenly Mount Zion. In Hebrews 12:22 it seems to be a synonym for the ultimate abode of the saints. In the end, every believer in Yeshua can rightly be called a 'Zionist' – at least a Heavenly one!

> But you have come to Mount Zion, to the heavenly
> Jerusalem, the city of the living God. You have come to
> thousands upon thousands of angels in joyful assembly,
> to the church of the firstborn, whose names are written
> in heaven. You have come to God, the judge of all men,
> to the spirits of righteous men made perfect, to Yeshua
> the mediator of a new covenant, and to the sprinkled
> blood that speaks a better word than the blood of Abel.[97]

Walking on the Stones of Fire

The word of God does not tell us about everything in Heaven and on earth. It wisely notes that, when all is said and done, "no eye has seen, no ear has heard, no mind has conceived what God has prepared for those who love Him."[98] The Bible is not an exhaustive thesaurus about the eternal order. Only tiny hints are scattered here and there across the leaves of Scripture. Students of the prophetic

---

96   Rev. 21:3; 22:3-5

97   Heb. 12:22-24; cf., Rev. 14:1-3 which could be describing earthly or Heavenly Zion.

98   1 Cor. 2:9

Scriptures who endeavor to grasp this complex subject are bound to run into some insoluble points, some thorny difficulties that cannot be smoothed out.

One of these eschatological tensions is found in Revelation 21:22's description of the New Jerusalem: "I did not see a Temple in the city, because the Lord God Almighty and the Lamb are its Temple."[99] The New Jerusalem does not have a Temple, yet the Bible plainly teaches that God Almighty abides in a Heavenly Temple. Why are the descriptions of Heaven and the New Jerusalem different in this regard? Has something happened to the Temple in Heaven? Has it somehow been transformed into a glorious city?

The first clue to solving this mystery might be found in Revelation 21:1. "Then I saw a new heaven and a new earth, for the first heaven and the first earth had passed away, and there was no longer any sea."[100] In this passage John seems to be contrasting the spiritual state of affairs on the first earth, our present earth – where Jerusalem is a localized and mostly Jewish city – to the spiritual state of affairs in the new creation, the new heavens and the new earth – where the New Jerusalem is the ultimate city, coming down out of heaven and perhaps landing on the new earth. If that is the case, then what John is saying might be the following: whereas the earthly Zion has been the abode of four Temples – where mankind could go on pilgrimage and meet God – the inhabitants of this New Jerusalem will have such close fellowship with God that the formalities of a Temple will be unnecessary.

The second clue comes from two Bible passages which discuss spiritual events prior to the creation of Adam and Eve. Isaiah 14 refers to Satan's fall from purity. His ambition caused him to reach for control over parts of Heaven which were reserved for God alone. "You said in your heart, 'I will go up to Heaven. I will raise up my throne above the stars of God. I will sit on the Mount of Appointed Gatherings, which is on the farthest northern side. I will ascend

---

99   Rev. 21:22
100   Rev. 21:1

above the tops of the clouds. I will make myself resemble the Most High.'"[101] Another passage dealing with the same event describes other places in Heaven.

> You were in Eden, the garden of God; every precious
> stone adorned you: ruby, topaz and emerald, chrysolite,
> onyx and jasper, sapphire, turquoise and beryl. Your
> settings and mountings were made of gold; on the day
> you were created they were prepared. You were anointed
> as a guardian cherub, for so I ordained you. You were
> on the holy mount of God; you walked among the fiery
> stones ... Through your widespread trade you were
> filled with violence, and you sinned. So I drove you in
> disgrace from the mount of God, and I expelled you,
> O guardian cherub, from among the fiery stones.[102]

These two descriptions refer to what seem to be geographical place names in Heaven – the Mount of Appointed Gatherings which is on the far northern side,[103] a mineral-filled Heavenly Garden of Eden, the Holy Mount of God, and the Court of the Fiery Stones. So little is clear in these passages, but there is enough to suggest that there are different geographical places in Heaven, and that perhaps the New Jerusalem is neither the very center of Heaven nor the 'transformed' Heavenly Temple of God. God was able to be simultaneously with His people in Solomon's Jerusalem Temple while still dwelling in His Heavenly Temple. Perhaps God can be with His people in the New Jerusalem while still dwelling in the Heavenly Temple on His Holy Mountain. These thoughts and suggestions are poor and stumbling attempts to describe the indescribable. These are at best meditations on heavenly realities and not the realities themselves.

Twelve Gates to the City

101　Isa. 14:14 my translation

102　Ezek. 28:13-14, 16

103　The Hebrews and Canaanites believed that the most sacred area of Heaven was its northern side. These beliefs are reflected in Job 37:15-22 and Psalm 48:1-2 and perhaps are based on Heavenly realities.

One of the richest passages in Holy Scriptures is John's description of *Yerushalayim shel ma'alah,* the New Jerusalem. In that city all the redeemed of all the ages, whether male or female, Jewish or Gentile, will move and breathe and have their being in the sunshine of God's love.

> And he carried me away in the Spirit to a mountain
> great and high, and showed me the Holy City, Jerusalem,
> coming down out of heaven from God ... It had a great,
> high wall with twelve gates, and with twelve angels at
> the gates. On the gates were written the names of the
> twelve tribes of Israel ... The wall of the city had twelve
> foundations, and on them were the names of the twelve
> apostles of the Lamb ... The wall was made of jasper, and
> the city of pure gold, as pure as glass. The foundations of
> the city walls were decorated with every kind of precious
> stone ... The twelve gates were twelve pearls, each gate
> made of a single pearl. The great street of the city was of
> pure gold, like transparent glass.[104]
> Then the angel showed me the river of the water of
> life, as clear as crystal, flowing from the throne of
> God and of the Lamb down the middle of the great
> street of the city. On each side of the river stood the
> tree of life, bearing twelve crops of fruit, yielding its
> fruit every month. And the leaves of the tree are for
> the healing of the nations. No longer will there be any
> curse. The throne of God and of the Lamb will be in
> the city, and His servants will serve Him. They will see
> His face, and His name will be on their foreheads.[105]
>
> Blessed are those who wash their robes, that they
> may have the right to the tree of life and may go
> through the gates into the city ... The Spirit and the
> bride say, "Come! And let him who hears say, "Come!
> Whoever is thirsty, let him come; and whoever wishes,
> let him take the free gift of the water of life.[106]

104   Rev. 21:10, 12, 14, 18, 21
105   Rev. 22:1-4
106   Rev. 22:14, 17

For all eternity the twelve gates of the New Jerusalem will be inscribed with the names of the twelve tribes of Israel, while the twelve foundation stones under the walls will always bear the names of Yeshua's twelve Jewish apostles. When all creation gazes at these gates, they will forever remember that "access to salvation is through Israel's covenant promises in general and through Israel's promised Messiah in particular."[107] When the citizens of heaven look at the foundation stones of the city, they will remember that these Jewish apostles "are the foundation of the church as they confess the Lamb, Jesus, as the Messiah, the Son of God (Matt. 16:18; Eph. 2:20)."[108]

In the eternal order God has wonderfully succeeded in 'dancing at two weddings simultaneously' – in displaying His distinctive callings on both Israel and the Gentiles, as well as His creation of a rock solid unity between both as His one beloved people!

---

107   David L. Turner, "The New Jerusalem in Revelation 21:1-25: in *Dispensationalism, Israel and the Church: The Search for Definition*, ed. Craig A. Blaising and Darrell L. Bock (Grand Rapids: Zondervan, 1992), p. 288.

108   *ibid.*

Conclusion

Pikuach Nefesh:
The Church's Threefold Commission
To Save Jewish Lives

During the Roman persecutions of Judaism in the second century AD, several rabbis developed a principle known as *pikuach nefesh*. Briefly stated, this principle says that danger to human life overrides the many Sabbath laws. From that point onward the principle of *pikuach nefesh* was codified into Rabbinic law. It permitted Jews to escape from situations where torture and certain destruction awaited them, even if those dangers occurred on their holy day of rest.

The Body of Messiah has been called to enter into the rest of God, according to Hebrews 4:9-10. We believers also have a divine commission to save Jewish lives, a Messianic principle of *pikuach nefesh* which has been codified in the Hebrew Scriptures as well as in the New Covenant. God Himself developed this principle in the courts of Heaven before the foundation of this world.

The first link in God's commission to the Church is *intercessory prayer* for the Jewish people. For Zion's sake the Church cannot hold its peace, and for Jerusalem it cannot remain silent. Day and night the Body of Messiah is to give God no rest and to give themselves no rest until He brings the Jewish people into the fullness of their national calling. "Save, O God, the remnant of Your people!" Pray for the peace of Jerusalem and that the Redeemer would come to Zion. Pray that the work of the gospel will prosper among the Jewish people, that God will lift the veil off of Israel's eyes, and that the Lord would bring a whole people into their prophetic national calling.

The second link in God's commission to the Church is *evangelism* to the Jewish people. How can Israel be saved unless they hear the gospel message, and how can the message be preached unless someone's evangelistic outreach is subsidized? Invest your time and money in Jewish evangelism. Do not be ashamed of the glorious gospel, because when you preach the message to the Jewish people first, you will discover that it is still God's power to bring salvation to everyone who believes.

The third link in God's commission to the Church is *saving Jewish lives*. The time will soon be upon us when mighty nations turn their backs on Israel and plot the Jewish state's downfall. Waves of satanic anti-Semitism are about to sweep across the face of the globe. Prepare now! Ask God to give you a strategy for rescuing and hiding Jewish refugees, for feeding Jewish families and for transporting them to ports and airports of safety, where they can be spirited away to Israel. Pray as God raises up a hidden network for this future Jewish 'underground railroad.' Get ready to extend a hand of comfort and blessing to God's chosen people as you help them on their way. And stock up on Bibles and literature sensitive to Jewish spiritual needs and questions.

The future redemption of the Jewish people holds the key to the liberation of Planet Earth. Stand up in the strength of God's courage and embrace His call on the Church to save Jewish lives. It is time to throw ourselves into the heat of battle. The God of Jacob is calling you. Stretch out your hands to Israel and unlock the door to world revival!